PARLIAMENTARY REFORM, 1785–1928

QUESTIONS AND ANALYSIS IN HISTORY

Edited by Stephen J. Lee and Sean Lang

Other titles in this series:

Imperial Germany, 1871–1918
Stephen J. Lee

The Weimar Republic
Stephen J. Lee

Hitler and Nazi Germany
Stephen J. Lee

The French Revolution
Jocelyn Hunt

The Spanish Civil War
Andrew Forrest

The English Wars and Republic, 1637–1660
Graham E. Seel

The Renaissance
Jocelyn Hunt

Tudor Government
T. A. Morris

The Cold War
Bradley Lightbody

Stalin and the Soviet Union
Stephen J. Lee

PARLIAMENTARY REFORM, 1785–1928

SEAN LANG

ROUTLEDGE

London and New York

First published 1999 by Routledge
11 New Fetter Lane, London EC4P 4EE

Simultaneously published in the USA and Canada
by Routledge
29 West 35th Street, New York, NY 10001

Typeset in Baskerville by Keystroke, Jacaranda Lodge, Wolverhampton
Printed and bound in Great Britain by TJ International Ltd, Padstow, Cornwall

British Library Cataloguing in Publication Data
A catalogue record for this book is available from the British Library

Library of Congress Cataloging in Publication Data
Lang, Sean
    Parliamentary reform, 1785–1928 / Sean Lang.
        p.   cm. – (Questions and analysis in history)
    Includes bibliographical references and index.
    1. Great Britain. Parliament–Reform–History. I. Title.
    II. Series.
    JN543.L36   1999
    328.41'0704'09–dc21   98-31486
                                                        CIP

ISBN 0-415-18399-5

CONTENTS

Series Preface   vii
Acknowledgements   viii

Introduction   1

1   The unreformed Parliament   5

2   The Great Reform Act   26

3   Chartism – the demand for universal suffrage   45

4   Disraeli and the Second Reform Act   67

5   The professionalisation of politics, 1867–1900   88

6   The Labour Movement and the growth of
    democracy   111

7   The decline of the monarchy and the fall of the
    House of Lords   129

8   Votes for women   151

    Notes and sources   173
    Select bibliography   179
    Index   184

SERIES PREFACE

Most history textbooks now aim to provide the student with interpretation, and many also cover the historiography of a topic. Some include a selection of sources.

So far, however, there have been few attempts to combine all the skills needed by the history student. Interpretation is usually found within an overall narrative framework and it is often difficult to separate out the two for essay purposes. Where sources are included, there is rarely any guidance as to how to answer the questions on them.

The Questions and Analysis series is therefore based on the belief that another approach should be added to those which already exist. It has two main aims.

The first is to separate narrative from interpretation so that the latter is no longer diluted by the former. Most chapters start with a background narrative section containing essential information. This material is then used in a section focusing on analysis through a specific question. The main purpose of this is to help to tighten up essay technique.

The second aim is to provide a comprehensive range of sources for each of the issues covered. The questions are of the type which appear on examination papers, and some have worked answers to demonstrate the techniques required.

The chapters may be approached in different ways. The background narratives can be read first to provide an overall perspective, followed by the analyses and then the sources. The alternative method is to work through all the components of each chapter before going on to the next.

ACKNOWLEDGEMENTS

Author and publisher are grateful to Addison Wesley Longman Ltd for permission to reproduce three tables from their book, *The Forging of the Modern State* by Eric Evans. They would be grateful to hear from holders of any copyright material they were unable to contact.

INTRODUCTION

The Victorians were fond of pointing out the marked contrast between the peace, general fairness and above all the stability provided by their own parliamentary system of government, and the apparent inability of their neighbours to set up anything to compare with it. While nineteenth-century Europeans resorted to revolution with alarming frequency, and even the Americans fell into fratricidal civil war, the ease with which Britain avoided civil strife of equivalent proportions seemed – and not just in Britain – transparently obvious proof of how successful she had been in developing and continuing to develop a workable system of government. Within their colonial territories the British either established mirror images of their own Parliament, as in the Dominion colonies like Australia or Canada, or else, as in India or areas of Africa, they looked into local customs for the nearest equivalent they could find to the House of Commons and based their governmental system upon that; where they found a hereditary ruler or tribal elders, they attempted to mould them into constitutional princelings and houses of lords, in both cases with – perhaps predictably – patchy success.

Parliament and its workings were enormously important to the Victorians. In towns and cities throughout the country there are statues they put up, often financed by public subscription, to local MPs: some – like Cobden and Bright in front of Manchester Town Hall or Earl Grey atop his column in Newcastle – of national significance, many others of more local importance and now long forgotten, but all deemed worthy of the sort of honour more usually accorded to military or revolutionary heroes. And it follows, logically enough, that the state of Parliament, who should sit in it, who should vote for people to sit in it, and what they should do when they got there, were never points of merely academic interest to the Victorians, but were of immense and immediate importance. Nearly all of the most important popular campaigns of the nineteenth century, from the agitation of the Peterloo years, through Chartism and the campaign for Irish Home Rule, to the long battle for female suffrage and the crisis over Lloyd George's People's Budget, were connected either directly or indirectly to the issue of reforming the workings of Parliament. Even the one major exception, the Anti-Corn Law League, can be said to prove the rule, in that its refusal to get involved in the issue was at least in part because it represented the classes who had benefited from the 1832 Act and who were in no hurry to force through a sequel.

The contrast with the twentieth century is striking. The twentieth century saw a series of major changes to the workings of Parliament, including universal adult suffrage, the virtual crippling of the House of Lords as a political institution, the lowering of the voting age to 18, and numerous changes to parliamentary procedure, not to mention innovations like direct elections to the European Parliament or television cameras in both chambers at Westminster; yet beyond the dogged attempts of the Liberal Party, later the Liberal Democrats, to introduce proportional representation, the issue of electoral reform has seldom attracted widespread interest since the days of the suffragettes. It is tempting to ascribe this twentieth-century general lack of interest in the issue to the sheer success of the nineteenth century in resolving it, rather as the civil war of the seventeenth century meant there was no need to fight one in the eighteenth; but the late twentieth century faces problems of parliamentary reform every bit as important as those which activated the Whigs and the Chartists. Scottish and Welsh devolution is as much an issue about the role of Parliament in a United Kingdom as it is about Celtic nationalism; the long period of Conservative rule under Margaret Thatcher and John Major (1979–1997) raised important issues about the role of Parliament in the face of an Executive apparently entrenched in power, an issue by no means resolved by the election in 1997 of a Labour government with an equally robust majority; above all, the issue of Britain's relationship with the European Union, which did so much to split and discredit the Conservative Party in the 1990s, remains as much a question about the sovereignty and future role of Parliament as it is about the economic benefits of membership. How right Peel was when he defended his opposition to the 1832 Reform Act by saying it would open a door that he saw no hope of ever closing!

One of the problems with studying parliamentary reform is that it is at once very familiar ground and also treacherously unfamiliar. Some of the highlights of the story, notably the Great Reform Act of 1832, used to be drilled into young children at school. More recently, children are more likely to be taught about groups like the Chartists or the suffragettes, but either way, parts of the story are well known and for essentially the same reason: because, one way or another, their efforts helped make things *better*. Definitions of 'better' have changed considerably, but the overall story of parliamentary reform still seems to be one of gradual but eventual – perhaps even inevitable – improvement, a view with which the nineteenth-century Whigs would have agreed heartily. The Whigs regarded the reformed Parliament as the envy of the civilised world, and if we would probably not go quite so far about our politicians today, we seem nevertheless broadly satisfied with the system within which they operate. In that sense, parliamentary reform seems a logical story or progress from an archaic system to a better system which we enjoy today.

The problem is that the aspirations of different groups involved in the story, even the very words they used, can often confound modern expectations. To modern eyes, what was wrong with the unreformed Parliament was that it was undemocratic; it is difficult to grasp that that was, to eighteenth-century eyes, *including those of many reformers*, one of the system's greatest assets. It is easy to assume that, since Disraeli did so much to enfranchise the urban working classes, he must have had some confidence in their sense of political responsibility; it can seem paradoxical at first to learn that Disraeli placed most confidence not in the working classes but in the aristocracy, the more blue-blooded the better. We assume, often wrongly, that the most important parts of Parliament were the House of Commons and the government front bench; it is easy to underestimate the importance of the House of Lords or the monarch. Simple words can be misleading. 'Party' meant very different things in the 1780s, or the 1860s, from what it came to mean in the twentieth century. It is an understandable mistake, but a mistake nevertheless, to assume that when an 'election' was held, voters, however few or unrepresentative they might be, living in their constituencies, however unevenly distributed, went to the polls and voted for candidates, however corrupt; the idea of *uncontested* elections takes some getting used to. Nowadays MPs who change party are relatively rare; the idea that virtually an entire cabinet could shift from one party to another, as Peel's did, and that this should be regarded as perfectly normal political behaviour (as indeed it was) will seem novel to many students. So too, no doubt, will the idea that ministers and even governments actually resigned not just after losing votes in Parliament, but after winning them by reduced majorities.

Yet the story of parliamentary reform remains relevant. In 1992 the Foreign Secretary, Douglas Hurd, appealed to the Conservative Party to avoid repeating – over the Treaty of Maastricht – the catastrophic split the Conservatives suffered in 1846 over the Corn Laws. His warning went unheeded; as so often, ignoring the past led to a repetition of its mistakes.

1

THE UNREFORMED PARLIAMENT

BACKGROUND NARRATIVE

Mediaeval parliaments were no more than a gathering of representatives of the three estates of the realm, Church, Lords and Commons. Parliament served the function of a high court, and could, if asked, make financial grants to the crown, but it was of no greater significance than many other institutions of the mediaeval state. Parliament began to play a more important role in the 1530s, when King Henry VIII used it to give a legal basis to the break with Rome. In theory this raised important questions about the relative importance of Crown and Parliament: was Henry's authority not sufficient on its own? But the issue remained essentially academic until the reign of Charles I. His attempt to impose taxation and to introduce religious changes without seeking the sanction of Parliament drove many of his opponents to declare that Parliament was not just the king's equal, but his superior.

The basis for Parliament's claim to sovereignty was that it represented the people, but did it? Cromwell closed down what was left (the 'rump') of the Long Parliament in 1653 because it was so long since it had been elected, and its membership was so decimated by the Civil Wars that in effect it was representative of nothing but itself. Parliament hit back. Well into the nineteenth century one of the most damaging accusations that could be made against a power-hungry politician was that he was setting out to make himself another Cromwell, riding roughshod over parliamentary sovereignty.

Parliament's moment of glory came in 1688 when James II was overthrown by a combination of parliamentary revolt and a Dutch invasion, and Parliament was able to dictate the terms by which the new monarchs, William and Mary, were to be allowed to reign. This 'Revolution Settlement' established Parliament and Crown on a basis of mutual dependence weighted in Parliament's favour, and was regarded throughout the eighteenth century and well into the nineteenth with almost holy awe. The delicate balance of the settlement might easily be ruined without constant vigilance on the part of all concerned, so that eighteenth-century politics always resembled a sort of constitutional egg-and-spoon race. There were many potential threats to the balance of the constitution, including foreign invasion, a return of the Stuarts, or concessions to Catholics (too inclined to autocracy) or Protestant dissenters (too radical), but all of these had been averted by the middle of the eighteenth century.

The danger of the Crown seeking to upset the balance of the constitution seemed remote: the first two Hanoverian kings, George I and George II, in particular were happy to leave Parliament largely to its own devices; they worked closely with ministers, like Sir Robert Walpole and the Duke of Newcastle, in whom they had confidence and who commanded the confidence of Parliament. The eighteenth-century Parliament therefore gradually evolved into the normal body of government. A form of cabinet government developed, as did a sort of political split between the supporters of the Hanoverians and of parliamentary sovereignty, known as Whigs, and those who (discreetly) hankered after a Stuart restoration and tended to support the Crown and the Church of England, known as Tories. Parliamentary business, like most public business in the eighteenth century, was fuelled by a system of patronage. Essentially, this meant that to obtain any post, however humble, in any branch of professional or public life, it was important to have the support ('enjoy the patronage') of someone higher up who either controlled the post directly, or could influence the appointment. Official appointments under the Crown or in the Church of England, commissions in the armed forces, or seats in Parliament were all subject to patronage. Some 'boroughmongers', like Sir John Lowther in the north-west of England, could control the selection of MPs for whole areas of the country. Many eminent politicians began their careers in this way: Pitt the Younger was first elected at Lowther's pocket borough of Appleby in Westmorland, and other major figures elected at pocket boroughs included Castlereagh, Burke and Canning.

The accession of the young King George III in 1760 threw the whole system into disarray. George sought a much more active role in politics than his predecessors, and Whig politicians quickly came to suspect his motives. The Americans blamed him for upsetting their delicate relationship with the mother country, and the Whigs accused him of seeking to upset the constitutional balance between Crown and Parliament. In 1780 the House of Commons even debated and passed a celebrated motion 'that the power of the Crown has increased, is increasing, and ought to be diminished'. By allowing a favoured minister to bestow the vast resources of Crown patronage on supporters, the king could in effect use the patronage system to keep his chosen minister in power. Conversely, by denying a ministry access to Crown patronage, the king could severely weaken its authority in Parliament. In 1783 King George set out to do just that to the controversial (not to say unlikely) coalition ministry set up by Lord North and the charismatic Whig leader, Charles James Fox.

The king denied the ministry access to royal patronage; Fox countered by sponsoring a bill to reform the workings of the East India Company, which would also, in effect, give the ministry control of the fabulously wealthy patronage available in India. The king could not prevent the bill passing the House of Commons with a large majority, but by threatening to withdraw royal patronage and favour from anyone who voted for it, he managed to defeat it equally heavily in the House of Lords. George dismissed Fox and North before the night was out.

Fox and his supporters were outraged: the king had interfered in the workings of the House of Lords to defeat and dismiss a ministry which had the clear and overwhelming support of the House of Commons. No leading politician would taint himself by association with such conduct, and George had to resort to the 24-year-old William Pitt to form a new ministry. Characteristically, Fox then so mishandled the business of opposition to Pitt, that by March 1784 Pitt, with the king's support (and patronage) behind him, felt confident enough to go to the polls, where he won a resounding victory. The Whigs saw the crisis of 1783–4 as the Crown's successful attempt to undermine the authority of Parliament; the electorate, especially in rural England, saw it more as George and Pitt rescuing the constitution, not to mention the wealth of the East India Company, from the greedy hands of Fox and his cronies.

Subsequent events merely served to confirm each side's view. For the Whigs, Pitt's long hold on power, his staunch opposition to the principles of the French Revolution, and his repressive wartime measures all confirmed that executive power was triumphant and Parliament had become an irrelevance: indeed, for a long time Fox gave up attending it at all. From Pitt's point of view, the Whigs' record merely confirmed their unfitness for office. Their cherished opposition to royal power disappeared pretty quickly during the king's illness in 1788, when it briefly looked as if they might benefit from a pro-Whig regency; above all, Fox was loud in his support for the French Revolution long after it had become clear how bloody and threatening the revolution had become. In 1794 the leading Whig patron, the Earl of Portland, led his supporters over to join Pitt, exasperated and alarmed by Fox's support for the French. During their long years in opposition, the Whigs began to see that their best hope of reducing the power of the Crown – and, incidentally, of returning to office – lay in cleaning up the system which enabled Pitt and George III to hold on to power, and so they were gradually wedded to a policy of parliamentary reform.

ANALYSIS (1): HOW REPRESENTATIVE WAS THE UNREFORMED PARLIAMENT?

To anyone familiar with democratic forms of government, the eighteenth-century parliamentary system seems transparently, even comically, chaotic. The distribution of constituencies was dominated by the English rural counties with a heavy weighting towards the south of England, while major new industrial centres like Birmingham or Sheffield were totally unrepresented; and borough electorates could be tiny, enabling wealthy patrons to buy and sell pocket boroughs like so much produce. In an extreme case, the parliamentary borough of Gatton in Surrey contained only six houses, and was frequently sold between borough-mongers. While in the counties the normal voting qualification was that of holding a freehold worth forty shillings a year, in boroughs the franchise qualifications varied erratically, from scot-

and-lot and 'pot-walloper'[1] boroughs, including Preston and Westminster where, in effect, anyone present at election time could vote, to burgage and corporation boroughs, where control over elections was frequently concentrated either in the local corporation or in wealthy landowners. Plural voting was common. Graduates of Oxford and Cambridge could vote both in the constituencies where they lived and in the two university seats; many borough electors also had a vote in elections in the county the borough was in. There are cases recorded of individuals who managed to amass impressive numbers of such plural votes in different constituencies, and with a bit of planning, given that elections were held over a fortnight, they could cast them all.

Above all, what really offends modern sensibilities is the corruption which pervaded the system, from widespread bribery at elections to the patronage circles and faction politics that operated at Westminster, not to mention the manifold opportunities at all levels for embezzlement or fraud. So obvious are the faults of the system that understanding it actually becomes problematic: it is hard to see how anyone other than those with a vested interest could seriously have defended it. But this is the wrong way to look at it. Until the very end of the eighteenth century there was no major drive to reform the system. Apart from the most blatant abuses, like the deserted boroughs of Old Sarum and Dunwich which still returned two MPs each, even radical writers had surprisingly little to say about parliamentary reform until the 1780s, almost a century after the Revolution Settlement of 1688. This lack of demand suggests an obvious conclusion, which is nevertheless generally overlooked by students, that by and large the system was working well and those involved were happy with it.

This point has been made by some historians. Norman Gash argued in *Politics in the Age of Peel* that until the 1820s the system enjoyed the support of all but the most extreme radicals and was, to all intents and purposes, working satisfactorily. Frank O'Gorman in *Voters, Patrons and Parties* went even further and argued that, contrary to much received opinion, the unreformed system was actually, in its own terms, rather a good one. 'Pocket borough', in his argument, is a misleading term. It suggests that the electorate merely followed the wishes of their local patron at election time, whereas in reality things were never so predictable, which was precisely why patrons spent such vast sums of money on wooing the voters. They were well aware that voters could and did show themselves staunchly independent.

Such arguments paint a refreshingly different picture of eighteenth-century electors, but they have not gone unchallenged. Derek Beales criticised O'Gorman for basing his analysis on six relatively large towns, untypical of the wider range of constituencies. He also pointed out that, however sturdily independent electors might be, it made little difference if the large proportion of uncontested elections meant that in practice they 'had fewer opportunities to cast a vote than to observe Halley's comet'.[2] D.C. Moore in *The Politics of Deference* argued that the voters he had looked at were much more inclined to defer to the wishes of local patrons than O'Gorman suggests, but then he was looking at rural areas whereas O'Gorman was concentrating on towns. Detailed studies of individual constituencies, of which there are many, make it even more difficult to reach satisfactory general conclusions. There could be major differences in what determined the outcome of elections even in neighbouring constituencies. Most elections were won or lost on local issues or rivalries, but sometimes a topical national issue could play an important role. Local rivalries might not follow supposed 'party lines', and there are cases of candidates changing their party colours in the course of an election campaign, or of voters electing for one candidate from each party; there was even a case, at Hertford in 1832, of voters cheerfully accepting the bribes offered by the Tories and then electing a Whig, though this caused quite a scandal and the borough came close to being disenfranchised. In short, the more deeply one looks at the unreformed Parliament, the harder it is to come up with any wholly acceptable general analysis of it.

What is clear is that the people who used the system generally thought that it worked, but that their conception of how it worked was very different from our own. The modern parliamentary system is seen as representing the electorate which is, to all intents and purposes, the adult population; the eighteenth-century Parliament was conceived of as representing the different 'interests' that constituted the nation. These might be economic interests, such as the woollen interest in East Anglia, or the farming interest, or it might be the Church of England or the armed forces. The nobility as an interest group was well represented, and not just in the House of Lords, but many lords had connections with one or more other 'interests' as well. Plantation owners in the Caribbean, who opposed the abolition of the slave trade for so long, were the 'West Indian' or 'Sugar' interest; those with investments in the East India Company were the 'Indian interest', and so on.

To eighteenth-century thinking, it was very important that all major interests should be represented in Parliament, but it was by no means necessary for them to be represented *directly*. As long as there were people in Parliament – in either house – to speak up for each particular interest, it did not matter which constituencies any of them happened to represent. When Radicals complained that huge sections of the population were not represented in Parliament, either because they did not have the vote or because they had no MP, the answer was that they did not need to be directly represented because they were *virtually* represented. This idea was common currency in the eighteenth century: until the 1760s it was quite happily accepted, for example, by the American colonists, even though not one of them had a vote or an MP. Neither Catholics nor slaves lacked voices in Parliament, often very eloquent voices, even though none of them had the vote. To eighteenth-century ears, to argue that everyone had to be represented directly was as illogical as it would be today to claim that an MP cannot represent children because they cannot vote, or cannot speak on behalf of constituents who voted for his opponents.

Virtual representation operated at the constituency level too. It was not necessary for everyone in a constituency to have the vote, as long as a selection of the local population could vote on everyone else's behalf. The forty-shilling freeholder, which was as near as the system came to a standard franchise, was generally regarded as the epitome of the stout-hearted Englishman, independent enough to make up his own mind, but close enough to his fellows to be able to speak for them. This was one of the reasons why voting was done in the open, on the hustings, in full view of the large crowds who habitually gathered at election time. It is often assumed that this was done in order to intimidate the voters, who would not dare vote against the wishes of the squire in case they got evicted from their cottage; in fact, cases of this actually happening are relatively few, even though there are plenty of examples of voters going against the squires' wishes. On the contrary, having open hustings was a safeguard *against* corruption. Voters were held to be answerable not to their landlords or patrons, but to the unenfranchised community as a whole, who had a right to know which way their 'representatives' were casting their votes. Elections were communal events, notoriously robust, not to say violent, and it was a foolish candidate (or voter) who ignored the crowd just because they did not have the vote; a wise patron would spend a lot of money on free beer and victuals for all and sundry. Perhaps the most apt comparison for the role of the crowd is with that of a modern crowd at a sports fixture or a rock concert, who give each event its distinctive atmosphere and who, as any player or performer will attest, can exert a major influence on what happens on stage or on the pitch.

It is tempting, therefore, to argue, in line with O'Gorman, that the old system has been misjudged and that, in its way, it was as representative as it needed to be and that its anachronisms are the result of modern hindsight. On the other hand, we cannot avoid the point that, however representative it may or may not have been, by the very end of the eighteenth century the system was coming under criticism, and contemporaries were beginning to perceive it as inadequate. The point about uncontested elections, for example, is an important one. Out of the 268 constituencies of England and Wales, 65 either saw only one electoral contest in the hundred years from 1734 to 1832, or never went to the polls at all. This does not necessarily indicate that *Parliament* was unrepresentative, since MPs sat for constituencies whether or not they had had to fight for their seats, but it does suggest that the *electoral system* was not as representative as its most zealous defenders might suggest. Linked with that is the point (by no means unknown even today) that MPs were notorious for their long absences from Parliament, or else for attending but never speaking (though most would attend when their particular interest was under debate), and this did not necessarily go down well at election time. Even when absenteeism was on principle rather than from inertia, as when Fox boycotted Parliament during the 1790s in protest at Pitt's repressive regime, it could arouse resentment, not least from those MPs who did make the effort to attend and speak.

Secondly, even by its own criteria, the House of Commons was becoming less representative of the actual interests of the country by the end of the eighteenth century. The obvious example, becoming more obvious almost by the day, was the rapid growth of the industrial and manufacturing interest: it was not so much that Sheffield or Manchester had no MPs, but rather that *none* of the major industrial centres were represented and so there were no MPs who could with any justification claim to speak for this important and wealthy interest. Some historians have also pointed out that some county MPs were alarmed that the growth of major cities within their counties, like Birmingham within Warwickshire or Leeds within Yorkshire, could distort the county electorates and make them much more difficult to influence; granting separate representation to the cities would therefore help preserve their traditional hold on the counties. At the same time, some of the interests represented in the old system had declined by the end of the eighteenth century, and could safely be dropped. Areas like Cornwall and East Anglia no longer produced the sort of wealth which had originally won them their extensive representation in Parliament; proposing to cut their representation down to size was simply recognising economic and social reality.

In conclusion, although it is difficult to generalise accurately about the representative nature of the unreformed Parliament, it does seem safe to say that it was at once a more complex and a less scurrilous system than superficial examination suggests. It did not represent the population in the manner of the modern Parliament because the whole concept of representation was conceived differently, in terms of virtual representation at all levels. In its own terms, the system was as representative as it needed to be for much of the eighteenth century; by the 1780s, however, the strains were beginning to show, as English society underwent a fundamental change and it was increasingly clear that the political system would need to change as well.

Questions

1. What are the grounds for claiming that the unreformed system worked effectively?
2. 'The unreformed Parliament was as representative as it needed to be.' How fair is this judgement?

ANALYSIS (2): WHO SUPPORTED, AND WHO OPPOSED, THE CAUSE OF PARLIAMENTARY REFORM 1785–1815, AND WHY?

No survey of political attitudes in this period can ignore the sweeping effects on Britain of the French Revolution and the long period of war that followed it. The French experience provided numerous examples and models to those in England already disposed towards reform: a written constitution, the Declaration of the Rights of Man, racial equality, the abolition of privilege, equality before the law – it is easy now to forget how exciting the events in France appeared at the time. The way in which the revolution departed from the optimistic pattern of its early days was also carefully noted in England. In the view of the Radicals, most of the blame lay fairly and squarely with King Louis: had he remained true to the constitution instead of intriguing with the Austrians and attempting to flee, France could have been stabilised as a constitutional monarchy and much bloodshed could have been avoided. Others drew precisely the opposite conclusion: the pattern of events in France showed that even moderate reform could easily descend into violence, anarchy and military despotism. The fact that Edmund Burke had predicted the course of events with such precision as early as 1790 in his *Reflections on the Revolution in France* merely seemed to confirm that the link between moderate reform and violent revolution was as close as it was inescapable.

The effect of the war on calls for the reform of Parliament was to polarise opinions sharply. The Foxite Whigs and the Radicals felt that the need for reform grew more imperative with each new piece of repressive legislation Pitt introduced in the 1790s. Pitt, who had himself introduced a limited reform measure in 1785 (though by doing so as a private member rather than making it a government measure he was virtually inviting the Commons to defeat it, which it did) believed that the threat posed by France made it far too risky to start stirring up the excitement and controversy that a Reform Bill was bound to provoke. On top of this, the tendency of Radicals and reformers to pepper their speeches and slogans with the language of the French revolutionaries made it even less likely that the government, let alone the king, would listen to their calls.

However, there were important distinctions and differences between those on either side of the debate. 'The Radicals' were not a single group, nor did they all argue along the same lines. The tradition of opposition to authority could be traced back at least to the seventeenth century – the Hampden Clubs which spread rapidly in the 1810s were named after one of the most celebrated of Charles I's rebellious subjects. John Wilkes' battle with the House of Commons and the king back in the 1760s to take his seat as MP for Middlesex had raised important questions about the electoral system for those who cared to ask them, though at the time few did. By the 1780s, however, there were important tensions between the radical reformers and more conservative advocates of change.

The most important of these more conservative movements was Christopher Wyvill's Yorkshire Association, which was established in 1780 to petition Parliament against the most blatant corruption and abuses and to petition for MPs to be more answerable to their electors. The Yorkshire Association's drive against sleaze chimed in with the spread of Methodism and the Anglican evangelical revival: reform of Parliament was seen as part and parcel of a more general cleaning-up of public morals. The most obvious beneficiary of this drive to improve standards in public life was Pitt, who enjoyed the support of all these movements in the crucial 1784 election. His clampdown on inefficiency, corruption and waste, and especially his stand against the French Revolution, ensured that their support remained rock-solid for the rest of his life. By contrast Fox, both in his private life and his public principles, epitomised everything the evangelicals and the Yorkshire Association abhorred, and the Whigs' deep attachment to Fox's memory alienated evangelical opinion well into the nineteenth century.

The more radical reformers included a breakaway group within the

Yorkshire Association led by John Jebb, who in turn owed many of his ideas to a radical-thinking militia officer, Major John Cartwright. Cartwright's basic premise was widely accepted: he argued that the Norman Conquest had wrecked the perfectly balanced constitution that had existed in Saxon times; in his view, therefore, parliamentary reform should seek to restore the *status quo* before 1066. Cartwright's ideas were revolutionary in the sense that they aimed to complete a full turn of a circle, but they also provided a basis to parliamentary reform which owed nothing to the French Revolution (and even less to any real knowledge of Anglo-Saxon England!) – indeed it could be argued that they were the ultimate in conservative policy. But the Radicals were not united. For Cartwright and Henry Hunt, reform meant universal suffrage; for their close colleague, Sir Francis Burdett, who enjoyed an extensive popular following, universal suffrage was not necessary, especially as demanding it was likely to stiffen resistance to any reform at all. Others looked more to the French for inspiration. Tom Paine fully agreed with Cartwright on the need to restore the Saxon constitution, but his way of doing so was to establish a sort of alternative Parliament, to be called a National Convention, which would represent the nation more fairly, and which would exist alongside the existing Parliament until, presumably, it usurped Parliament's place by force. Inevitably, the implications of Paine's ideas alienated at least as many as they attracted, but they were the staple diet of underground radical groups like the London Corresponding Society, which also debated them with their counterparts in France.

These more radical reformers often attracted support among the new industrial workers. William Cobbett addressed his ideas directly to the working classes through his newspaper, the *Political Register*, and many other radicals of the war years, of whom Hunt was the most celebrated, actively cultivated working-class support. The large public meetings which Hunt and others addressed were carefully choreographed performances, with all the trappings of popular showmanship. Hunt was known by his trademark white hat, and would ride round the field in a splendid open carriage, shamelessly playing to the gallery. Apart from acting as a forum for rousing speeches, which would be relayed to the further reaches of the crowd by callers strategically positioned around the ground, these meetings were often held to choose representatives to sit in a proposed National Convention, a working-class anti-Parliament of the sort that Paine had proposed. We need to be careful, however, before concluding from this that there was widespread working-class support for Radical demands for parliamentary reform.

Few, if any, of the Radicals could be described as working-class: they were nearly always aspiring members of the new middle classes, often with a touch of the dandy about them. Their ideas often did not reflect working-class concerns. William Cobbett felt deep contempt for 'Old Corruption', the system of bribery and jobbery which kept the landed classes in power, and he loudly lamented the spread of industry and the disappearance of old rural crafts, but he had little interest in the details of factory reform or conditions in the industrial cities. In Birmingham, Thomas Attwood argued for parliamentary reform because he hoped it would lead to a more stable monetary policy; in Manchester, the middle-class reformers wanted to break the power of the landed classes because they were the people who had introduced the Corn Laws; in Leeds, Edward Baines, editor of the *Leeds Mercury*, campaigned for parliamentary reform as a necessary precursor to social reform legislation, though in practice he seemed keener on the former than the latter. There was, in other words, no unity of purpose either within middle-class reformers or between them and the working classes, and it is hardly surprising that these differences came out into the open once the Reform Bill was passed.

The Whigs' approach to reform was even more circuitous. It is quite wrong to imagine that they had a long-standing commitment to it. Fox embraced the rhetoric of reform, but he was never an enthusiast for its substance, which he saw as either unnecessary or too radical. In his youth, Charles (later Earl) Grey had been an enthusiastic reformer, and had associated himself with the radical group the Society of Friends of the People; yet by 1814 Grey seemed to have lost either hope or interest, and he let down his audience badly at a big 'Fox dinner' in Newcastle by omitting any reference to parliamentary reform: four years later he was advocating only very moderate change. The Whigs' interest in parliamentary reform really dated only to the political crisis of 1783–4 which killed off the Fox–North coalition. What it seemed to show was that the existing system had failed utterly to prevent the Crown from clawing back a huge amount of executive power from Parliament, and the electoral system had allowed the king to get away with it. Pitt promptly set about using the system to swamp the House of Lords with his own supporters, reversing or suspending the very rights which Parliament had spent so much time and blood in winning from the Stuarts: freedom of speech, freedom of assembly, freedom of the press, even habeas corpus. Little wonder that the Whigs came to recognise that the system needed overhauling.

But there was a big difference between agreeing on the need for reform and agreeing on what form it should take, even allowing for the awkward fact that the Whigs were in no position to start implementing policies on anything. Fox himself blew hot and cold on the issue, and disappointed the radicals among his followers and beyond by his lukewarm support. The issue proved highly divisive for the Whigs, nearly all of whom, after all, owed what parliamentary seats they held to the old system. By the 1810s and 1820s, even the bogey of unlimited Executive power and the crisis of 1783–4 was looking rather tired, and it had much less appeal to the younger generation of Whigs who entered Parliament after Fox's death in 1806. Reform was a useful weapon to use against the Tory governments of the war years and after, but its use was as a slogan rather than as a detailed proposal for action. Not until much later, perhaps as late as 1830, did the Whigs as a body adopt parliamentary reform as a definite policy.

On the other hand, opposition to reform was widespread and often well grounded. Although different interest groups inevitably had different agendas, there was a strong *prima facie* case against reform which all its opponents could share, which was based in the common experience of the whole nation between 1793 and 1815. Britain had been at war for nearly a quarter of a century against an enemy – France – who, had she conquered Britain as she had conquered nearly all the rest of Europe, would have overthrown the monarchy, abolished Parliament and completely destroyed the whole constitutional structure of the nation. Instead of that, the constitution had proved both strong and flexible enough to survive the biggest invasion threat since the Armada, a major rebellion in Ireland in 1798, serious unrest at home, and the resultant need to curtail civil liberties; and it had emerged at the end of the war apparently even stronger than at the start. Parliament now governed Ireland directly, and Linda Colley argues in *Britons* that the long experience of war with France had a profound effect in binding classes and nationalities together in a new British national identity. To suggest that such an obviously successful system was in need of radical change seemed grotesque. Moreover, there was so little agreement among those who advocated reform about what form it should take that there could be no guarantee that conceding to moderate demands would not provide an opening that more radical reformers could exploit. Above all, there was a genuine fear that giving in to calls for reform would lead to disorder and bloodshed on a scale with which, let us not forget, the early nineteenth century was much more familiar than we are today.

This view was particularly strongly held by the landowning classes who felt, not without reason, that they had made a major contribution to the war effort, not least in paying tax on their landed income, and who now looked forward to enjoying the benefits of peace. The Corn Laws, the Game Laws and the abolition of income tax, all passed in the two years immediately following Waterloo, were a sort of shot across the bows to warn off would-be reformers. Nor was it just the richer land-owners who saw no need for reform. Even in 1831, 159 Oxfordshire freeholders felt strongly enough to petition Parliament against reform, describing it as 'hostile to the interests of our excellent constitution, and particularly injurious to the agricultural interests'. A cynic might comment that the rural communities were rather too accustomed to identifying the nation's interests with their own, but there was opposition to reform in the new industrial areas too. In the 1780s a commentator noted opposition to reform among the industrial middle classes in Manchester, and right up until the passage of the Reform Bill some manufacturers remained sceptical about the commercial benefits of reform. Workers too were sometimes indifferent, or even hostile, to reform. In Leeds, working-class support switched from the reformer Baines to his opponents, Michael Sadler and Richard Oastler, both fierce opponents of reform but tireless workers for factory reform, which interested the Leeds working men rather more (though, since the working men did not have the vote, the reformers got in anyway!). In Glasgow the working classes saw no necessary connection between parliamentary reform and social reform, and Scottish MPs were well known and formidable enemies of reform.

As so often with parliamentary reform, once one looks at the detail, general patterns begin to disintegrate. There were many different groups who argued for reform between 1785 and 1815, but beyond this it is very difficult to trace any consistency between them. Some, like the Yorkshire Association, sought merely to clean up the existing system; others, like Cartwright and his followers, looked to a mythical version of the past for a model for reinventing Parliament; others, following Tom Paine, sought to set up a democratic rival Parliament along French lines; many more were prepared to be persuaded of almost any scheme that seemed likely to promise them affordable food and a living wage. Against these was the overwhelmingly strong case that Britain's triumph in the war seemed to obviate any need for far-reaching reform, and there was a sort of 'silent majority' at all levels of society, from the greatest landowners to the poorest industrial workers (and, importantly, including the king) which simply did not see that there was any particular need for reform. By the 1820s even enthusiastic and optimistic reformers like Lord John Russell were realising that, until this view changed, no measure of parliamentary reform was likely to make any headway at all.

Questions

1. 'The French Revolution did not make the need for reform any less urgent, but it did make it less likely.' Is this judgement adequate?
2. How far were the reformers themselves to blame for failing to achieve reform by 1815?
3. Who, by 1815, were more representative of the wishes of the British people, the reformers or their opponents?

SOURCES

1. THE UNREFORMED ELECTORAL SYSTEM

Source A: approximate size of the electorate in England and Wales (1831).

Counties	201,859
Boroughs	164,391
Combined	366,250

Adult male population of England and Wales in 1831: 3,463,250
Reprinted by permission of Addison Wesley Longman Ltd.

Source B: contested elections in England.

Year	Number of contests	Total constituencies	Percentage contested
1784	72	243	29.63
1790	76	243	31.28
1796	60	243	24.69
1802	73	243	30.04
1806	65	243	26.75
1807	71	243	29.22
1812	57	243	23.46
1818	93	243	38.27
1820	73	243	30.04

Reprinted by permission of Addison Wesley Longman Ltd.

Source C: parliamentary seats (1801).

	England	Wales	Scotland	Ireland	Total
County seats	80	12	30	64	188
Borough seats	405	12	15	35	465
University seats	4	0	0	1	5
Totals	489	24	45	100	658

Reprinted by permission of Addison Wesley Longman Ltd.

Source D: from a legal brief drawn up in 1762.

For a long series of years the family of Carlisle has been accustomed to name the Members of Parliament [*for the borough of Morpeth*]. From this almost uninterrupted possession they began gradually to regard it as part of their private property and . . . having previous to the late elections treated the freemen *de haut en bas** and in such manner as they judged tyrannical and an insult upon their liberties, the whole corporation and those who wished well to it were in an uproar . . . To such a height had this political contest inflamed the minds of the freemen, that any opponent of the family of Carlisle would have been received in Morpeth with open arms.

(Quoted in John Brooke, *The House of Commons, 1754–1790* (1968))

*condescendingly, in a highly patronising manner.

Source E: Sir Robert Inglis MP in the House of Commons (1 March 1831).

Such, generally speaking, as the House of Commons is now, such it has been for a long succession of years: it is the most complete representation of the interests of the people, which was ever assembled in any age or country. It is the only constituent body that ever existed, which comprehends within itself, those who can urge the wants and defend the claims of the landed, the commercial, the professional classes of the country; those who are bound to uphold the prerogatives of the Crown, the privileges of the nobility, the interests of the lower classes, the rights and liberties of the whole people. It is the very absence of symmetry in our elective franchises which admits of the introduction to this House of classes so various . . . How far, under other than the present circumstances, the rights of the distant dependencies, of the East Indies, of the West Indies, of the Colonies, of the great Corporations, of the commercial interests generally . . . could find their just support in this House, I know not.

Questions

1. Explain briefly the following references:
   a) 'University seats' (Source C) [1]
   b) 'to name the Members of Parliament' (Source D) [2]
   c) 'the very absence of symmetry in our elective franchises' (Source E) [2]
2.* How adequate are Sources A–C as evidence of the representative nature of the unreformed Parliament? [6]
3. How far does Source D support the analysis of the political system in Source E? [7]
4. Using these documents and any other evidence known to you, assess the view that the unreformed Parliament was less representative after 1815 than before it. [7]

Worked answer: Question 2

No set of statistics can be taken as adequate historical evidence on its own. The population figures are based on census returns, which were still relatively novel in the 1830s and are best treated as an approximate guide. It is particularly difficult to be precise about the numbers of voters because of the immense complexity of the franchise, and because of the sharp practice which created extra electors when they became necessary. To add to the electorate it was only necessary, for example, to create a new batch of borough freemen, or to spend a night in Preston at election time. The overall picture, of an electorate of about 11 per cent of the adult male population, is in line with estimates at the time, but does not convey the deep division of opinion amongst reformers as to whether all of this potential electorate *ought* to be enfranchised. For all but the most radical reformers, the issue was not one of round figures, but of deciding *which* further sections of the population to enfranchise.

In many ways Sources B and C are more useful. The relatively low percentage of contested elections was a major drawback to the system, though the figures perhaps reflect wider issues: the low figure for 1812 coincides with a period of major anxiety at the height of the war with Napoleon and the outbreak of Luddite activity in the north of England; the much higher figure for 1818 perhaps reflects the widespread criticism of Lord Liverpool's government in the period of radical meetings leading up to Peterloo, which was carried forward into the popular opposition to the government over the Queen Caroline affair. If so, then it could be said that the figures are some sort of guide to public opinion of the government. Source C underlines the extent to which the House of Commons was dominated by English boroughs; it does not reveal the extent to which those boroughs were themselves in the hands of boroughmongers and patrons.

The limitations of the figures lie in what they do not reveal: the corruption and sharp electoral practice, the pocket boroughs, or the unbalanced geographical spread of the representation. On the other hand, they do give actual figures to support general analyses, and in that sense they are useful supplementary evidence.

SOURCES

2. ARGUMENTS FOR AND AGAINST REFORM, 1785–1793

Source F: Pitt introducing his Parliamentary Reform Bill (18 April 1785).

MR PITT: Those who, with a sort of superstitious awe, reverence the constitution so much as to be fearful of touching even its defects, had always reprobated every attempt to purify the representation. They acknowledged its inequality and corruption, but in their enthusiasm for the grand fabric, they would not suffer a reformer, with unhallowed hands, to repair the injuries which it suffered from time. Others who, perceiving the deficiencies that had arisen from the circumstances, were solicitous of the amendment, yet resisted the attempt, under the argument, that when once we had presumed to touch the constitution in one point, the awe which had heretofore kept us back from the daring enterprize of innovation might abate, and there was no foreseeing to what alarming lengths we might progressively go, under the mask of reformation. Others there were, but for these he confessed he had not the same respect, who considered the present state of representation as pure and adequate to all its purposes, and perfectly consistent with the first principles of representation.

Source G: from the debate on Mr Flood's parliamentary reform motion (4 March 1790).

MR FLOOD: But I am told this is not the time. And why? because, forsooth, there are disturbances in France. Now first I say, that if those disturbances were ten times greater, than with every exaggeration they are represented to be, yet that mass of confusion and ruin would only render the argument more completely decisive in favour of a timely and temperate reform here. And why? because it is only from want of timely and temperate reform there that those evils have fallen upon France.

MR WINDHAM: But, Sir, were I even disposed to approve of the right honourable gentleman's notions of reform, I should still feel it my duty to object in the strongest manner to the time in which he has thought proper to bring them forward. What, would he recommend you to repair your house in the hurricane season?

MR FOX: His honourable friend had asked, Would any man repair his house in the hurricane season? He would be glad to know, what season was more proper to set about a repair in, than when a hurricane was near, and might possibly burst forth.

Source H: Pitt replying to Charles Grey's reform motion (30 April 1792).

MR PITT: He had seen with concern that those gentlemen of whom he spoke [*Charles Grey and his associates*], who were members of that House, were connected with others, who professed not reform only, but direct hostility to the very form of our government. This afforded suspicion, that the motion for a reform was nothing more than the preliminary to the overthrow of the whole system of our present government; and if they succeeded, they would overthrow what he thought the best constitution that was ever formed on the habitable globe.

Source I: Charles Grey MP introducing a parliamentary reform petition from the Society of Friends of the People (2 May 1793).

MR GREY: The business of reform appeared to have slept from 1785 to 1790, when it was again brought forward by Mr Flood. At that time, the internal convulsion in France had but just begun; and it was then asked, whether we would think of repairing our house in the hurricane season. But he should, no doubt, be told that the danger was now greater than ever this country experienced, by many degrees, for the dangers talked of at other times were held to be all of no account, when compared with the danger of what were called French principles. If, however, there was ever any danger to this country from the propagation of French principles, or from the increased dominion of France, that danger unquestionably was completely at an end; for it was impossible that any set of men, who had not actually lost their senses, should ever propose the French revolution as a model for imitation. No argument, therefore, drawn from the situation of France could apply to the kind of reform which it was the wish of those with whom he acted to introduce.

Note on language

These extracts all come from the parliamentary History of England, the precursor of the modern record of parliamentary debates, Hansard. Until the late nineteenth century, speeches were not recorded verbatim, but in reported speech, i.e. instead of it reading 'MR PITT: I believe this bill to be a disaster . . .' it would read 'MR PITT: Said he believed this bill was a disaster . . .', where 'he' refers to Mr Pitt, and not to some other person. In addition, it reflects the conventions of parliamentary language. Where there is a reference to another MP, he is referred to as 'the right honourable gentleman' or some similar form of words. Speeches in the House of Commons are technically addressed to the Speaker of the House, and this occasionally comes across in the use of 'Mr Speaker' or 'Sir', as in the extract from Windham's speech in Source G. In all these extracts 'that House' refers to the House of Commons.

Questions

1. Explain the following references:
   'They acknowledged its inequalities and corruption' (Source F) [2]
   'MR FOX' (Source G) [1]
   'French principles' (Source H) [2]
2.* Compare the reasons given in Sources F and G for opposition to reform. [6]
3. How well do Sources F–H reflect the changing arguments against parliamentary reform in the 1780s and 1790s? [6]
4. Using these documents, and any other evidence known to you, how far would you agree that in the period c.1785–c.1815 there was general consensus on the need to reform Parliament; the major disagreement was on when to do it? [8]

Worked answer: Question 2

Comparison questions are common in examinations, but frequently misunderstood by candidates: as well as looking at the similarities and differences in what the extracts contain, it is important to consider their context, their authors and any other relevant factor.

Source F is a speech of a prime minister with an electoral triumph, a strong majority in the Commons, and the staunch support of the king behind him; on the other hand, he could not afford to alienate powerful interests. Both of these considerations are shown in Source F. Pitt identifies three main types of objection: those who acknowledge the need for reform but who fear that implementing it would wreck the constitution; those who feared that beginning the process of reform, necessary though it might be, would inevitably start a process towards radical change which it would be difficult to stop; and those who saw no need for reform at all. Although Pitt points out the inconsistency of admitting the need for reform but doing nothing about it, and he injects a hint of gentle mockery ('a sort of superstitious awe', 'unhallowed hands'), it is clear that Pitt treats the first two views with some respect, while he frankly admits that he has less respect for the third view. His conflicting needs, to pass the bill but to keep the support of the back-benchers, lead him to adopt a conciliatory tone towards all but the most trenchant of his opponents.

In Source G on the other hand, Fox and Flood, as whig members in a minority opposition five years later, have no such tactical considerations and are freer to speak their minds. They are contemptous ('forsooth', 'every exaggeration') of the main argument against their reform proposal, reiterated by Windham, that with revolution under way in France ('the hurricane season') it is too dangerous to reform Parliament. Yet, although this appears to be a very different argument from those Pitt outlined in Source F, there is a similarity. The views in Source F suggest that reform would lead to unrest; five years later, but well before the situation in France had got truly violent, Pitt and Windham are arguing much the same thing.

2

THE GREAT REFORM ACT

BACKGROUND NARRATIVE

During the long wars with France, between 1793 and 1815, there was little hope of parliamentary reform being passed. Fear of revolution, seen as a particular risk given the growth of the new industrial areas, grew rather than diminished in the years after Waterloo, and Lord Liverpool's government (1812–27) resorted to a policy of strict repression. This, coupled with the serious economic hardship of the 1810s, prompted the Radicals to demand parliamentary reform, and universal suffrage in particular, and their calls received widespread working-class support. The situation reached its peak in 1819, with the famous 'Peterloo' massacre in Manchester; after Peterloo, radical activity declined, partly because leading Radicals were imprisoned, partly because the use of troops in Manchester scared many would-be demonstrators, and partly because the economy picked up in the 1820s and, as Cobbett pointed out, it is difficult to agitate a man with a full stomach.

The 1820s also saw political change. To all intents and purposes the Tories divided into two groups: the followers of William Huskisson, who were keen to address the question of parliamentary reform; and a more conservative group which included the die-hard 'Ultra-Tories' and those, notably Robert Peel, who were strongly opposed to the idea. After Liverpool's resignation in 1827 and the death of his successor, George Canning, these differences came into the open. The Huskissonites quickly became disillusioned with the leadership of the Duke of Wellington and left the government. The chances of their rejoining it, never strong, disappeared when Huskisson was killed in a railway accident in 1830.

Meanwhile, Wellington's government had been manoeuvred into an astonishing reversal of policy over Ireland. The Irish nationalist leader, Daniel O'Connell, had stood for and won the by-election in County Clare; as a Catholic he was debarred from sitting in Parliament, but such was the government's fear of a general uprising in Ireland if O'Connell were not allowed to take his seat that it hurriedly passed a Relief Act granting Catholics full political emancipation. Peel and Wellington were bitterly criticised for this, particularly by their own political supporters, who felt badly betrayed over the issue. The Tories suffered in the general election that followed in 1830 on the accession of the new king, William IV, though they retained a majority. It was widely expected, not least by many Tories, that the government would address parliamentary reform; when Wellington announced that he had no intention of doing so, the government was defeated and forced to resign.

The Whigs took office under Earl Grey, and immediately set about drafting a Parliamentary Reform Bill, which they introduced in the Commons in 1831. The bill was more radical than had been expected, and it was defeated after its second reading. The Whigs persuaded the king to dissolve Parliament, and a second general election, which was fought on the issue of reform, gave the Whigs a working majority. The bill now passed the Commons but was promptly defeated in the House of Lords. Public anger at this spilled over into serious riots in Nottingham, Derby and Bristol. The Whigs defiantly introduced a third bill, slightly modified to take some objections into account, which again was passed by the House of Commons. To overcome the anticipated opposition to the bill in the Lords, Grey then asked the king to promise to create enough peers, probably between fifty and sixty, to force it through. The king refused, and Grey and the Whigs tendered their resignations. The Duke of Wellington tried to put a government together but could not gather enough tory support, and the king was obliged to invite the Whigs back into office and to agree to create the necessary fifty Whig peers. In the end he did not need to because, rather than allow themselves to be swamped by Whigs, the Lords decided to let the bill pass. It became law (with separate measures for Scotland and Ireland) in 1832.

The Act disfranchised 56 boroughs (listed on Schedule A) and cut down 31 boroughs from two MPs to one (Schedule B). In addition

22 new two-member seats and 21 one-member seats were created and distributed among the new towns and cities; exactly the same number of seats were given to the English and Welsh counties. A further 8 seats went to Scotland and 5 to Ireland. In the counties, the 40s. freeholder remained the basic franchise, along with £10 copyholders, £10 long leaseholders and £50 tenants-at-will; in the boroughs, the £10 householder became the basic franchise, though most holders of ancient voting rights retained their vote for the duration of their lifetime. Borough voters could no longer vote in county elections.

ANALYSIS (1): WHY, BY 1830, HAD THE CASE FOR PARLIAMENTARY REFORM BECOME SO STRONG?

Although reform had been debated in Parliament on many occasions over a period of half a century by the 1830s, there was nothing inevitable about the process by which it was finally passed. In a sense, the question is wrong: the *case* for reform by 1830 was no stronger or weaker than it had been in 1820 or 1810: it was the likelihood of *achieving* reform which changed, though it seemed, if anything, more remote by the 1820s than at any time since Pitt. During the war years there had at least been the argument (whether or not one agreed with it) that it was too dangerous to engage in parliamentary reform for fear of provoking revolution, and this argument held sway until the early 1820s. However, by the mid-1820s fear of revolution had receded, and the economy had recovered enough for the government to moderate the operation of the Corn Laws, yet the campaign for parliamentary reform seemed stuck in the doldrums. Whigs and Radicals alike despaired, not so much because of the opposition of staunch Tories, which was to be expected, but because the sort of people who had gone along to protest meetings in the 1810s seemed, ten years later, to have lost interest. Yet at the end of the decade, reform became the single most important issue in British public life. Reform split the Tories, united the Whigs, brought down Wellington's government and provoked (arguably) the most serious constitutional crisis since 1688.

The speed with which reform changed from being the hobby-horse of a few backbench bores into an issue that obsessed the nation and shook the constitution requires some explanation, and there have been many conflicting theories. For a long time it was believed that the July Revolution in Paris had an important influence on events, and on the

1830 general election in particular; this view was challenged by Norman Gash, who pointed out that news of the revolution was announced in the British press too late for it to influence the polls. More recently Roland Quinault has in turn challenged Gash, pointing out that there is abundant evidence that Radicals and reformers had been following events in France very closely, and that they were consciously influenced by what was happening across the Channel.[1] There is disagreement about the role of extra-parliamentary pressure. Michael Brock, in his detailed account *The Great Reform Act*, accorded relatively little importance to the political unions which sprang up during the crisis of 1831–2 on the model of Attwood's Birmingham Union; others argue that they were much more significant than Brock allows; others still argue that the threats of these groups, like Francis Place's famous call 'To Stop the Duke, go for Gold!' were never as serious as they looked.[2] Most importantly, there is strong disagreement over whether the reform crisis was the outcome of a long process of development, or essentially a piece of glorified crisis management. Jonathan Clark, in *English Society, 1688–1832* is quite adamant: 'Reform was not the culmination of a well-informed campaign of enquiry and planning, but the hurried and confused consequence of [Catholic] emancipation'; Norman McCord (*British History, 1815–1906*) argues precisely the opposite: 'The reform of the representative system in 1832 was not a hastily planned device improvised to meet a crisis. It embodied conceptions of reform which had been discussed for many years.'

To find a way through the arguments, we need to address two subsidiary questions. Firstly, why were the opponents of reform, with all their immense powers of patronage and influence (including a large majority in the House of Lords), unable to stop a Reform Bill put forward by the same people, with the same arguments, as they had been resisting successfully for over fifty years? The answer lies in the deep divisions in the Tory party which came into the open after Lord Liverpool's retirement in 1827. Canning was a divisive and controversial figure, not least because of his support for Catholic emancipation, but the Duke of Wellington was to prove even more so. Wellington had a general's appreciation of the need to beat the occasional strategic retreat, but he lacked the politician's instinct for doing it diplomatically. Wellington quickly alienated the more liberal wing of the Tory party, associated with Huskisson. The issue which divided them was a sort of precursor in miniature of the reform crisis: the question of what to do about the shamelessly corrupt parliamentary boroughs of Penryn and East Retford. Huskisson was keen for them to be disfranchised and their four seats to be transferred to the industrial cities, but the cabinet would not go along with this. The compromise was for East Retford to be enlarged, to make it less easy to control, and for Penryn's seats to go to Manchester or Birmingham. When the House of Lords protested against the principle of transferring a parliamentary borough's seats to another borough the cabinet decided to drop the proposal for Penryn altogether, and Huskisson resigned in protest.

However, Wellington went on to anger his natural allies, the Ultra-Tories, even more than he had the Huskissonites. This time the issue was religion. Repealing the anachronistic Test and Corporation Acts, which limited public office to Anglicans only, infuriated many Tories, who took the defence of the Church of England very seriously, but it was the way Wellington and Peel forced Catholic emancipation through Parliament in 1829 which proved most damaging. Lord Winchilsea fought a duel with Wellington over the matter; Peel and Wellington were fiercely denounced as 'rats' for betraying their deepest principles (the dowager Duchess of Richmond even decorated her bedroom with stuffed rats named after the members of the cabinet!); above all, it looked as if Wellington, of all people, had given in before the threat of violence in Ireland. Many English Radicals took careful note of the success of Daniel O'Connell and his Catholic Association, noticing especially their mixture of daring but legal action with the threat, ill-defined but none the less real for that, of violence.

The consequences of Catholic emancipation were very serious indeed for the Tories. Brock argues, convincingly enough, that the traumatic experience of emancipation stiffened Peel's determination not to 'rat' again, and the obvious issue on which he might be tempted to do so was parliamentary reform. However, at exactly the same time the case for reform was beginning to be argued in an unlikely quarter: the Ultra-Tories. Taking their lead from the Marquess of Blandford, they argued that emancipation made reform suddenly necessary, if only in order to prevent Parliament from being swamped by Irish Catholics (even though emancipation was accompanied by an increase in the Irish county franchise from 40s to £10). Some Tories favoured a moderate measure of reform to steal the Whigs' thunder, but others, including Peel, were staunchly opposed to any concessions. Wellington's position was unclear. He tried hard for a reconciliation with the Huskissonites, and he also sounded Grey out about a coalition, either of which courses would have entailed introducing some sort of reform. The Tories' divisions were not helped by the strong personal animosity which emerged between Peel and Wellington after emancipation, nor by the embarrassment caused by Peel's hurriedly arranged election at Westbury, one of the most notoriously corrupt pocket boroughs in the country.

On top of all these troubles, the Tories lost one of their most important allies in the most inconvenient circumstances. King George IV lay dying through the spring and early summer of 1830, which meant that the government knew that a general election would have to be called, but could not, with any propriety, prepare for it while the king was still hanging on. The Whigs had no such problems, and consequently went into the 1830 election unusually well prepared. They were also buoyed up by the knowledge that the new king, William IV, was sympathetic to them rather than to the Tories. On paper, Wellington's ministry won the election, but there was an uncomfortably large number of MPs who were not committed to either party. Moreover, it was clear that some Tories were prepared to desert Wellington if he proposed reform, and others if he did not.

Nevertheless, as the reform crisis developed in 1830–32, the Tories showed themselves able to give the Whigs a very good run for their money. They defeated the first bill in the Commons; despite being trounced in the election that followed they fought back, this time in the House of Lords. They were able to pass amendments to the bill, notably the famous Chandos clause which gave the vote to £50 tenants-at-will, who were popularly supposed to be the most dependent and pliable pocket voters. When Grey started talking about creating whig peers, the Tories successfully stiffened the king's resistance to the idea, which led briefly to the Whigs' resignation from office. Even when they finally gave in to reform, they did so in order to preserve their hold over one of the two houses of Parliament.

But this cannot disguise the fact that time and again the Tories' best efforts against the bill were frustrated by their own deep divisions. Many Tories supported Wellington in 1830 in the expectation that he would introduce a measure of reform, and they were surprised and angry at his rejection of any measure of reform when he addressed the House of Lords after the election. Wellington, for his part, had no idea of the strength of feeling on the matter among his own followers. He did not expect the hostile reaction to his initial declaration against reform, and then later, when the Whigs offered their resignation in May 1832 and he tried to take office on the basis that he would introduce reform, he could not understand why so many Tories accused him of inconsistency and refused to serve under him.

By contrast, the Whigs and Radicals were able to sink most of their differences, at least for the duration of the crisis, in order to get the bill through. There were some differences of approach among the Whigs: the earliest proposals for the bill, which came from a special task group chaired by Lord John Russell, included vote by ballot and a proposal to shorten the length of parliaments, both of which proposals were quickly rejected by the cabinet. However, although the Whig government was itself a coalition, with old Whigs like Grey, younger, more reform-minded Whigs like Althorp, Huskissonites like Palmerston and Melbourne, radical Whigs like Lord Brougham and even an Ultra-Tory in the Duke of Richmond, they were able to hold together on the one issue which had brought them together in the first place: parliamentary reform. The Whigs were also astute in deciding to press for a relatively radical measure, startling enough to provoke scenes of disbelief when Russell introduced it into the Commons. A less radical measure might have passed more easily, but it would have stood no chance of being accepted as the 'final' solution to the problem that Grey intended the bill to be. By going for a radical approach, the Whigs were able to assure themselves of the support of the sort of middle-class interest groups which they wanted to see represented in Parliament, and whose MPs they hoped would be sitting on the government benches.

The Whigs were fortunate to enjoy the support of all the major Radicals. Prices were rising again and the sort of economic conditions which had helped produce radical activity in the 1810s seemed to be recurring. Even though the bill in each of its three versions fell far short of universal suffrage, Hunt, Cobbett and Burdett all decided that it would be better to get it passed rather than to withdraw their support and run the risk of its being defeated. Although the Tories criticised the Whigs' links with the Radicals, especially when they got wind of letters passing between Russell, Althorp and Thomas Attwood, the idea that the Whigs were dupes or stooges of the Radicals was never likely to be convincing. Since coming into office, the Whigs had been vigorously pursuing the 'Swing' rioters in the countryside, and using troops to do it. The political unions formed in many English cities amalgamated into the National Union of the Working Class (NUWC), modelled on O'Connell's Catholic Association; but although Grey accepted the NUWC's support, he did so warily and discreetly, and never owned up to any formal connection. In this way the Whigs enjoyed the support of the unions, most noticeably in the 1831 election ('The Bill, the Whole Bill and Nothing but the Bill') and in May 1832 when the unions organised the famous run on the banks ('To Stop the Duke'), yet they did not suffer by being seen to associate with dangerous radicals.

The Whigs were fortunate in other respects as well. The king proved a very willing ally. After the first bill was defeated in the Commons, William IV could not have been more accommodating to the Whigs: sweeping protocol aside, he raced to Westminster to dissolve Parliament, cramming the crown onto his head even though he had not yet been crowned, and threatening to go in a hackney carriage if no state coach was available. There is no doubting the value to the Whigs of the king's support. But when William drew back from the Whigs, unwilling to create large numbers of Whig peers simply in order to force the bill through the Lords, the Tories' failure to form an alternative government forced William to take the Whigs back on their own terms. Whether or not William would have got away with sacking the Whigs had the Tories not been so divided must remain a matter for speculation; he certainly failed when he tried again two years later, though that was after the bill had been passed. On the whole, it seems likely that while the Whigs certainly benefited from the king's support, they were not unduly hampered by his opposition.

How did the circumstances of 1831–2 affect the arguments for and against reform? In one sense, they did not: rotten boroughs were just as rotten, Old Sarum as deserted and Dunwich as wet as they had ever been. But the events of 1829–30 did significantly affect the counter-arguments in favour of the *status quo*. It had always been held that the constitution was so finely balanced, so delicate a construction, that it would not survive major change, however desirable that change might be. This was what lay behind the Ultra-Tories' predictions of ruin and desolation if reform were to be passed. It was this argument that was utterly ruined by emancipation. It was true that there had been an unspoken threat of violence in Ireland if it were not passed, but the fact remained that Catholics had been allowed into Parliament, and yet the constitution had survived. On a scale of perceived threat to the established order, parliamentary reform scored high, but Catholic emancipation was at least as feared, if not more. At a blow, therefore, a central argument against reform disappeared, and as we have seen, some of its most ardent opponents became instantly converted to the need for it, if only to maintain their position of dominance in Ireland. Small wonder that John Cannon describes Catholic emancipation as 'the battering ram that broke down the old unreformed system'.[3]

Lastly, it is impossible to ignore the enormously high hopes that were held of reform up and down the country. Radicals told their readers and their audiences that reform would pave the way to further change, in living conditions, in food prices, in social justice, as indeed some of the younger Whigs hoped that it would. This heightened public level of expectation had its effects during the reform crisis itself: it explains Brougham's triumphant election as MP for Yorkshire in 1830, an unprecedented achievement for a non-Yorkshireman; it also helps explain the serious rioting that broke out in Bristol and Nottingham when the Lords rejected the second bill. This level of unrest reinforced the case for immediate reform now, rather than later: it was quite simply too dangerous to delay any longer. Just as Wellington and Peel had granted emancipation to avoid a rising in Ireland, so the Whigs and the 'waverers' on the tory benches should grant reform as the lesser of two evils. This was the message of Macaulay's famous speech in the Commons, and was eventually the reasoning behind the Lords' decision to abandon their opposition to the bill. Whether or not Britain was really in danger of revolution in 1830 is less important than the fact that enough of the people who mattered believed that she was, and passed the bill accordingly.

In conclusion, therefore, the reason that reform was so pressing a cause in 1830, as opposed to at any earlier point, was not because of some inevitable process working itself out, but rather because the end of the decade brought a unique combination of factors which ensured that reform would happen. A divided Tory party faced a coalition of Whigs and Radicals, which enjoyed both popular support and the support of the king. The experience of emancipation suggested that reform might not be as dangerous as some feared; on the other hand, Radical activity and disturbances in the country suggested that failure to reform might be very dangerous indeed. Historians do not agree on whether the old system was worth preserving, but even those who think it was, like Norman Gash, conclude that 'the unreformed system had by 1830 one gross demerit. It was not regarded as satisfactory by the bulk of informed and influential opinion in the country.'[4] It could not go on.

Questions

1. How strong was the link between the passage of Catholic emancipation and the passage of the Great Reform Act?
2. How important to the Whigs was the support they received from: i) the Radicals and political unions, and ii) the king?

ANALYSIS (2): 'REFORM THAT YOU MAY PRESERVE' (MACAULAY). WHAT DID THE 1832 REFORM ACT REFORM, AND WHAT DID IT PRESERVE?

Macaulay was not a well known figure when he made his famous speech on the Reform Bill (he was unfamiliar enough for *Hansard* to misspell his name), but he made his name on the issue because he put the essential case for reform so succinctly and eloquently: Brougham, the Whig Lord Chancellor, made a similar case, with rather more melodrama, falling to his knees in the House of Lords. There is ample evidence, from the details of the bill in its various forms, to phrases and statements they made in innumerable letters, speeches and conversations and faithfully recorded by society diarists to show that the Whigs felt that they were acting in a spirit of preservation. Grey made no bones about it: 'the most aristocratic measure that ever was proposed in Parliament' he called it; and, indeed, one only has to look at the cabinet putting the bill forward to realise that they were hardly likely to propose anything too drastic. Yet the fact remains not only that many people of different political persuasions expected (whether in fear or in anticipation) that the bill would be a radical measure, but that when Lord John Russell introduced the first Bill in the Commons the reaction among MPs was of mounting disbelief: Peel sank his head into his hands in despair.

In order to judge how far this reaction was justified, we need to address a problem of language. The Bill certainly changed many things, but that does not by any means necessarily mean that it *reformed* those things that it changed. Concepts of 'reform' have changed considerably since the 1830s. For instance, it is often held against the Whigs that the bill had the effect not only of limiting the working-class franchise, but of reducing it, in some areas by a considerable margin. To modern, democratically-inclined minds this sounds like a step backwards; at the time, however, restricting the working-class franchise was seen as essential in order to limit the influence of wealthy patrons, whose money was such a strong temptation to poor and ill-educated voters. In Whig eyes, in other words, it could be viewed as a reform. Similar considerations applied to the redistribution proposals. Where we might think that granting representation to any sizeable town would constitute reform of the system, contemporaries saw things differently. Once a particular interest group had been catered for in the redistribution, there seemed no merit in enfranchising other towns, which would merely duplicate the influence the interest group already enjoyed. There were protests against enfranchising watering places like Brighton and Cheltenham, on the grounds that they represented no interest group worthy of the name, and their enfranchisement would only add to the general level of corruption within the system.

It is perhaps better to ask what the Whigs *thought* they were reforming. The main pattern seems clear enough: they were enfranchising new interest groups, principally in manufacturing; they were addressing the issue of the sort of extreme rotten boroughs which tended to bring the whole parliamentary system into disrepute; they were reinforcing the county representation in Parliament, long regarded as the bulwark of independence both of thought and of means; and they were redressing the balance of the constitution between Crown and Parliament. D.C. Moore argues that both the redistribution of seats and the franchise qualifications were designed for the new middle classes, in a sort of tactical regrouping by the governing class to retain its own position. This may be a bit too conspiracy-based a theory, especially given the hard bargaining that went into the final form of Schedules A and B, but it is true that the new seats were distributed according to the traditional criteria that both Whigs and Tories understood. The towns that received representation were chosen in order to represent very specific interests, like the woollen cloth trade (Frome) or shipping (Whitby). Some of the largest newly enfranchised towns had considerable electorates: 6,700 in Manchester, 4,000 in Leeds and Birmingham, 3,500 in Sheffield, and a formidable 34,000 in the new London boroughs. The sheer numbers alone would make the cost of trying to 'manage' elections in the traditional manner prohibitively expensive. At the same time, Schedule A abolished all the most notoriously rotten boroughs, like Old Sarum or pocket boroughs like Appleby, closing many familiar doors to aristocratic influence.

This had a number of repercussions for the electorate. To start with, it was much bigger, some 800,000 as against 495,000 before the Act. Moreover, the rates of actual participation in elections shot up after 1832. In fact, in due course the changes actually went further than the Whigs can either have intended or anticipated. Inflation made 40s. freeholds less of a guarantee of respectability; the boom years of the mid-century helped more people to meet the franchise qualifications laid down in 1832. In some areas, like Oxfordshire, voters proved more independent and less inclined to defer to the wishes of wealthy patrons. In due course Radical and even Chartist MPs would sit in the reformed Parliament. When Peel declared that reform opened a door that he saw no prospect of ever closing again, or Tories moaned about the thin end of the wedge, they did so with some justice.

The constitutional subtext of the Act was that, by 'purifying' Parliament, it would render it less open to 'corrupt' royal and executive influence, the cause so dear to Fox's heart and kept alive after his death at Fox dinners, in Fox clubs and in all the iconography with which the Whigs decorated their houses and educated their children. The Act's success appeared to be proved more quickly and more precisely than the Whigs could ever have hoped for. In 1834 William IV tried to impose conditions on Melbourne's appointment as prime minister, requiring specifically that Melbourne should negotiate a coalition with Peel. When Melbourne refused, the king seized the opportunity of Lord

Althorp's elevation to the Lords to sack the whole ministry. It seemed like 1783 all over again. As his father had done with Pitt, William IV imposed Peel on the Commons at the head of a minority ministry, and supported him in the election which Peel called the following year. But history did not repeat itself: although the Whigs lost about 100 seats, they still had a majority of over 100 over Peel, and promptly turned him out. This looks like a victory of a 'purified' Parliament over an unrepentant, unreconstructed king (an impression no doubt reinforced for many by the fire which destroyed the old Parliament buildings in 1834). Unfortunately, it is harder to be certain whether the lesson of the episode is that Parliament was less open to corruption, or simply that the Whigs were more popular with the electorate than either Peel or the king.

Nevertheless, the constitutional implications of 1832 were indeed considerable, though not necessarily in the way the Whigs intended. More than the provisions of the Act itself, the way in which it was passed constituted a very worrying precedent for both the monarchy and the House of Lords. Both had succumbed to pressure from the government (apparently abetted by violent mob action outside Parliament) to comply with the wishes of the Commons. In order to pass the bill, Grey had been perfectly prepared to use the monarch's powers, of dissolution and of creation of peerages, like so many spanners in a tool box. More worryingly for the conservatively-minded, the king had been forced to submit to Grey's wishes after failing to get rid of him, and the House of Lords had given in when it knew it stared defeat in the face. Even though it would be years before the implications of this were worked through, they were there for anyone to read at the time: the passage of the Great Reform Act (rather than its content) proclaimed the supremacy of the House of Commons within the constitution, and with it, the supremacy of the electorate. Ironically, in the end the Whigs would be as threatened by this process as anyone. It was why the Duke of Wellington, more astutely than he has been given credit for, saw the Reform Bill as marking the end of the power of the aristocracy, a view shared by Disraeli and reiterated by Norman Gash: 'The most revolutionary aspect of the reform crisis of 1831–2 was not the Reform Bill itself, but the coercion of the House of Lords'.[5]

If we turn to what the bill preserved, here too we face a problem of language. There were many features of the unreformed system which *survived* 1832, but these were not necessarily deliberately *preserved* by the Whigs. For instance, the obligation on ministers to stand for re-election before accepting office survived largely because the Whigs were too engrossed with other things to remove it, though they soon regretted not having dealt with it when they had the chance. There is no shortage of examples of electoral sharp practice after 1832: landlords would raise their tenants to 40s. freeholds, or else voters would tout for business among competing political patrons, but it would be unfair to ascribe the widespread survival of malpractice to a deliberate Whig policy of preservation. Rather, the Whigs sought to preserve what they perceived to be under threat which, apart from the threat to parliamentary sovereignty from the Crown, was essentially a social balance which seemed to be under threat from the mob.

It is tempting to cite the Bristol and Nottingham reform riots as evidence here, and indeed these were serious disturbances; but whether or not they constituted a threat to the constitution is more debatable. In each case they were sparked off by a specific combination of local factors, such as the arrival in Bristol of the vociferous opponent of reform, Sir Charles Wetherall, who also happened to be Recorder for the city. Although riots were undoubtedly unpleasant and dangerous, they had happened before without threatening revolution. The Gordon riots in 1780 engulfed London for a week, and the anti-war riots of the 1790s, or the Spa Fields riot of 1816, even military action at Peterloo, had not in the end undermined the constitution. Violent riot, arising suddenly on a local or national issue and dying down again as suddenly as it broke out, was virtually a feature of urban life in the period. In any case, the Whigs showed themselves just as capable as the Tories of taking a tough line on urban riots: their reaction to the Coldbath Fields riots of 1833 was likened by the Radical press to the worst excesses of Peterloo or Tolpuddle.

What was much more worrying was the outbreak of 'Captain Swing' riots in the south-east in 1830. These were rural, they appeared to be organised and co-ordinated, presumably through an underground network of cells, they involved threats aimed at named individuals, and they set about the systematic destruction of landed property. It would be hard to come up with a better combination of factors guaranteed to scare the nineteenth-century landed classes out of their wits. The Whigs were as determined as any other landowners to preserve their position against this sort of threat, and they mobilised all the forces at their disposal, including cavalry and spies, to put it down. This fear of subversion in the rural areas no doubt helps explain the government's uncompromising stance in the Tolpuddle case in 1834.

In this sense, the bill sought to preserve the country from violent revolution. The Whigs were aware of the support among working people for the bill, indeed they benefited from it in the elections of 1830 and 1831. However, they were also quite determined not to allow the working classes to hold any sort of dominant position in the new electoral system. Passing the bill therefore saved the country from risings and rebellion; the content of the bill saved the country from the 'evils' of democracy. Needless to say, disappointment among the working classes was likely to be intense once they realised how little they had gained from the bill, but by then they would have lost their middle-class allies, won over to the system by the bill, and would be powerless to do anything about it.

Macaulay spoke of reforming that you may preserve; it would have been more accurate to point out that reforming and preserving were, to all intents and purposes, two sides of the same process. The Whigs reformed the old system in order to preserve it in something like its original, purer shape. The system they were trying to establish through the Great Reform Act was essentially the same parliamentary system, suitably modified to meet the changed situation of the 1830s, that had flourished in the time of the elder Pitt and Fox, the system as it had been before George III had so hastened the growth of executive power. In that sense, it was a 'final' measure, ending a particular phase in the story of Parliament. Sadly for the Whigs, there were plenty of others who did not regard the Great Reform Act as a final measure, and it was the Whigs' own tactics in pushing the bill through which provided the model for pressing ahead to the next stage in the drama.

Questions

1. What considerations governed the redistribution of seats in the Great Reform Act?
2. How did the Great Reform Act help to redress the constitutional balance between king and Parliament?
3. How successful was the Reform Act in preserving the established political and social order in Britain?

SOURCES

1. THE REFORM CRISIS, 1831–2

Source A: Thomas Babington Macaulay MP, speaking in the debate on the first Reform Bill (2 March 1831).

Turn where we may, within, around, the voice of great events is proclaiming to us, reform, that you may preserve. Now, therefore, while everything at home and abroad forebodes ruin to those who persist in a hopeless struggle against the spirit of the age; now, while the crash of the proudest throne on the Continent is still resounding in our ears; now, while the roof of a British palace affords an ignominious shelter to the exiled heir of forty kings; now, while we see on every side ancient institutions subverted and great societies dissolved; now, while the heart of England is still sound; now, while old feelings and old associations retain a power and charm which may too soon pass away; now, in this, your accepted time; now, in this your day of salvation, take counsel, not of prejudice, not of party spirit, not of the ignominious pride of a fatal consistency, but of history, of reason, of the ages which are past, of the signs of this most portentous time. Pronounce in a manner worthy of the expectation with which this great debate has been anticipated, and of the long remembrance which it will leave behind. Renew the youth of the state. Save property, divided against itself. Save the multitude, endangered by its own ungovernable passions. Save the aristocracy, endangered by its own unpopular power. Save the greatest, and fairest, and most highly civilised community that ever existed from the calamities which may in a few days sweep away all the rich heritage of so many ages of wisdom and glory. The danger is terrible. The time is short. If this bill should be rejected, I pray to God that none of those who concur in rejecting it may ever remember their votes with unavailing remorse amidst the wreck of laws, the confusion of ranks, the spoliation of property, and the dissolution of social order.

Source B: Doherty's *Voice of the People*, a radical newspaper (1 January 1831).

Tell us not that the people have no power but in the field – no authority but with the pike or the pistol. Tell us not that they must wait to be led to the conflict for freedom by the wealthy and the influential. The Catholics of Ireland have taught us how to control and to command governments without battle and without blood . . . The gallant artisans of Paris have shown us the way to victory without the aid of the proud and pampered . . . aristocrat.

Source C: the *Edinburgh Review*, a Whig journal (June 1831).

Many . . . do not dread the progress of republican principles, but they are afraid the Reformed Parliament will be driven by the popular impulse to effect great changes in the system of our jurisprudence by wholesale, and without sufficient deliberation. Is there any solid foundation for this fear? We apprehend that the House of Commons will be influenced by the sentiments prevailing, not among the whole multitudes sometimes assembled at public meetings, but among those who constitute the body of electors; that is, the middle classes as well as the upper; those possessing some property, and tolerably well informed upon political matters.

Source D: the *Quarterly Review*, a Tory journal (February 1831).

One calls for reform, because it is to be the precursor of unbounded freedom of trade; another sees in it the triumphant revival of the old system of protecting duties and monopoly; – the bullionist relies on a reformed parliament for the defeat of all future attempts to tamper with the metallic currency; while the champion of paper trusts that it may yet save the nation by a copious issue of one-pound notes; – the people of Liverpool hail in its advent the total and instant downfall of the East India Company; – the saints* the equally total and instant emancipation of the West Indian slaves; – to the Whig it is the millennium of office . . .

What can be the motive of all these sudden conversions to the cause of parliamentary reform? The answer is short enough, and must be on the lips of every one who is not afraid to look at the truth. It is the *dread of physical force*.

*Saints: the popular nickname for the evangelical movement within the Church of England, prominent in the campaign against slavery.

Questions

1. Explain the following phrases:
   i 'the crash of the proudest throne on the Continent' (Source A) [2]
   ii 'property' (Source A) [1]
   iii 'The Catholics of Ireland' (Source B) [2]
2.* Comment on the use of language and tone in Source B. [3]
3. Evaluate Source C as evidence of whig expectations of reform. [4]
4. Compare the analysis in Sources A and D of the reasons for passing the Reform Bill. [6]
5. Using these documents and your own knowledge, how real was the threat of serious social upheaval if the Reform Bill were not to be passed? [7]

Worked answer: Question 2

As a radical newspaper, the *Voice of the People* adopts a suitably defiant ('Tell us not . . . ') and scornful ('proud and pampered . . . aristocrat') tone towards those who would oppose the Reform Bill. The extract is peppered with the language of violence – 'pike', 'pistol', 'conflict for freedom', 'battle', 'blood', and so on, yet the message is more subtle and, in its way, more threatening. It is saying that the people can act on their own initiative and use the *threat* of violence (but a threat which can easily be carried out) to gain their ends. To convey this, the author deliberately uses language guaranteed to alarm the landed classes and inspire his working-class readership: 'conflict for freedom' and the 'gallant' revolutionaries in Paris on the one hand, and the inspiring (or chilling) spectacle of O'Connell's Catholic Association showing the working classes 'how to control and to command governments' on the other. It would galvanise a tavern or cause a Tory to choke on his breakfast.

SOURCES

2. THE IMPACT OF THE GREAT REFORM ACT

Source E: Charles Greville's diary.

15 March 1831

When it [*reform*] comes into operation how disappointed everybody will be, and first of all the people; their imaginations are raised to the highest pitch, but they will open their eyes very wide when they find no sort of advantage accruing to them . . . Then they will not be satisfied, and as it will be impossible to go back, there will be plenty of agitators who will preach that we have not gone far enough; and if a Reformed Parliament does not do all that popular clamour shall demand, it will be treated with very little ceremony.

Source F: Lord Eldon, speaking against the second reading of the Reform Bill in the House of Lords (7 October 1831).

LORD ELDON: The Bill will be found, I fear from my soul, to go to the length of introducing in its train, if passed, universal suffrage, annual Parliaments, and vote by ballot. It will unhinge the whole frame of society as now constituted . . . with this Bill in operation, the Monarchy cannot exist, and . . . it is totally incompatible with the existence of the British constitution.

Source G: *Hansard's Parliamentary History* (4 June 1832).

THE EARL OF WINCHILSEA said, he suffered a pain of mind greater than he could express in thinking that he had lived to that hour to witness the downfall of his country. That night would close the first act of the fatal and bloody tragedy. It would close the existence of that House as one branch of the Legislature, for its independence, which was its brightest ornament, had fallen, and without that independence it might be considered as having ceased to exist.

Source H: the *Westminster Review*, a Tory journal (1833).

The landed interest must always exercise great sway in public affairs; for that class alone have much leisure to meddle in them. The intelligence of the other classes is absorbed, if not exclusively, yet in a great degree, in the business of money-making . . . The men who have the leisure for intrigue, from whose coteries the ministries are formed, and whose leisure finds no other occupation than to tattle on the politics of the day, to clog the steps of officials, and flutter from club to club – are of the landed interest.

Source I: Charles Greville's diary.

December 4, 1835

Lord Segrave has got the Gloucestershire Lieutenancy, and this appointment, disgraceful in itself, exhibits all the most objectionable features of the old borough-mongering system, which was supposed to be swept away. He was in London as soon as the breath was out of the Duke of Beaufort's body, went to [*Lord*] Melbourne, and claimed this appointment on the score of having three members, which was more than any other man in England now returned.

Questions

1. Explain the following references:
   i 'annual Parliaments, and vote by ballot' (Source F) [2]
   ii 'the most objectionable features of the old system' (Source I) [2]
2. To what extent does Source I confirm the outlook in Source E? [3]
3. How justified are the arguments in Source F against reform? [4]
4.* Account for the different views on the power of the landed classes expressed in Sources G and H. [7]
5. Using these documents and your own knowledge, who can be said to have lost most from the Great Reform Act, the working classes or the House of Lords? [7]

Worked answer: Question 4

Both extracts present the Tory view of events, but the most obvious difference between them is that Lord Winchilsea is speaking in the House of Lords in despair and desperation as he sees the Reform Bill about to pass into law, while the *Westminster Review* is being written in calm reflection a year after the event. There is nothing in the extract from the *Westminster Review* with which Winchilsea would disagree, except perhaps its confidence that the power of the landed classes would last, for in 1832 Winchilsea, and he was far from alone in his view, considered that the days of the landed aristocracy were numbered.

The reason why the *Review* was able to take a more optimistic view so soon after the bill's passage was essentially because the bill itself did not materially affect the power of the aristocracy – indeed, the Whigs specifically intended that it should not. Despite the gains made by the middle classes in 1832, the *Review* is essentially right in seeing that the landed classes had retained their position at the head of government and society for so, at that date, they had. Winchilsea, on the other hand, was inclined to look more deeply at the changes Parliament was introducing (it was he who fought a duel with Wellington over Catholic emancipation). Although we may make allowances for the emotion of the occasion, his basic message, that by allowing itself to be coerced by the Commons into passing the bill the House of Lords was surrendering its independence, was to be fully justified in the longer term. In a sense, then, although the *Review* was written as a sober analysis in the aftermath of the bill, its view was actually more short-term and superficial, more deceived by appearances, than Winchilsea's impassioned plea issued in the full heat of the moment.

3

CHARTISM: THE DEMAND FOR UNIVERSAL SUFFRAGE

BACKGROUND NARRATIVE

Chartism remains probably the best known of the Victorian working-class movements. It has remained the subject of historio-graphical debate and argument, not just because historians debate such things anyway, but because the story of Chartism still has the power to arouse passions, especially in politically conscious writers.

In the years between the Great Reform Act of 1832 and the revival of parliamentary reform as a major political issue in the 1860s, it was the Chartists who kept the reform question alive and in the public eye. The 1834 Poor Law Amendment Act had provoked widespread fury among the working classes, and there followed a series of concerted attacks on workhouses – 'Bastilles' as they were often termed. The campaign against the new Poor Law was a forerunner of Chartism, though its immediate origins lay in the collapse of Robert Owen's Grand National Consolidated Trades Union, which was killed off after the famous Tolpuddle case in 1834. Tolpuddle's fate discouraged ambitious national movements for a while, and instead there was a spread of locally-based associations of working men.

One of these was the London Working Men's Association, founded by William Lovett in 1836. Lovett soon saw that better conditions for working men would only come from a Parliament prepared to listen to them; he therefore put forward proposals for a radical overhaul of Parliament, and framed them in a Charter, a word which for Victorians carried thrilling overtones of Magna Carta and the long battle for English liberty. The Charter's main proposals were summarised in the famous six points of the chartist programme: universal (male) suffrage, vote by secret ballot, equal electoral districts, annual parliaments, payment of MPs, and the abolition of the property qualification for sitting in Parliament. The programme quickly won considerable popular appeal, and within a year the Charter was presented to Parliament supported by a huge petition – parliamentary petitions of awesome size being a feature of popular political activity in this period.

Parliament, as alarmed by the swell of popular support for the Charter as it was by its actual demands, refused even to accept the petition but, nothing daunted, the Chartists set about gathering signatures for a second one. The process of doing so saw some remarkable political activity. The Chartists developed a sophisticated organisational structure, foreshadowing those of later political parties, with carefully thought-out propaganda, a chartist news-paper, large public meetings and a pool of effective speakers, administered centrally, to travel round the country to address them. The Chartists set up a National Convention (whose name had more unsettling connotations with the French Revolution) as a sort of alternative Parliament. Lovett's leadership was enhanced by powerful and charismatic figures like Feargus O'Connor and Bronterre O'Brien. But despite all its efforts the movement's second attempt to petition Parliament, in 1842, met the same fate as the first.

After the failure of 1842 disillusion set in. Popular support for Chartism died away. Many Chartists channelled their energies into other movements, like the early trade unions, or else tried to establish land-holding schemes or schools on Chartist principles; others travelled abroad in search of the opportunity to fulfil their ideas, especially to the western United States. The revolutionary year 1848 brought an unexpected opportunity to have another attempt at pressurising Parliament, and a huge Chartist meeting was held on Kennington Common to be followed by a march to Westminster with yet another 'monster' petition. This time

Parliament, which had brought in troops and enrolled special constables to protect London from revolution, agreed to receive the petition; however, on examination the charter proved to contain a large number of obviously false signatures, including names like 'Mr Punch', 'Victoria Rex' and the Duke of Wellington. After all the build-up, this revelation proved too humiliating for the Chartists, and their cause was effectively, not to say literally, laughed out of Parliament. To all intents and purposes, Chartism as a movement was dead.

ANALYSIS (1): WAS CHARTISM A REVOLUTIONARY MOVEMENT?

It would be hard to conceive of Lord John Russell and Karl Marx agreeing on much, but they were as one on their view of Chartism: they each, from their different perspectives, saw it as a potentially revolutionary movement. Marx, who knew England well, was convinced that Chartism embodied the reaction of the working class against their economic exploitation: first they would demand political power, then social equality, until eventually they would cause the entire capitalist system to collapse. Russell and other leading politicians, though they would not have carried their analysis as far as Marx, nevertheless felt they knew a revolutionary movement when they saw one. Russell, Palmerston and Peel were all born in the late eighteenth century, and knew about the fears of French revolutionary ideas at first hand; more recently they had seen revolution sweep Latin America (admittedly to Britain's economic advantage), destabilise Italy, bring down another French regime in 1830, sweep the Dutch from Belgium, and cause appallingly bloody civil wars in Portugal and Spain.

Just like the post-Waterloo generation of Radicals, the Chartists seemed to relish revolutionary language and symbols, guaranteed to make the propertied classes' flesh creep. They staged vast public meetings, which threw up shades of Peterloo or O'Connell's Catholic Association in Ireland; they seemed to have more regard for their National Convention, whose members even proudly put MC (Member of the Convention) after their names, than for Parliament itself; and throughout the period of the chartist movement, never far from the surface, was the threat of violence. This is what lay behind the refusal of governments, Whig or Tory, to listen to Chartist petitions until by 1848 they felt it was no longer safe to refuse; it was also why the authorities were so ready to call out troops in response to Chartist activity, to the point in 1848 where the Duke of Wellington was called out of retirement to supervise the defence of London.

On the whole, although their reasons also differ, historians have required more to convince them of Chartism's revolutionary credentials. In 1918 Mark Hovell in *The Chartist Movement* argued that Chartism was essentially a moderate movement, a sort of precursor of Lloyd George's style of Liberalism, and that it would probably have succeeded had it not been misdirected by hotheads like O'Connor. Hovell was almost certainly indulging in wishful thinking, and his analysis has not survived into more recent writings. Asa Briggs in *Chartist Studies* (1959) looked in depth at the local manifestations of Chartism, and, perhaps not surprisingly, he saw the movement as more of a network of local, essentially separate protest movements rather than anything like a co-ordinated attempt at revolutionary change. Gareth Stedman Jones concentrated on one of the more telling aspects of Chartism: its use of revolutionary language and symbols.[1] Jones disagreed with Briggs in that he saw Chartism very much as a national movement; however, he ageed that it was not a revolutionary one. Jones argued that Chartism's use of language, along with its red caps of liberty and white hats of the sort favoured by Henry Hunt in the 1810s, was simply continuing the traditional language of protest against 'Old Corruption' which went back well into the eighteenth century, and was therefore not really a reflection of class consciousness at all.

Other historians, on the other hand, have been more inclined to agree with Marx or Russell. D.J.V. Jones, who studied the Newport rising in detail, observed that it was a major incident, with more people killed (twenty-two) than in any comparable incident in the nineteenth century.[2] He pointed out that it was both planned and politically motivated: 'It was an overt exercise in direct action, with Newport gaol as the Winter Palace'. If that seems a rather dramatic view (though that does not mean it is wrong), Dorothy Thompson would certainly agree with it: she stresses the importance of political motives in Chartism, as opposed to economic or social ones, and she sees the movement's fate as the result of a straightforward class-based political battle which it was unable to win.[3] The Chartist programme, she argues, was very radical, even revolutionary, in its implications: for example, the demand for annual parliaments, often passed over quickly even by sympathetic historians because it seems so naive and impractical, was in fact a serious attempt at mass participation in politics, effectively rule by referenda.

Edward Royle has pointed out that the 1830s saw elections in

1830, 1831, 1832, 1835 and 1837, which was getting on for the chartist ideal.[4] However, these were exceptions: two elections (1830 and 1837) were occasioned by the death of the monarch, one (1831) by the reform crisis and one (1832) by the need to implement the terms of the Great Reform Act, leaving one (1835) which was in effect triggered by William IV's unexpected dismissal of the Melbourne ministry in 1834. In other words, these elections are very much the exceptions rather than the rule, and, if anything, the fact that frequent elections were a feature of a decade of political crisis and instability underlines the radicalism of the Chartists' demand for them to be made annual events. Indeed, for Dorothy Thompson, Chartism failed precisely *because* it was so revolutionary: the authorities were determined to kill it.

There is no reason why all, or at any rate most, of these views should not be right, or at least compatible. It is, for example, perfectly possible for the march on Newport Gaol to have had revolutionary intentions which the rest of the movement did not share. It is in any case difficult to judge the revolutionary potential of Chartism precisely because it did fail: many movements only really develop into fully-fledged revolution once they have succeeded in gaining power – the French Revolution is a good example of this, as is the English Civil War. To judge the revolutionary nature of Chartism we need to consider its aims, its leaders and supporters, and the methods it adopted to put its message across.

The Chartists' aims are so familiar to anyone who studies the period, and with the exception of annual parliaments, they are so easily accepted in today's democratic system that it is difficult to conceive how they could have been regarded as revolutionary, either by the reform-minded Victorians or by communists like Marx and Engels. For one thing, their demands were not necessarily unreasonable, by the standards of even the time. By no means all the features of Parliament they wanted to change were as ancient as is (and was) often supposed. The property qualification for MPs, for example, only dated from the early eighteenth century, and the insistence that it should be landed property had been dropped as recently as 1838 without apparent threat to the fabric of the constitution. Vote by ballot was a frequently raised issue, and in 1839 over 200 MPs had voted in favour of it. In their writings the Chartists went to considerable lengths to calm fears that they were set on a revolutionary path. Nevertheless, the fact that they felt they had to defend themselves against this accusation is itself an indication of how radical their programme was.

It would be overstating it to say that any one of their demands was perceived as a threat to the Constitution, but taken all at once, as the

Chartists intended them to be taken, the demands were not so much for a reform of Parliament as for a complete change in its purpose. Payment for MPs and the abolition of the property qualification, for example, would not only allow the working classes to sit in Parliament, but would undermine the entire system of parliamentary patronage. Even so apparently innocuous a demand as equal electoral districts carried profound implications: it threatened the traditional county constituencies, still regarded as the bedrock of English independence; coupled with a secret ballot it also suggested that MPs should be much closer, and therefore more answerable, to their constituents. The traditional role of MPs had been defined by the eighteenth-century political philosopher, Edmund Burke: he argued that they were elected as representatives, chosen for their personal and political qualities and, once elected, they were trusted to act and vote as they saw fit. The logic of the Chartists' demands, on the other hand, was that MPs would become mere delegates, voting on every issue as their constituents wished, and obliged to refer back to them frequently. There will always be argument about whether this constituted a *threat* to the constitution, but Parliament was surely right to recognise in the Chartist programme a blueprint for a complete, root-and-branch *overhaul* of the parliamentary constitution as it then existed.

Nervous politicians, scared by the radicalism of the Chartists' aims, were not likely to be reassured by the Chartists themselves. For one thing, the Chartist leaders were not newcomers to radical political activity. Lovett and Bronterre O'Brien had been active supporters of Robert Owen's movement, O'Connor had been a leading figure in the long and bitter battle against the Poor Law Amendment Act (when the Houses of Parliament burned down in 1834 it was widely interpreted as divine retribution for the introduction of the workhouse). The Charter was drawn up by Lovett in conjunction with the experienced Radical MP Francis Place, who had engineered the repeal of the Combination Laws, and the up-and-coming Radical John Roebuck. Other fiery Radicals included J.R. Stephens and John Frost. Early on, the movement enjoyed the support of the financial reformer, Thomas Attwood, who had built up a novel and sophisticated urban political organisation, the Birmingham Political Union. Chartism, in other words, combined experienced Radicals who knew a thing or two about political campaigning, with the very latest techniques in large-scale political mobilisation. Not until after the 1867 Reform Act would the mainstream political parties have anything to match the Chartists' powers of organisation.

The Chartists' techniques were imaginative and often audacious.

Political unions on the Birmingham model were founded in Leeds and Newcastle; when their petitions were rejected, the Chartists employed strike action and, in the 'Plug Plots', industrial sabotage; when Church leaders spoke out against Chartism, Chartists took to packing churches (arriving early, so as to occupy rich parishioners' private pews) and trying to persuade the vicar to preach on a suitably Chartist text. When O'Connor was released from prison in 1841 he was carried in triumph in a carriage in the shape of a conch shell, pulled by six white stallions decked out in pink and green velvet – it was precisely the sort of crowd-pleasing showmanship that Henry Hunt had engaged in in the days before Peterloo. Above all, the *Northern Star* and the Chartist Convention showed Parliament that here was a movement that not only sought parliamentary reform, but actually rejected Parliament's very authority: the *Northern Star* even referred to it as 'the Imperial Parliament' to distinguish it from the Chartist Convention, the 'real' Parliament.

The radicalism of Chartism is further underlined by its failure to maintain any sort of long-term alliance with more moderate groups. Attwood himself, never an enthusiastic supporter of universal suffrage, quickly disassociated himself from Chartism. Although they were opposed to the Corn Laws, the Chartists remained very wary of Richard Cobden and the Anti-Corn Law League and only entered into what proved abortive negotiations to combine forces with the greatest reluctance. This was largely because they perceived the League as a middle-class, employer-dominated association which would be unlikely to offer much more than temporary support to a working-class movement like Chartism. On the other hand, the Chartists were quite happy to seek the support of women. It had originally been intended that the Charter should simply demand universal suffrage, though this was soon altered to universal male suffrage: female suffrage was thought too radical a proposal even for the likes of O'Connor or O'Brien. Nevertheless, women continued to play an important role in Chartist activity, and the movement was one of the most important vehicles for female political activity before the suffragettes.

However, for contemporaries, the most telling evidence of the radical nature of Chartism was its propensity for violence. The most notorious example was the Newport rising, but there were plenty of other examples, most of them local though some, like the Birmingham Bull Ring riots, of national significance. Many historians have, rather rigidly, divided the Chartists into 'physical-force' Chartists, who advocated violence, and 'moral-force' Chartists who did not. Clearly some Chartists did relish violence: the Newport marchers were carrying large numbers of guns, and some Chartists, especially Irish immigrants, used the language of violence and threat in their speeches. But in fact nearly all Chartist leaders sanctioned the use of force at one point or another. O'Connor and O'Brien are well known for it, but even William Lovett, usually regarded as the epitome of the respectable, 'moral-force' Chartist, was capable of using violent language and condoning the use of force in the face of provocation by the authorities. It was this drift towards what seemed to be a more violent approach which alienated Thomas Attwood, and helped him decide to drop out of the movement. Nor can we entirely ignore the obvious point that the governments of the day clearly regarded Chartism as a potentially violent movement and took defensive measures accordingly.

However, the evidence simply is not there to make Chartism into a revolutionary movement bent on the use of force to overturn the constitution. If we cannot ignore the views of the Whig and Tory governments of the 1840s, neither, in all fairness, can we ignore the protestations of the Chartists themselves that they intended no violence. In fact, perhaps the most telling objection to the proposition that Chartism was a violent movement is that Chartist violence was so spasmodic and ill-planned, especially if we compare it with other movements which clearly were more violently inclined. There was no attempt at any time to erect or defend barricades in the street (except, of course, by the government in 1848), as contemporary European revolutionaries did almost on instinct; nor, despite the Plug Plot, was there anything to compare with, say, the systematic use of violence against property and persons employed later by the suffragettes. Chartism's major weapon throughout was the perfectly respectable and constitutional petition, in which the Chartists were following the precedent set by, amongst others, Christopher Wyvill's impeccably Tory Yorkshire Association in the 1770s. When violence broke out it was invariably in reaction to moves by the authorities, such as the arrest and incarceration of John Frost at Newport in 1839, or Parliament's refusal even to look at the mammoth 1842 petition, which sparked off a further and serious round of riots and disturbances.

Of course it might be said that when the Chartists wanted to fight they seemed to have suspiciously easy access to the weapons with which to do it, but we need to remember the age in which they were living. It is not that England in the 1840s was a particularly violent society – it was not – but it was neither as difficult nor as remarkable for people to get hold of weapons as it is today. In the countryside hunting weapons were commonplace, and in the towns a certain number of muskets and pistols seem to have come home with soldiers from the

Napoleonic Wars, not to mention fresh supplies available at any gunsmith's. However, the weapon most commonly mentioned by those who would make the Chartists into violent subversives is the pike. Whenever rumours spread that the Chartists were arming, it was usually in terms of large numbers of pikes – relatively easy for any blacksmith worth his salt to fashion from household or agricultural tools.

In fact, pikes seem to have been a common theme of nineteenth-century insurrectionary plans: the American abolitionist, John Brown, for example, put in an order for thousands of pikes to arm the vast army of slaves he confidently expected would come running to his side when he seized the federal armoury at Harper's Ferry in 1859. Why pikes? Apart from the obvious point that they were cheaper than firearms, we need to consider what pikes might be used *for*. They would be of little use as an offensive weapon against troops armed with muskets; on the other hand, they might be a very effective *defensive* weapon against cavalry. Since cavalrymen usually used their sabres in battle, whether against an armed foe or (as the Chartists knew only too well) against the civilian population of Manchester, pikes would either deter a cavalry attack altogether or, if that failed, allow for a fight on more equal terms. Every precedent screamed at the Chartists that the authorities would use force, and that the most likely form it would take would be cavalry action. It is not only that we can hardly blame the Chartists for arming themselves in advance: it would have been foolish, not to say irresponsible, of them not to.

Does this mean that Chartism cannot be considered a revolutionary movement? Inevitably, when a word like 'revolutionary' appears in this sort of context much hangs on the definition that is given to it. In the sense in which the word was generally used and understood (and practised) in the 1840s, that is, a violent upheaval of the working classes, with support and leadership from the radical middle classes, aimed at destabilising and overturning the existing regime, Chartism, despite a certain superficial resemblance, did not qualify as a revolutionary movement. In due course, Marx came to realise this, and it is no coincidence that the next movement which excited his expectation was the much more radical (and violent) Paris Commune of 1870–71. But if Chartism's methods were less revolutionary than they appear at first sight, its aims were, perhaps, the other way round: they seem more revolutionary the closer one looks at them. Of course, in many ways Chartism was a very conventional, one could even say conservative, movement: it sought to reform Parliament, not to abolish it: although there were republicans among the Chartists, on the whole Chartism refrained from attacking the monarchy, and a republican constitution was never one of its aims. The Chartists had little but contempt for the peerage, and not without reason, but there is no argument for abolishing the House of Lords, or even reforming it, in the Chartist programme.

Perhaps most remarkably, unlike contemporary movements in Europe, the Chartists did not even argue for a written constitution as such, except in the relatively limited form of the Charter itself. But then, perhaps with the Charter they did not need to, for the Charter, had it been accepted when it was presented, would have constituted a radical enough change in Parliament's function in society. From being a sort of club through which the ruling classes maintained their rule and from which the great mass of the population was excluded, the Charter would have changed Parliament, or at least the Commons, into a national assembly, to which the people at large had ready access (abolition of property qualification, payment of MPs, equal electoral districts) and over which they would have been able to exercise considerable control (universal suffrage, annual parliaments, vote by ballot). It would have meant breaking at a stroke the landed classes' patronage system both at local and at national level, and it would have brought British politics closer to the American system, where anyone could aspire to the highest reaches of the legislature or executive, and democracy was truly (and to many British eyes, appallingly) open. Most of the establishment's opposition to Chartism was instinctive, but those who thought about it more deeply found even more compelling reasons to set their faces firmly against it. And against those stern unyielding faces, Chartism broke.

Questions

1. To what extent do historians' interpretations of Chartism depend on whether they look at it from a national or a regional perspective?
2. What were the main reasons in the 1840s for regarding Chartism as a potentially revolutionary movement?
3. Why were both the Chartists and the authorities prepared to resort to the use of force?

ANALYSIS (2): WHAT DID CHARTISM ACHIEVE?

Chartism is usually deemed a failure, even by sympathetic historians. In terms of the aims which it set itself and repeated frequently, it is hard to see how else the movement can be regarded. Despite all its activity in

1838–42 it did not even manage to persuade Parliament to look at its petitions, and its revival in 1848 was more due to a further downturn in the economy than to any particular efforts of the Chartists themselves. In fact, many commentators at the time and since have described Chartism as a 'knife-and-fork question', that is, one which only attracted support when people were hungry and food prices were high; there was no depth of support for its aims and, when things got better, popular support for Chartism died away. Although all the Chartist demands except annual parliaments were eventually granted, the first, abolition of the property qualification for MPs, did not happen until 1858 and Chartism can claim little direct credit for it. In its own terms Chartism failed and failed conclusively, particularly when one compares it with other, equally well orchestrated campaigns, such as the anti-slavery movement, and especially the campaign against the Corn Laws. Chartism joins a long line of defeats for the workers, from the 1848 revolutions, through the Paris Commune and the General Strike right up to the 1984 miners' strike.

This fact seems so inescapable that the main line pursued by historians sympathetic to Chartism is not to present it as a success, which it patently was not, but to save the movement from scorn and ridicule. Clive Behagg, who has written extensively on Chartism, entitled one of his articles 'Taking Chartism Seriously' (*Modern History Review*, 7 (4) April 1996), and it is not hard to see why. When the 1848 petition flopped, there was a reaction of immense relief amongst those who had been so fearful of Chartism, and while part of this took the form of vilifying the chartist leaders and the so-called 'physical-force' element, another part of it viewed the rank-and-file Chartists as well-meaning but naive figures, rather touching in their simple affectations, such as putting MC after their names or presuming to address the House of Commons on equal terms. And, of course, female Chartists were widely regarded as figures of great fun. Chartism was subjected to that peculiarly English treatment by which a conservative establishment patronises and gradually grows more indulgent towards, even fond of, its bitterest opponents. Small wonder, then, that left-wing historians have sought to extricate the memory of Chartism from being smothered in a sort of patronising sentimentality.

However, instinct suggests that Chartism cannot be left there. The movement was simply too big, too well organised and orchestrated not to have any further significance. At the very least, it was remarkably prescient in its aims and would merit attention for this on its own. But beyond that, it seems unlikely that such a large movement of the working class, operating on such a wide scale in the Britain of the

1840s, should not have achieved anything. And indeed, there are a number of achievements with which Chartism can be credited, many of which came well within the lifetimes of most of those who participated in Chartist activities and all of which were of important long-term significance.

The first is the effect of Chartism on the parliamentary reform issue. Let us not forget that the 1832 Reform Act was widely regarded as a final measure, thanks to which the question of the reform of Parliament would never have to be revisited: Lord John Russell earned his famous nickname 'Finality Jack' for putting forward precisely this view. And in the terms in which the Great Reform Act was conceived, he was right. The question of the balance between the power of the Crown and the Executive on the one hand and the power of Parliament on the other did not have to be addressed in any of the Reform Acts that followed. What the Chartists did was to move the debate on from an essentially eighteenth-century constitutional agenda to a nineteenth-century democratic one. At precisely the time that the Whigs were congratulating themselves that, whatever else they might have got wrong, at least they had reformed Parliament properly, the Chartists pointed out that it was the reformed Parliament that was so inequitable in its composition and disreputable in its conduct. Naturally, the members of that *reformed* Parliament were not keen to hear this message, but in terms of determining thinking about Parliament and its representative function, the Chartists did have an important influence.

In 1839 and 1842 the House of Commons, even though it voted to reject the Chartist petitions, nevertheless debated the issue of the Charter and its demands at considerable length, and no MP in the 1840s can have been unfamiliar with the arguments in favour of an extension of the franchise into the working classes. Sure enough, by the 1850s reform was back on the agenda again, and the decade 1850–1860 saw no fewer than four bills, three of them proposed by 'Finality Jack' Russell himself. These bills differed in their details, and in particular in their attitude towards redistribution of parliamentary seats, but they all contained proposals for extending the franchise into the upper reaches of the urban working class: it was not by any means the Chartist idea of universal suffrage, but it did mean that within a few years of Chartism's collapse politicians on both sides were putting forward proposals to enfranchise the very sort of people who had supported it. In fact, it would not be stretching things too far to say that, if not from the death of Chartism then from very shortly after it, the main question over the future of parliamentary representation was not whether or not to enfranchise the working class, but when, and how much of it.

Secondly, Chartism was of undoubted importance as a model of how a working-class movement might operate. This was clearly true of its network of speakers and meetings, but Chartism's land and education schemes were also significant here. Chartism was always more than just a parliamentary reform movement: its origins lay in the philosophy Robert Owen had enshrined in his mill at New Lanark, whereby with goodwill on all sides it was possible to create a more equitable and just society. Owen achieved it on a local scale but failed on the national scale. The Chartists failed too on the national scale, but after that, the logical move was to return to the local level, and to try to set up what a later generation would term the New Jerusalem within the imperfect society of Victorian England. This was the idea behind the Chartist settlements, carefully planned in every small detail and given names like O'Connorville or Charterville. Again, these have tended to be dismissed by historians as naive attempts by the Chartists to mix with affairs they did not understand, and there is some evidence to support this view. The Chartists of O'Connorville, near Rickmansworth, did not know how to plough properly or to make their own bread, and most of them ended up on parish relief. Within six months of Charterville's foundation in 1848 the residents were in revolt against the exorbitant rents they were expected to pay, and two years later we see the sorry sight of O'Connor sending the bailiffs in to evict 68 allottees in the village. Nevertheless, the land scheme was not a complete failure: the Gloucestershire settlements at Snig's End and Lowbands did particularly well, and for all its troubles Charterville seems to have flourished better than its surrounding neighbours. The schemes aroused much more attention and expectation than their rather dismissive treatment by historians might lead us to suppose, and in some ways their example was to prove one of the Chartists' most important legacies.

The obvious evidence for this lies in the movements that sprang out of Chartism, either figuratively or directly, as former Chartists turned their attentions to other aspects of working-class activity. In 1844, when Chartism seemed dead after the failure of the 1842 petition, a group of former Chartists in Rochdale set up a co-operative society, which flourished and became a model for similar movements around the emerging industrial world. The idea was simple enough: by paying into a central pool, members of the co-operative could enjoy in common the benefits bought with the fund. The initial purpose was to provide cheap groceries (the origin of the modern Co-op shops), but the idea could be adapted to support in times of sickness or unemployment, and in due course to insurance against both. The Rochdale Pioneers, as they became known, found their ideas spreading rapidly as first the friendly societies and later trade unions adopted the Rochdale model. In 1859 Samuel Smiles' best-seller, *Self-Help*, gave a sort of philosophical basis to the movement, as did the strong work ethic of the nonconformist churches. Asa Briggs points out that the middle years of the century saw quite a vogue for literature exhorting people to set their lives in order, and the same idea was at the root of the great move to emigrate to the United States or to colonies like Australia or South Africa.[5]

But although going overseas got round the problem of the entrenched attitudes one encountered at home, nevertheless a way had to be found to build the New Jerusalem in, to quote Blake's famous phrase (much used at the time), 'England's green and pleasant land'. Some of these schemes were the work of individuals or families, like Titus Salt's industrial community near Bradford, which he christened Saltaire, or the model community set up by the Cadbury family of chocolate manufacturers at Bournville, outside Birmingham. On a more general scale, the most obvious manifestation of this search – one might almost say crusade – were the trade unions, who did indeed use this sort of semi-religious language to describe their aims. The unions of the 1850s and 1860s, known as New Model Unions, owed much to Chartism, in terms of their organisation, their methods, and in many cases their membership. And the sober and dignified stance of these New Model Unions, who represented the skilled 'aristocracy' of labour, such as the engineers and the boilermakers, did much to influence thinking in Parliament when in 1867 it finally agreed to grant the vote to this more prosperous end of the working class. And later still, we can see how ideals first widely expressed and circulated by the Chartists influenced the work of municipal authorities to provide the basic amenities of decent life for their electorates – proper sewers, cheap public transport, free public libraries and baths, what became known, in a significant phrase, as Gas-and-Water Socialism.

This last example shows the important link that the Chartists perceived between political enfranchisement and social reform: it was only when local councils started being elected on a more democratic basis that they started taking their obligations to the electorate more seriously. This brings us back to Chartism's political legacy, and the lessons that were to be learnt from its failure. Chartism's importance can hardly be overestimated in the story of the growing political consciousness of women. Women joined the Chartist movement in large numbers and played an important and active part within it. For their time, the male Chartists were surprisingly advanced in their thinking about women's political rights: as we have seen, they had originally intended to campaign for genuine universal adult suffrage, and only substituted male suffrage on the grounds that it was a more feasible political aim (even the European revolutionaries of 1848 – male and female – were the most part dying and fighting for the cause of universal *male* suffrage). On the other hand, they were not twentieth-century feminists in embryo: Chartists supported the rights of women, but upheld the rights of husbands over their wives – since, after all, many male Chartists were themselves husbands with wives. The reform movements which followed on after Chartism's collapse, such as the Reform League or the Manhood Suffrage Associations, did not bother themselves with the issue of female emancipation;[6] it was not until the 1860s that the philosopher John Stuart Mill argued the case for female suffrage. Only in 1869 did women win the right to vote in municipal elections, and in 1870 they won the vote in elections to the local boards set up to oversee the new elementary schools. So if any movement deserves the credit for raising the issue in the first half of the century, and sowing seeds that were to grow to fruition in the second, it is Chartism.

But more immediately, Chartism's most important legacy was that it was a genuine working-class movement, perhaps the largest and best organised that there had ever been. Apart from a brief flirtation with the idea of joint action, the Chartists had steered well clear of the middle-class Anti-Corn Law League, and although the League proved much more successful in its aims than Chartism, there is no evidence that the Chartists blamed their movement's collapse on a failure to work with the middle classes. In that sense, Chartism was highly significant, and it helps explain Marx's keen interest in the movement, for Chartism marks the point at which the political alliance of working classes with the middle classes, to whom they had previously looked for leadership, broke down. As a sort of corollary to this, the repeal of the Corn Laws can be seen as the point when the middle classes were able to overcome the last remaining obstacle which stood in the way of their absorption into the ranks of the landowning classes of the old ruling order.

After Chartism the working classes were increasingly prepared to take a stand different from, or even opposed to, that of their middle-class employers. During the American Civil War, for instance, when the Federal north's blockade of southern (Confederate) ports starved the Lancashire mills of cotton and threw thousands of workers into unemployment and hunger, there was strong support among the upper and middle classes for the south. The mill workers of Manchester, however, addressed a dignified letter of support to Abraham Lincoln, which he called 'an instance of sublime Christian heroism', heroic because, as Lincoln well knew, the men were holding to their principles in the face of the dire effects of the blockade and in defiance of the stance of their employers. In this action they owed more to the Chartists than perhaps they knew.

Questions

1. How can Chartism be credited with influencing the parliamentary reform debates of the 1850s and 1860s?
2. What was the significance of the Chartist land scheme?
3. In what ways did Chartism advance the cause of women's emancipation?

SOURCES

1. CHARTISM AND VIOLENCE

Source A: Feargus O'Connor reported in the *Northern Star* (5 January 1839).

MR O'CONNOR: . . . He [Mr O'Connor] had been called a destructive, a revolutionist, and a firebrand; but it would be his duty to prove to them the bloodthirstiness and the anarchical feelings of those who were the enemies of the repeal of the Corn Laws; and he would further show them that their repeal, without accompanying measures, would only lead to bloodshed, strife, and civil war. (Loud and long cheers.) On the other hand, he would satisfy them that in seven days after the other measures had been obtained, the repeal of the Corn Laws would follow as a matter of course.

Source B: extract from a resolution of the Chartist National Convention, drawn up by William Lovett (5 July 1839).

1st. – That this Convention is of opinion that a wanton, flagrant, and unjust outrage has been made upon the people of Birmingham by a bloodthirsty and unconstitutional force from London, acting under the authority of men who, when out of office, sanctioned and took part in the meetings of the people; and now, when they share in public plunder, seek to keep the people in social slavery and political degradation.

Source C: 'The Designs of the Chartists and their Probable Consequences' published in the _Leeds Mercury_ (3 August 1839).

There is one consideration which at once proves the wickedness of the instigators among the Chartists and the deplorable folly of their dupes, namely, this, that _if their cause be really a good one, it is certain to be carried by peaceful and constitutional means_, and therefore the resort to violence is wholly without excuse. With a free Press, the right of Meeting and Petition, and a Representative Government, no honest cause ought to be despaired of. Has not the present generation had the strongest proof that this is true? Have we not seen the most extraordinary victories of truth and right over prejudice and self-interest? Did not a Legislature wholly Protestant concede the privileges of the Constitution to the Roman Catholics? Did not a Legislature consisting almost entirely of Churchmen grant their rights to the Dissenters? Did not a Parliament of Boroughmongers abolish the Rotten Boroughs? Did not a Parliament of Englishmen, many of them slave-owners, extinguish slavery in our colonies, and even vote Twenty Millions to purchase the freedom of the Negroes, though they were nearly as defenceless and destitute of influence as the cattle in the field? And after all this, and when so many of the working classes themselves have votes for Members of Parliament, can any one doubt that Universal Suffrage will one day be carried if the people should be generally fit for the exercise of the Suffrage? But it would not suit the professional agitator to wait for the peaceful and solid victories of truth. Violence is the element of these men, and confusion their harvest.

Source D: Friedrich Engels, _The Condition of the Working Classes in England_ (1845).

[The bourgeoisie] gave the command to fire upon the crowd in Preston, so that the unintentional revolt of the people stood all at once face to face, not only with the whole military power of the Government, but with the whole property-holding class as well ... The fruit of the uprising was the decisive separation of the proletariat from the bourgeoisie. The Chartists had not hitherto concealed their determination to carry the Charter at all costs, even that of a revolution; the bourgeoisie, which now perceived, all at once, the danger with which any violent change threatened its position, refused to hear anything further of physical force, and proposed to attain its end by moral force, as though this were anything else than the direct or indirect threat of physical force. This was one point of dissension, though even this was removed later by the assertion of the Chartists (who are at least as worthy of being believed as the bourgeoisie) that they, too, refrained from appealing to physical force.

Source E: from a Bradford councillor to the Home Office (25 May 1848).

Bradford would be a dis-affected town for a good many years in consequence of the largest body of workmen in the town and its immediate vicinity being thrown out of employment by the introduction of combing machines, inventions that had already thrown some thousands of wool combers out of employment. One firm, Messrs Walker & Co., used to employ 1,700 combers, now they do not employ 400 – their machines now do the work of 1,000 men. They attribute their unfortunate position to what they call class legislation and that the Charter would find them plenty of good work and good wages if it became the law of the land. Milligan, the Mayor of Bradford, is like the Mayor of London described by Charles Dickens in *Barnaby Rudge*. Nothing can induce him to put a stop to the illegal meetings, drillings, and secret armings of the tumultuous mob who even hold their meetings and perambulate the streets on the Sabbath day, marching in military style with their captains in red and green caps and divided into sections and companies, keeping step with true military precision carrying tricoleur flags and others bearing abominable inscriptions such as 'more pigs and less parsons', 'down with the aristocracy'.

Source F: Ben Wilson, *The struggles of an old Chartist: what he knows and the part he has taken in various movements* (1887).

The Chartists were becoming very numerous in this district, and throughout the country great alarm was caused by the large numbers who were arming themselves. A meeting of delegates was held in Yorkshire to name the day when the people should rise; November of that year was fixed, and Peter Bussey was appointed leader. John Frost, a magistrate of Newport, was chosen leader in Wales; but when the time came, Peter Bussey had fallen sick and had gone into the country out of the way, or, being a shopkeeper, he was hiding in his warehouse amongst the sacks. Henry Vincent was arrested and imprisoned at Newport; the Chartists determined to release him, and, in a drenching storm in November, they assembled in thousands, armed with guns, pikes, etc., with Frost as their leader; and marched towards the prison; on their way they met the soldiers, a scrimmage took place in which 10 men were killed and between 40 and 50 wounded. Frost, Williams and Jones were arrested and sentenced to be hung, but afterwards reprieved and transported for life.

Questions

1. Explain the following references:
   'the repeal of the Corn Laws would follow as a matter of course' (Source A) [2]

'the people of Birmingham' (Source B) [1]
'proposed to attain its end by moral force' (Source D) [2]

2. How strong is the case put forward in Sources A, B and D that the blame for violent clashes lay with the authorities? [5]

3.* Compare Sources C, E and F as evidence of Chartist violence. [7]

4. Using all these documents, and any other evidence known to you, how far would you agree with the view that the Chartists harmed their own cause by the violence of their actions and of their language? [8]

Worked answer: Question 3

Although all three sources were written by men who lived through the chartist experience at first hand, only E and F, in their different ways, contain actual eye-witness accounts of violent or potentially violent incidents. Source C, from the well informed but conservative *Leeds Mercury*, argues that Chartist violence was essentially the result of impatience; the councillor in Source E sees it arising from economic distress; while the old Chartist reminiscing in Source F is vague about the plans for a general rising, yet is very precise in showing that the Chartists would resort to violence in order to free a chartist leader wrongly imprisoned.

Source C, being from a newspaper (which, like all newspapers at the time, was designed in part to be read aloud), depends almost entirely on rhetoric – 'the wickedness of the instigators', 'violence is the element of these men' – to make its case against Chartist violence. It takes a very simplistic view: its list of successful non-violent campaigns includes two, Catholic emancipation and parliamentary reform, which were carried partly because of the fear of violence if they were not. The councillor in Source E is reporting on an alarming situation to the Home Office (and, no doubt, hoping to do Mayor Milligan a bit of no good) and therefore takes a more analytical approach than the *Leeds Mercury*. The fact that the writer of Source E, who is clearly deeply alarmed by the Chartists, nevertheless recognises the very real economic distress which has helped attract working people to the movement, adds to the source's credence.

Ben Wilson's memoirs in Source F tally with our general picture of Chartism, and give the impression that grand plans for general insurrection were not fully thought through. However, apart from one or two minor details, like Peter Bussey's cold feet, the document does not actually tell us a lot more about the movement than would have been fairly common knowledge at the time it was written: in its way, therefore, and despite being written by an ex-Chartist, this document is not a lot more useful as evidence of chartist violence than the *Leeds Mercury* extract. The best evidence of Chartist violence, or at least of preparation for violence, lies in Source E.

SOURCES

2. THE WIDER SIGNIFICANCE OF CHARTISM

Source G: *Hansard*, debate on the Chartist petition (3 May 1842).

MR MACAULAY: I conceive that civilisation rests upon the security of property, but I think, that it is not necessary for me, in a discussion of this kind, to go through the arguments, and through the vast experience which necessarily leads to this result; but I will assert, that while property is insecure, it is not in the power of the finest soil, or of the moral or intellectual constitution of any country, to prevent the country sinking into barbarism, while on the other hand, while property is secure, it is not possible to prevent a country from achieving prosperity.

MR HUME: He would ask the right hon. Gentleman [Macaulay] to point to any request amongst those demands which could in any way injure either public or private property. They demanded the electoral suffrage, and he would ask, was it fair, that men who are liable to be called on to defend their country by sea and by land, and also obliged by taxation to contribute their share to the support of the Government of the country, should be deprived of their constitutional rights in that and in other respects?

Source H: 'W.R.', an informer, reporting on a Chartist meeting in Bradford, to the Home Secretary (28 May 1848).

[He said that] it was now the duty of all Irishmen who were at present leaders in the Chartists ranks to double our exertions and keep them up to the mark by every means in our power, and by keeping up the Agitation more and more it will prevent the Government from sending any more troops to Ireland.

Source I: *The Times* (10 April 1848).

The present [Chartist] movement is a ramification of the Irish conspiracy.

Source J: John Livesey, 'Mechanics' churches – a letter to Sir Robert Peel on church extension in the populous towns and manufacturing districts' (c.1843).

The wealthier classes, in tolerable numbers, are found occupying the pews; but the free seats are too often thinly tenanted. To what shall we attribute this indifference to Divine ordinances? . . . The prevailing reason, I am assured, is the force of inveterate habit . . . they tread in the steps of their fathers, and are neither impressed with the obligation, nor feel the desire, of obtaining religious instruction . . . There is indisputable evidence, that the ramifications of the late Chartist conspiracy were deep and numerous in this district.

Source K: H.D. Traill (ed.), *Social England: a record of the progress of the people* (1897).

It was soon seen that the number of Chartists in favour of physical force, and willing to risk their lives in armed rebellion, was insignificant. The panic passed away, but not the discontent. It smouldered on, varying in intensity with the popular distress and other contingencies. Socialism, Secularism, Teetotalism, Trade Unionism, Co-operation, Vegetarianism, and other movements got mixed up with Chartism in some degree. But its main factor continued to be a bitter sense of injustice and misery, with a conviction that the rich were in some way responsible. The upper and middle classes repaid hatred with hatred, and generally regarded the Chartists as brutal and desperate men, coveting the wealth of others, without belief in God, and without reverence for their social superiors or the rights of property.

Source L: Mary Ann Walker, addressing a Chartist meeting in High Holborn, London (10 December 1842).

There never was a time when England possessed such abundance as at present. (Hear.) How was it, then, she would ask, that two-thirds of the population were, in the face of such a fact, without food! (Hear, hear hear.) . . . Why, she would further ask, were the people of this country ground down as they were, taxed to keep a Queen Dowager – Queen Adelaide? who, besides the Royal Manor and Palace of Hampton Court, the park and domains of Bushy, also Marlborough House in Pall Mall, two parks and three Royal Palaces, drew from the taxes of England £100,000 a year, £274 per day. (Shame, shame.) Why was that? And she (Miss Walker) would ask how 'an old lady' could spend it. (Hear, and cheers.)

Questions

1. Explain the following references:
   'the Irish conspiracy' (Source I) [2]
   'the late Chartist conspiracy' (Source J) [2]
2.* Evaluate the argument in Sources H and I that Chartism contributed to conflict in Ireland. [5]
3. Compare Sources G, J and L as evidence that Chartism challenged the established social order in Britain. [8]
4. Using all these sources, and any other evidence known to you, how strong is the case that Chartism's greatest significance lay outside its campaign for the franchise? [8]

Worked answer: Question 2

The idea of a link between Chartism and Irish nationalism in the 1840s looks (and looked at the time) superficially attractive. The Chartists openly acknowledged that they had learnt a lot from the Catholic Association's successful campaign for emancipation, and many Chartists were Irish, including some of the leaders, like O'Connor and O'Brien. However, the sort of evidence put forward in Sources I and J simply is not enough to establish a close link between the two movements, still less the sort of co-ordinated action the sources seem to suggest. Source H was written by an informer, and although there undoubtedly were individuals who said the sort of thing 'W.R.' reports, we cannot be certain: the reliability of spies' and agents' reports is notoriously difficult to gauge. Spies certainly see and report, but they are also well known for reporting what their masters want to hear. In this case, Source H feeds into the sort of hysterical reaction to Chartism that seemed to reach its peak in 1848: in this context, the idea of radicals with different aims working in cahoots with each other seemed logical enough, and explains the sort of conspiracy-theory approach evident in Sources H and even in the normally sober *Times*, Source I. In reality, O'Connor himself showed little interest in Irish nationalist politics, and in Ireland Daniel O'Connell was deeply suspicious of Chartism. Although universal suffrage would have helped empower the Irish Catholics, equal electoral districts would have drastically reduced the Irish representation at Westminster. In any case, by 1848 Ireland was in the throes of the terrible potato famine and had little time to indulge in nationalist, let alone chartist, politics. In short, the case in Sources H and I does not amount to anything substantial.

4

DISRAELI AND THE
SECOND REFORM ACT

BACKGROUND NARRATIVE

The Second Reform Act of 1867 was pure Disraeli. The way in which it was passed was so riddled with contradictions that historians still have difficulty conveying Disraeli's sheer effrontery to the modern reader. The Act is often (wrongly) described as having given the vote to the urban working class. It is true that Disraeli, as a young novelist, had coined the famous phrase 'The two nations' in reference to the rich and the poor, but he had never shown any particular interest in the social welfare or political aspirations of the working classes: he was a firm believer in the merits and leadership of the landed aristocracy, never happier than when hob-nobbing with dukes. On the other side of the House, the coalition of Whigs such as Russell and Peelites such as Gladstone, which was about to evolve into the Liberal party, was slowly and uncertainly taking up the cause of reform; but it held back from open support at least partly because of the reluctance of its leader, Lord Palmerston, to tackle the issue. However, Palmerston must soon have been spinning in his grave, for no sooner had he died than Russell put forward a bill to extend the franchise into the upper reaches of the working classes. The Conservative attack on the bill in the Commons was led by Disraeli, but the main credit for killing the bill went to a group of disgruntled and grudge-holding Whigs led by Robert Lowe (and likened by Disraeli to the Cave of Adullam, where grousers against the biblical King Saul had gathered; and thereafter referred to by historians as either the Adullamites or the Cave).

Defeat on an issue of such importance brought Russell's government down in 1866, and the Conservatives took office under the Earl of Derby, with Disraeli as chancellor of the exchequer and the principal government spokesman in the Commons. The defeat of Russell's bill was not well received outside Parliament, and a large protest march organised by the Reform League degenerated into violence when the police tried to keep the marchers out of Hyde Park. Once in office, however, Derby and Disraeli gave notice that they intended to introduce a Reform Bill of their own, and Disraeli was given the task of drafting it. There was much humming and hawing in the cabinet about whether it should be a radical or a moderate bill, with three ministers, led by Lord Cranborne, threatening to resign unless the bill were very moderate indeed. With only ten minutes to go before details of the proposed bill had to be announced to the party, Disraeli plumped for a moderate measure in order to placate the dissident ministers; but once the bill started being criticised in the Commons for being too moderate he withdrew it, substituted a much more radical measure, and simply let the disgruntled ministers resign.

As the bill went through its parliamentary stages Disraeli accepted amendment after amendment, from either side of the House, with the exception of those proposed by Gladstone. The most striking example was Disraeli's calm acceptance of an amendment proposed by an obscure backbencher named Hodgkinson, which had the effect of enfranchising compound-ratepayers (discussed below, p. 72), whom Disraeli had consistently described as unfit for the vote. Disraeli repeatedly said he would not accept the principle of household suffrage in the boroughs, that is, a vote going to every male head of household; but as soon as it looked as if the Commons might insist on it he accepted it without turning a hair. The upshot was that Disraeli's 1867 Act was far more radical, and enfranchised many more people, than the Whig–Liberal bill he had so vigorously opposed only the year before. Moreover, Disraeli went on to present this piece of blatant political opportunism as a deliberate re-launching of the Conservative party on new principles: an appeal to the working classes that Lord Randolph Churchill would later christen 'Tory Democracy'. Gladstone was quite dumbfounded at Disraeli's political chicanery. In his diary, which was for the most part simply a record of his movements and appointments, he felt moved not only to comment on Disraeli's audacity but to employ uncharacteristically strong language: 'A smash,' he called it, 'perhaps without example'.

ANALYSIS (1): WHY, DESPITE GENERAL CONSENSUS ON THE NEED FOR FURTHER REFORM OF PARLIAMENT, WAS NO REFORM MEASURE PASSED UNTIL 1867?

The cross-party consensus on the Second Reform Act of 1867 is one of its most striking contrasts with the Great Reform Act of 1832. Although 1867 did see considerable drama, it was a complex, parliamentary drama, quite unlike the sense of national emergency which had characterised the crisis of 1831–2. No-one in 1867 was threatening to create large numbers of peers to force the bill through or to put pressure on the queen; instead, the Act was the result of a long and complicated process of parliamentary manoeuvring which had contemporaries as bemused and confused as many modern readers. Not the least confusing element in it was that the parties were engaged in bitter parliamentary battle on an issue on which not only were they to all intents and purposes in agreement, but on which they clearly and frequently recognised themselves to be in agreement.

This had not always been the case. Immediately after 1832 there was indeed a consensus, but it was *against* further reform, not for it. Lord John Russell, who had introduced the first two drafts of the Great Reform Act, declared the 1832 Act a final settlement of the issue. Nevertheless, it was he who first tried to introduce further reform, in 1849. It is not too difficult to see why. The 1832 Act had been designed to redress the balance of the constitution, to remove the most obviously venal elements and to strengthen the more robustly independent elements, like the counties and the new industrial interests, as a counter-weight to the power of the Crown and the Executive. The Chartists had argued, with impressive levels of public support, for Parliament to take on a more directly representational character, and one did not have to be a Chartist to recognise that they had a point. The 1832 Act was essentially an eighteenth-century measure passed to deal with an eighteenth-century problem, but by the 1850s times had changed considerably. The nineteenth century had already seen rapid and breathtaking achievements in technology and industry, celebrated in the Great Exhibition of 1851 in which half the exhibits came from the British Isles. In this Brave New World the claims of what were termed

Capital and Labour to play their part in determining the future of the country could hardly be dismissed or ignored.

These were the years of what was known as the Condition of England Question: heart-searching over horrifying official reports into cholera or sewerage, fuelled by the pen of novelists like Mrs Gaskell. Closely linked to this was a growing sense of anger at the culture of amateurism and inefficiency in official circles which produced this misery. The indolence of the Civil Service was satirised by Charles Dickens' description in 1855 of the 'Circumlocution Office' in *Little Dorrit*: competitive examination had just been introduced for the Imperial Civil Service, but despite the recommendations of the 1853 Northcote-Trevelyan report, it would be another twenty years before the same thing was introduced in the Civil Service at home. Above all, the Crimean War revealed to an appalled Victorian public the depths of muddle and incompetence to which the hierarchy of the armed forces and the War Office could sink in time of crisis: it is hardly surprising that the two most celebrated individuals who emerged from the war, Florence Nightingale and the *Times* journalist William Howard Russell, both earned their fame by fighting against this culture of amateurism and stupidity. In the context of the 1850s, therefore, it did not take a particularly radical outlook to recognise that a largely agricultural and rural Parliament, still heavily influenced by patronage and the interest groups of the previous century, and overseeing the fortunes of the world's foremost industrial nation, was more of an anomaly with every passing year.

Nevertheless, reform proposals, put forward with impressive tenacity by Russell in 1849, 1852 and 1854, by Derby in 1859 and by Russell again in 1860 and 1866, all failed, and even proved divisive. Russell's 1854 bill almost prompted Palmerston to resign as home secretary, and his 1866 bill prompted the Adullamite revolt. One of the bitterest attacks on Derby's 1859 measure came from the Radical MP John Bright, an enthusiastic supporter of reform, but not of Disraeli and Derby's version of it. The problem was that the consensus that was beginning to emerge was in favour of reform as a general principle; but, as soon as discussion progressed to specific detail, it fell apart. There was general agreement, for example, that the post-Chartist groups like friendly societies and trade unions had demonstrated that there was a responsible, politically literate and active section of the working class who deserved, in Gladstone's phrase, to come within the pale of the constitution. These were essentially the skilled workers who constituted what became known, perhaps rather misleadingly, as the 'labour aristocracy', men such as the boilermakers whose work literally drove Britain's industrial production, or the engineers (the ASE), whose union membership certificate carried images of antiquity, Christianity and the great entrepreneurs of the industrial revolution. On the other hand, a great mass of the working population was unskilled, illiterate, uneducated and decidedly not respectable: these were the low characters whose appalling living conditions were exposed in Henry Mayhew's *Life and Labour of the London Poor*, and who were often referred to, rather less sympathetically, as 'the residuum'. The residuum also encompassed what Victorians referred to as 'the criminal classes': it was popularly believed that there were identifiable 'criminal types' to be found among the urban poor, and poor people in custody were liable to find themselves put in front of a camera or to have their skulls measured, all in the interests of further research.

'Democracy', as the term was understood, meant giving the vote to the residuum, including the 'criminal classes', and no-one outside the most radical ranks proposed this. British politicians looked with ill-concealed horror at America, where giving the vote to all (white) adult males had produced a populist style of politics which was notorious for its corruption and demagoguery: it was his experience of a similar situation in Australia, for example, which inspired Robert Lowe's determined opposition to further reform. But how, for the purposes of legislation, could a line be drawn between the 'respectable' and the 'unrespectable' working class? Despite the interest in such things sparked off by Darwin's Origin of Species, which had appeared in 1859, no-one seriously proposed basing the franchise on the shape of the skull or the distance between a prospective voter's eyes; on the other hand, union membership was an equally unreliable guide, partly because the legal status of trade unions was uncertain and partly because they were still regarded as potentially dangerous organisations: the climax of the reform campaign coincided with the 'Sheffield outrages', a series of bomb attacks on the homes of strike-breakers.

The obvious solution lay in the familiar field of tenure of property, which had always been the main criterion for deciding the franchise, though the idea of looking for different criteria survived in the form of the 'fancy franchises' proposed by Disraeli in 1859 and 1867 as a way of counter-balancing the influence of the new working-class voters. But using property tenure raised as many questions as it solved. Everyone but the most radical agreed that the vote was not a right: it had to be earned, but the threshold should be low enough for earning it to be a realistic ambition. Thus lodgers, for example, by common agreement were to be excluded from the franchise because by definition they did not possess independent means, though with time and hard work they might do so. Similarly, it was generally agreed that the county franchise would need to be different from the borough franchise, because agricultural labourers were less well educated and likely to remain so.

Beyond this, however, there were major disagreements. Was it more 'respectable' to pay rates or to pay rent? Disraeli argued that the real mark of respectability, and hence of social and moral responsibility, lay in 'personal payment' of rates, in other words actually answering in name to the local council for payment, but this excluded a whole class of perfectly respectable tenants known as 'compound-ratepayers' who paid a joint sum compounding their rent and their rates to their landlord, who then included his tenants' rates in his own payments to the council. Why should these people be denied the vote? It was an issue that seriously threatened the progress of the 1867 bill until Disraeli unexpectedly accepted Hodgkinson's Amendment, which effectively outlawed the whole process of compound ratepaying. And even if the parties could be got to agree on the categories of voter, what size of property or level of rate or rent should be taken as a sign of social and moral responsibility? Russell's proposals had tended to set the level lower than the Conservatives were prepared to go: he had set rating levels of between £5 and £7 a year in his proposals from 1852 to 1866, whereas Derby and Disraeli in 1859 had favoured more substantial property, rated at £10 a year. So much was deemed to hang on the issue that at one point in the debates on the 1867 bill there were questions about the number of rooms that constituted a 'household', and even their exact dimensions. It is not difficult to recognise a sense of general relief when Disraeli finally broke with the assurance he had consistently given throughout the debates and accepted the principle of simple household suffrage.

The issue proved so complicated and divisive that it is small wonder that there was no parliamentary campaign for reform of any major significance until right at the end of the period. The usual explanation given for this is the influence of Palmerston. In fact, Palmerston was much more open to suggestions for social and administrative reform than he is usually given credit for – his ministries brought in important reforms in health, education, law and order, and poor relief – but he was never in favour of reform for the sake of it, and given the detailed difficulties parliamentary reform carried, the case for it would have had to be overwhelming if it were to get the backing of such an experienced politician. There was very little to persuade Palmerston that the case *was* overwhelming. Russell had been raising the issue for twenty years without exciting any particular interest within or outside Parliament. The

Conservatives had raised the issue themselves in 1859, transparently with a view to getting a franchise and redistribution package which would benefit themselves, but again without stirring up any major public support.

Under the existing provisions of the 1832 Act, substantial numbers of the 'respectable' working class were already qualifying for the franchise, and there seemed no guarantee at all that any further extension would necessarily benefit the Whig–Liberals. On the other hand, there seemed every prospect that raising the reform issue would destroy the delicately-poised coalition of Whigs and Liberals that Palmerston was skilfully holding together. It can hardly have endeared reform to Palmerston that it was proposed by the two ministerial colleagues whom he found it hardest to take entirely seriously, first Russell and then Gladstone; and even Gladstone came round to reform very slowly, causing considerable surprise and not a little irritation with his 'pale of the constitution' speech in 1864. In short, even though most of the proposals were coming from his party, there was no pressing reason either of political principle or of party advantage for Palmerston to embark on the divisive and potentially destructive course of parliamentary reform.

On the Conservative side, the case looked even weaker. Although Derby developed a personal interest in reform, and his voice could hardly be ignored, it was never going to be an issue which would unite the Conservatives; and neither, until 1866, were they in a strong enough political position to envisage tackling the political battles that passing it would entail. The Conservatives were still suffering from the after-effects of their traumatic defeat over the Corn Laws, and insofar as there was any uniting element in the party it was a sort of hankering after the legacy of Sir Robert Peel, a stance which both Gladstone and Disraeli attempted to adopt. Peel's example was something of a two-edged weapon: on the one hand Peel was a strong anti-reformer; on the other hand his career seemed to demonstrate the danger of changing political principles too often and too suddenly. There was considerable caution in Conservative circles at the idea of enfranchising the working classes, and similarly strong scepticism about any suggestion that there were Conservative votes out there to be won.

The Conservative sceptics could also take solace in their leaders, who included General Peel, Sir Robert's brother, who could fairly claim to stand for the continuation of his brother's principles (though Disraeli made fun of him, describing him as 'very placable, except on the phrase "household suffrage", when his eyes light up with insanity'). The only area where it was generally felt that the Conservatives might benefit from changes to the constitution lay in redistribution, since Liberal-voting towns were tending to 'contaminate' their neighbouring Conservative-voting counties, and indeed the Conservatives were to gain some twenty-two seats from the redistribution provisions of the 1867 Act. But the case for this was not so strong that it impelled a reform movement within the Conservative party, and this can only be said to have started at Derby and Disraeli's initiative after they had defeated Russell's 1866 measure.

The question still remains, however, why the agitation for reform got going in 1866 when it had been dormant for so long. Royden Harrison saw the crisis of 1866–7 as the result of pressure from Edward Beales' Reform League and the Hyde Park rioters, which helped to produce a revolutionary turnaround in the Victorian constitution;[1] few historians have agreed with him. Since the decline of Chartism, working-class movements had fought shy of parliamentary reform, and had taken to campaigning on issues of social reform and working conditions instead. The only real evidence for outside pressure playing a part in pushing reform through Parliament is the pattern of events surrounding the Reform League's Hyde Park meeting in May 1866. This was clearly not a revolutionary or subversive gathering, and the trouble that ensued was essentially the product of an over-zealous Metropolitan Police superintendent who liked banning meetings, and a weak and indecisive home secretary, Spencer Walpole.[2] Nor was political violence at all unusual: rowdy and violent elections were still regular features of political life and were, if anything, getting more violent rather than less.

Even so, it is clear that the violence in Hyde Park did help to produce an impetus and a sense of public expectation for an issue which had hitherto lacked both. It also no doubt helped frighten enough back-benchers into considering the consequences of not reforming. There were more than enough examples of recent violent political uprisings, from Garibaldi's successful invasion of Sicily to the American Civil War, to lend credence to fears of the consequences of entrenched opposition to the will of the people. In particular two risings within the British Empire had concentrated MPs' minds: the appalling violence of the Indian 'Mutiny' of 1857–8, and a serious rising in Jamaica in 1866 whose suppression provoked a lot of controversy in Britain. One recent historian has pointed out that MPs were debating the closure of Jamaica's representative House of Assembly at precisely the same time that they were debating widening the franchise at home.[3] The age of revolution was by no means over, and the success of the 1832 Act in seeing Britain safely through the turbulent century added weight to the idea that further reform might have the same effect.

In terms of parliamentary tactics, the death of Palmerston in 1865 undoubtedly helped to settle the timing of the measure, but John Walton argues, plausibly enough, that the deciding factor was Gladstone's conversion to the cause, since this meant that the rising figure and probable next leader of the strongest party was committed to reform: it then became a question not of whether Reform would pass, but when and in what form.[4] The Hyde Park affair, coupled with other violent outbursts, helped to underscore the idea that it would be better to keep the goodwill of the respectable workers than to alienate them. There was a widespread hope that granting the franchise might, in many ways, act as a channel for moral and social improvement among the newly enfranchised classes, and even – by acting as an incentive to them to improve – among those without the vote. In that sense, it is peculiarly appropriate that Gladstone's should have been the deciding voice in bringing the issue to the fore, and peculiarly inappropriate that Disraeli should have passed it.

Questions

1. Why did it prove so difficult to decide the precise franchise qualification for the urban working class?
2. What political considerations hindered the cause of parliamentary reform between 1832 and 1867?
3. How significant was extra-parliamentary pressure in securing the passage of the 1867 Reform Act?

ANALYSIS (2): 'LESS THE RESULT OF DISRAELI'S OPPORTUNISM THAN OF GLADSTONE'S POLITICAL INCOMPETENCE'. HOW FAR WOULD YOU AGREE WITH THIS JUDGEMENT ON THE PASSAGE OF THE 1867 REFORM ACT?

Historians and students enjoy hurling accusations of opportunism at figures of political history. Clearly some element of opportunism is an important asset for any politician, but – equally clearly – with some politicians it can appear to become a substitute for anything resembling a political philosophy, and this is the sense in which it tends to be thrown at Disraeli. Modern historians and contemporary commentators alike have pointed the finger of inconsistency at Disraeli. The Conservative *Quarterly Review* in December 1867 was scornful of attempts to suggest that Disraeli had been following some sort of clever policy aimed all along at household suffrage, pointing out that 'this theory is of very modern date . . . It was not until that troublesome stalking-horse [the compound-householder] had been removed that it was found necessary to discover the antiquity of a Conservative belief in household suffrage.' Maurice Cowling's study of the 1867 Act, published to mark its anniversary, did indeed present the passage of the Act as a testament to Disraeli's political skill: Disraeli may not have known exactly where the measure was heading, but he steered it through the Commons and ensured that it reached its destination in a Conservative vessel.[5]

But other voices have been more critical, notably Disraeli's most eminent, and usually supportive, biographer, Robert Blake. Blake has no time for Disraeli's and Derby's claim to political consistency, pointing out that 'this was quite untrue and laid them open to the charge of deliberate deception, surely worse than mere inconsistency'.[6] However, the problem raised by the charge of opportunism and inconsistency on Disraeli's part is not so much whether or not he was guilty of them, for he clearly was, but whether or not it matters. Much the same could be said – and was said – of Peel over Catholic emancipation and the Corn Laws, and of Gladstone over Irish Home Rule, yet Peel's and Gladstone's inconsistencies resulted from conversions to what are usually regarded as noble causes. To some extent Disraeli's U-turn in 1867 escapes censure for the same reason, but only if one accepts Cowling's view of him as a sort of pilot who weathered the parliamentary storm. But was Disraeli's command of events as secure as this suggests?

Robert Blake, who clearly admired Disraeli's skill in steering the bill through the Commons, nevertheless stated that he 'lived from crisis to crisis, improvising, guessing, responding to the mood of the moment'. This need not be read as a criticism. The Conservatives were in a minority, attempting to pass a measure on one of the most divisive issues of the day, and which duly produced a split in the cabinet; Disraeli was not a figure around which the party would naturally rally; and Disraeli's insistence on using the issue to inflict a major defeat on Gladstone was producing a paradoxical situation which left many inside and outside Parliament confused, and which demanded nimble footwork from the party leadership. Russell's 1866 measure had been moderate, and a moderate measure still commanded considerable support from within the Whigs and Liberals including, crucially, Gladstone.

If Disraeli were to present anything different from what the Whigs had presented only the year before (and he could hardly present an identical measure because he had opposed Russell's bill so strongly), it had either to be much more moderate or much more radical: the Whigs had effectively occupied the middle ground. Disraeli's 'ten-minute' bill of February 1867 set a slightly lower level for the borough franchise than Russell had proposed, but a much higher level in the counties along with all the 'fancy' franchises as safeguards for the balance of the constitution. This proposal achieved its main purpose of keeping the party and cabinet together but this was of little consequence if the measure itself did not pass the Commons. If the bill failed, the Conservatives would be forced back into opposition, where they had been with only two brief intervals for the past twenty years; it was certainly inconsistent and opportunist of Disraeli to ditch the ten-minute bill in favour of a more radical measure, but given what was at stake inconsistency must have seemed a price well worth paying.

The more radical bill which Disraeli introduced on 18 March 1867 was to form the basis of the Act. Its proposals for the controversial borough franchise were all to be subject to substantial amendment: the two-year residence qualification was brought down to one year; personal ratepaying was widened to include the much-argued-over compound-ratepayer and to become, in effect, the franchise for every head of a household; the carefully crafted balancing franchises – an extra vote for those who paid 20 shillings in tax or held £50 in a savings bank, and a franchise based on educational qualifications – were all to disappear during the course of debate; nevertheless, this was to remain by common consent a Conservative measure, for which Disraeli and Derby retained the credit. To do this it was imperative that it should not appear to be a Whig–Liberal measure, and this meant resisting any amendments proposed by Gladstone or by his closest supporters, *however much they might appeal to the Conservatives*. However, since it was equally important to get the bill passed, this in turn meant that the amendments Disraeli would accept (and with a parliamentary minority he would have to accept some) would have to be radical ones. In other words the logic of his absolute opposition to Gladstone forced Disraeli to follow the risky course of outflanking Gladstone not on the right but on the left.

This in turn raises the question of whether Disraeli was pursuing a course of flexible principles merely in order to pursue a personal vendetta with Gladstone. The relationship between Disraeli and Gladstone cannot be summed up in simple terms, though there was clearly at least as much personal animosity as there was political opposition. On Gladstone's part, it was Disraeli's very lack of steady principle which animated his dislike, and especially his memory of how Disraeli had brought Peel down in 1846. Disraeli came to detest Gladstone – and certainly regarded him as a pompous humbug whom he delighted in provoking, rather as he had treated Peel in the 1840s – but there is no evidence that he took the line that he did on reform simply in order to score points off Gladstone. Had that been his primary intention, he would presumably have made his move earlier; as it was, Disraeli was to some extent 'bounced' into reform by Derby's insistence on it; and once Derby had decided that the Conservatives should pass a Reform Bill it was down to Disraeli, as the government spokesman in the Commons, to draw one up which stood a chance of actually passing. The fact that this could be combined with the happy task of snubbing Gladstone at every opportunity was clearly welcome, but it was not Disraeli's main motivation. Of course it also had the hardly invisible effect of promoting Disraeli's own cause within the Conservative party, and indeed he was soon to succeed Derby as party leader and prime minister, reaching the top, in his famous phrase, of the 'greasy pole'. Cynics will always see a personal motive in politicians' actions, and only the naive will entirely deny this; nevertheless, it is stretching the point too far to suggest that the only reason Disraeli supported reform was to advance his own career. As chancellor of the exchequer he was already Derby's number two, with twenty years of experience in acting as the Conservative spokesman in the Commons: Derby was already in ill health, and it did not take a crystal ball to see Disraeli as his most likely successor, with or without a Reform Act.

A more substantial criticism of Disraeli's rush for reform in 1867 is that he squandered the opportunity it opened up at the general election that followed. This was certainly the feeling among his own party after their defeat in 1868, and they placed the blame fairly and squarely on Disraeli. Not until his Manchester and Crystal Palace speeches in 1872 was he able to re-establish his hold over the party: in the meantime he was open to the criticisms of opponents like Lord Cranborne, later Lord Salisbury, who had resigned in protest at reform and who acted as a mouthpiece for Disraeli's critics. There is rather more substance in this line of argument, not only because it confronts a tangible result – the Conservative election defeat – but because, for all their rhetoric about leaps in the dark and educating their party, Derby and Disraeli made no attempt to mobilise Conservative support in the people for whom they had won the vote. Gladstone, on the other hand, fought a galvanised campaign and won such a handsome majority that Disraeli conceded defeat without bothering to meet the House of Commons. It is not entirely easy to see why Disraeli allowed himself to be so badly beaten:

it is tempting to put it down to complacency, or even fatigue, but Disraeli cannot escape all of the blame. For example, he squandered the considerable Irish Catholic vote, which could have been his for the asking, by rushing to the defence of the Irish Church against Gladstone's threats of disestablishment. All of which raises the question of Gladstone's tactics: why was the man who was able to win so decisively in 1868 so comprehensively outmanoeuvred in 1867?

The criticisms levelled at Disraeli after 1867 were as nothing compared with those hurled at Gladstone. The *Saturday Review* was merciless:

> Another blunder is added to the long list of Mr Gladstone's blunders. There can be no doubt that he thoroughly mistook the feelings of his party . . . Mr Gladstone lays down the law, and will hear no-one who attempts to dissent.[7]

Historians have tended to agree. Of Gladstone's recent biographers, E.J. Feuchtwanger blames Gladstone's 'High Anglican, Peelite priggishness' for a style of leadership in the Commons that 'was in many ways disastrous',[8] while Roy Jenkins[9] simply points out some of the bare facts of Gladstone's record: with a Liberal majority in the Commons of 77, Gladstone's own amendment to the bill, to set the borough franchise at £5, was defeated with a government majority of 21 thanks to the Liberal 'tea-room revolt' which led to 43 Liberals voting against their own leader and 20 more absenting themselves. A leader of the opposition with a commanding majority in the House, putting forward an amendment in line with his party's consistent policy, who yet manages not only to lose the vote but to lose 63 of his own supporters into the bargain, certainly does appear a leader who is unequal to the task. Nor is it enough to say that, since Gladstone wanted reform he cannot be blamed for letting Disraeli pass it, because Gladstone had never wanted a reform measure quite as radical as Disraeli's Act eventually proved. Somewhere along the line, Gladstone had miscalculated badly; but equally clearly he recovered quickly and was able to take office a year later with a majority of 116 and embark on one of the most important programmes of social and administrative reform of the century. If Gladstone can be accused of incompetence in 1867 it was of a short-lived variety: it certainly pointed to some major drawbacks in his leadership style but it did not indicate any deep-rooted political incapability.

John Vincent[10] argues that Gladstone came to reform in the first place by a circuitous route, as his relationship with John Bright developed and deepened, and that he was forced to take a more radical stance than he might otherwise have done by Robert Lowe's opposition to even the most moderate proposals. This suggests that Gladstone was just as much a victim of the 'flow of events' in 1866–7 as anyone else. More to the point, he was facing the issue at a particularly difficult time for his party. Within months of winning the 1865 election the Liberals had lost Palmerston, their single most popular electoral asset, whose personality alone was often credited with having won the two most recent general elections. Russell was a figure more respected than liked, an uninspiring leader who had led them to disaster and resignation over his 1866 Reform Bill, and that defeat had itself been the result of a revolt in the Liberal ranks. To take over the leadership of a party in such a state would have been a challenge for the most tactful of men, but tactful leadership was not one of Gladstone's many virtues.

Although Gladstone's Old Testament prophet style of politics went down well with the Victorian public, it did not lend itself to the sort of compromises and sweet-talking that would be necessary to get the Liberals to unite on parliamentary reform. And it can hardly be denied that Gladstone was badly caught out by Disraeli's tactics. Many Liberals were in favour of a more radical measure than Russell had proposed, and Disraeli was offering them one; others recognised that Disraeli's measure was bound to enfranchise large numbers of Liberal voters; either way, there did not seem to be much point in opposing Disraeli's bill if it effectively delivered what the Liberals wanted. There was a certain amount of fun to be had in trying to catch Disraeli out by pointing out contradictions between what he was saying in 1867 and what he had said in opposition to Russell's measure, but apart from that the best policy seemed to be to lay down supportive amendments to the bill and to let it go through. Gladstone seems only half to have seen this, and he never made any serious attempt to hail the bill for what it could plausibly be seen as: a Liberal measure. Of course, politicians who suddenly take over their opponents' policies frequently wrong-foot those opponents, but it is not quite so rare that their opponents can be entirely excused, and Gladstone certainly knew enough of Disraeli not to have been entirely surprised.

In the end, Disraeli needed to pass the 1867 Reform Act rather more than Gladstone needed to defeat or influence it. The Conservatives had presented the Whigs with a lacklustre opposition since the Corn Law crisis of 1846; it had taken twenty years to put together a credible front bench, and in 1866 they were still in a minority. In all that time they had achieved nothing of political note: Palmerston's Pax Britannica, the annexation of the Punjab, the Great Exhibition, the Crimean War, direct rule for India, the *Trent* and *Alabama* incidents with the United States, the unification of Italy, the Fenians, Prussia's war with Denmark – in not one of these major events had the party of Pitt, Castlereagh and Peel played any major role. Inevitably, the Whig and Liberal benches were full of men with long years of ministerial experience behind them, not least Gladstone himself who, had ten years' experience as chancellor of the exchequer alone.

In many ways parliamentary reform presented the Conservatives, and Disraeli himself, with a make-or-break opportunity: it was their one chance to pass a really weighty piece of legislation, and a complex one at that, which would establish them again as major players in the political field, and their leaders as statesmen. In this sense it is certainly accurate to accuse Disraeli of opportunism, as long as it is understood that this does not of itself diminish his achievement in either political or tactical terms. Gladstone is certainly open to criticism for missing his opportunities, and if one wants to be uncharitable he might be accused of incompetence; however, the circumstances were neither normal nor easy, and he was soon able to recover his political poise and to turn the political tables on the very man who had set them up.

Questions

1. Why was Disraeli obliged to introduce a more radical bill than the one he had defeated in 1866?
2. On what grounds might Gladstone, in 1867, be accused of a 'long line of blunders'?

SOURCES

1. ARGUMENTS AGAINST DEMOCRACY

Source A: Disraeli speaking in the debate on the 1859 Reform Bill.

If you establish a democracy, you must in due season reap the fruits of a democracy. You will in due season have great impatience of the public bodies combined in due season with great increase of the public expenditure. You will in due season reap the fruits of such united influence. You will in due season have wars entered into from passion, and not from reason; and you will in due season submit to peace ignominiously* sought and ignominiously obtained, which will diminish your authority and perhaps endanger your independence. You will, in due season, with a democracy find that your property is less valuable and that your freedom is less complete.

*ignominiously = humiliatingly

Source B: Robert Lowe, MP, speaking against the first reading of the Reform Bill (13 March 1866).

If you want venality*, if you want ignorance, if you want drunkenness, and facility for being intimidated; or if, on the other hand, you want impulsive, unreflecting and violent people, where do you look for them in the constituencies? Do you go to the top or to the bottom? . . . We know what those persons are who live in small houses – we have had experience of them under the name of 'freemen' – and no better law, I think, could have been passed than that which disfranchised them altogether. The Government are proposing to enfranchise one class of men who have been disfranchised heretofore . . . If experience proves that corruption varies inversely as the franchise, you must look for more bribery and corruption than you have hitherto had . . . The second [result] will be that the working men of England, finding themselves in a full majority of the whole constituency, will awake to a full sense of their power.

*venality = corruption, openness to bribery

Source C: Hansard (13 March 1866).

MR ACLAND: The extension of the franchise to the working classes ought always to move in accordance with their self-organization, and he should have been glad, if it had been possible, to introduce a franchise founded on the provident societies and clubs of the working men, which were always regarded by them as the test of forethought and respectability, the members embracing the most intelligent portion of that class. Education also, ought to be recognized as a test of qualification.

Source D: Disraeli introducing the Reform Bill (18 March 1867).

If this bill be a proposal that Her Majesty shall be enabled to concede to her subjects, with the advice and concurrence of her Parliament, a liberal measure of popular privileges, then there may be many of its provisions which will be regarded as prudent, wise, and essentially constitutional. If, on the other hand, it be looked upon as a measure having for its object to confer democratic rights, then I admit much that it may contain may be viewed in the light of being indefensible and unjust. We do not, however, live – and I trust it will never be the fate of this country to live – under a democracy. The propositions whch I am going to make tonight certainly have no tendency in that direction.

Source E: *Quarterly Review* (July 1867).

Last year the attempt was to enfranchise the class whose leading principles and ideas are illustrated by the transactions of Trade Unions. This year we have at least in some degree avoided this risk by swamping the skilled artisan in an element of which we do not even know that it has in it any political life at all. We seek to escape the evils of unbridled democracy by the evils of unbounded corruption . . . We call upon the Radicals to save us, we blush to say it, from the Tory Government, and they are gradually taking up the position of a Conservative opposition against the measures of Lord Derby and Mr Disraeli.

Source F: *Quarterly Review* (December 1867).

There can be no doubt that, as far as those who had no official reasons for passing a Reform Bill were concerned, the one dominant feeling of the present year has been a feverish anxiety to 'settle the question' . . . The meetings in the manufacturing towns, and the riots in Hyde Park, had had their effect. The comfortable classes had no stomach for a real struggle.

Questions

1. Explain briefly the following references:
   a) 'We know what those persons are who live in small houses' (Source B) [2]
   b) 'We seek to escape the evils of unbridled democracy by the evils of unbounded corruption' (Source E) [2]
2. Explain the reasons given in Source A for Disraeli's opposition to democracy. [3]
3. Assess Sources E and F as evidence of the reasons for conceding working-class household suffrage in 1867. [6]
4. Compare the views of the working classes given in Sources A and B with the view in Source C. [6]
5.* How far do these documents support the view that the passage of the 1867 Reform Act was due to fear of the working class? [6]

Worked answer: Question 5

There is certainly plenty of evidence of fear in these documents, from Disraeli's fears in Source A about the influence the uneducated masses might exert over policy, through Lowe's deep disapproval in Source B of the working classes' morals and the threat they pose to the constitution, to the *Quarterly Review*'s denunciation of the 'comfortable classes' in Source F for having given in to the Hyde Park rioters. But the picture is not an even one. Firstly, Source C obviously takes a very different view of the working classes anyway, and places trust in their responsibility and good sense. Even if we write Mr Acland off as an exception (though he was far from the only MP to hold this view), the fears of Disraeli, Lowe and the *Quarterly Review* are not all of the same type. Disraeli in Source A and D rules out a democratic franchise, but in each case he was putting forward a Conservative reform proposal designed to bring about just that; and Source D specifically suggests that anyone who expected democracy in the 1867 bill was going to be disappointed.

Lowe, on the other hand, takes a more pessimistic view of the morals of the working classes in the first place, with his talk of corruption, venality and violence, and his brand of fear led him to fight the 1866 Reform Bill, as he would fight the 1867 one, tooth and nail. The *Quarterly Review* reads even more hysterically: in Source E it is even appealing to the Radicals to stop Disraeli (presumably on the basis that 'my enemy's enemy is my friend'). Source F offers no evidence for its claim that the Hyde Park riots, if that is what they were, forced the bill through, and it is not easy to think of any evidence that it might have offered. Since Source E was written after the bill had passed it is probably best regarded as a sour grumble at the result rather than a reliable analysis. Overall these documents do give evidence of fear animating the bill's opponents, but not that it was the major factor among its supporters.

SOURCES

2. HODGKINSON'S AMENDMENT AND THE COMPOUND-HOUSEHOLDER

Hodgkinson's amendment, which proposed adding a proviso to the Reform Bill to end the actual practice of compound-ratepaying, was debated in the House of Commons on Friday 17 May 1867. Except where indicated, these sources are taken from that debate.

Source G: Disraeli introducing the Reform Bill (18 March 1867).

The question arises, ought a compound-householder to have a vote? Well, Sir, in our opinion, assuming that the House is of the same opinion that the foundation of the franchise should be rating and a payment of rates, and that that is adopted by the House, not as a check, as some would say, but, on the contrary, as a qualification, and because it is the best evidence of the trustworthiness of the individual, we have no hesitation in saying ourselves that we do not think that the compound-householder, as a compound-householder, ought to have a vote.

Source H: Disraeli speaking against Gladstone's amendments to the Reform Bill (12 April 1867).

As far as the borough franchise is concerned, I must repeat, at the risk of wearying the House, what I have said from the first, that the franchise in our plan is founded upon principles from which we cannot swerve. And the House has always in its discussions accepted that; nor is it a novelty when we say that personal payment of rate and residence are the only conditions upon which we consent to this arrangement of the borough franchise.

Source I: The Leader of the Opposition supports Hodgkinson's Amendment.

MR GLADSTONE: I therefore hope it may be consistent with the views of the Government to accept my hon. Friend's [Hodgkinson's] Amendment, as it is not in the slightest degree inconsistent with the principles of the measure they have in hand. To make this appeal is upon our part a complete waiving* of the ground upon which we have stood. It is the only way in which we can depart from that ground with propriety and honour; and as far as I am concerned, I am ready to take the responsibility of doing it for the sake of peace.

*waiving = dropping, doing away with

Source J:

MR CHILDERS* . . . could not help drawing the conclusion that Her Majesty's Government entirely approved the proposal of his hon. Friend [Hodgkinson]. Yet in neither of the Reform Bills they had brought forward during the present Session had that principle been embodied. This, then, was the third change of policy on the part of Her Majesty's Government in reference to the Reform Question, though it was one with which he would not quarrel.

*Childers was a Liberal MP and a close associate of Gladstone

Source K:

VISCOUNT CRANBORNE*: He [Disraeli] has announced a change of startling magnitude, a change which involves the certain admission, instead of the contingent and doubtful admission, of some 500,000 people to the franchise. Of this policy I express no opinion; but I say it is entirely an abnegation** of all the principles of his party.

* Viscount Cranborne, eldest son of the Marquess of the Salisbury, held a courtesy title which did not entitle him to a seat in the House of Lords. He therefore sat as a Conservative MP in the House of Commons.

** abnegation = denial

Source L: Disraeli

THE CHANCELLOR OF THE EXCHEQUER: Her Majesty's Government can have no opposition whatever to [Hodgkinson's Amendment]. It is the policy of their own measure – a policy which if they had been masters of the situation they would have recommended long ago for the adoption of the House. But . . . I do not think myself, as far as I can form an opinion on the subject – and it is one to which I have given long and painful thought – that it would be desirable or possible to deal with this question merely by a proviso in the Reform Bill . . . My opinion is that separate legislation would be the better course. You will, otherwise, cause great delay, impede the progress of the Reform Bill, and I doubt not so efficiently deal with the question.

Source M: Disraeli, speaking on Monday 20 May 1867.

THE CHANCELLOR OF THE EXCHEQUER: We [the Government] have given that subject consideration; and it is our opinion that the policy recommended by the Proviso can be effected* by clauses in the bill before the House, and if it can be so accomplished, it shall be.

*effected = brought about

Questions

1. Explain briefly the following references:
    i   'compound-householder' (Source G) [1]
    ii 'personal payment of rate and residence' (Source H) [2]
    iii 'if they had been masters of the situation' (Source L) [1]
2. Outline the reasons given in Source G for denying the vote to compound-householders. [3]
3.* Account for the different views of Hodgkinson's Amendment presented in Sources L and M. [3]
4. Compare the criticisms made of Disraeli in Sources J and K. [4]
5. How far do Sources G, H and L support Source J's accusation of inconsistency on Disraeli's part? [5]
6. How far do these documents, and any other evidence known

to you, support the view that the Liberals determined the final shape of the 1867 Reform Act? [6]

Worked answer: Question 3

Disraeli had always opposed giving the vote to compound-householders, on the grounds that they did not fulfil the criterion of personal payment of rates, but the issue had proved far more con-tentious than he seems to have realised, and looked in danger of holding up the whole bill. Under Hodgkinson's Amendment compound-householders would qualify for the vote as householders, but *not* as *compound-householders*, which is why Disraeli claims in Source L that the proviso is in line with the principles of the bill. On the other hand, Hodgkinson was a Liberal MP, and this was a Friday at the end of a long week: conceding too easily was bound to look either as if Disraeli had been beaten or that he had no principles. In Source L, therefore, Disraeli seems to be playing for time by proposing postponing the matter to a separate measure. In Source M, however, Disraeli has a weekend's reflection behind him; he would also have had a chance to consult the cabinet. He is therefore able to concede the point quickly, without having to be forced to a vote or appear to have suffered a defeat.

5

THE PROFESSIONALISATION OF POLITICS, 1867–1900

BACKGROUND NARRATIVE

Although we need to be careful not to exaggerate its significance from the point of view of enfranchising the working classes, the 1867 Reform Act did nevertheless mark a sea-change in British political life. A substantial section of the urban working class was now enfranchised, and each party was keen to capture these new votes. Doing so required a much greater degree of organisation at local level than the parties had been used to. Potential voters had to be identified, encouraged or cajoled down the appropriate political path, sometimes even taken to the polls. The introduction of the secret ballot in 1872 ended much of the traditional rowdiness of open hustings, but elections could still be very violent affairs and were often as brazenly corrupt as ever – indeed, some thought the Ballot Act made them more corrupt rather than less, since the more venal voters could now accept bribes from both parties without either knowing how they actually voted. Not until the passing of the 1883 Corrupt Practices Act was the bribery of electors effectively tackled.

Nevertheless, creating some 700,000 new voters effectively ruled out the sort of large-scale 'treating' that the old borough-mongers had practised. The new way ahead was pioneered in Birmingham by the work of Joseph Chamberlain. Chamberlain worked out a scientific and tactical route through the complex local electoral structure, in such a way as to return the maximum number of Liberals at both local and national elections. It required precise planning, constant communication with the voters, who had to know exactly what was expected of them, and formidable organisation. Although Chamberlain's critics, particularly within his own party, sneeringly compared his Birmingham Liberal Association to the sort of party 'caucuses' that were springing up in America, with their attendant showmanship and block-voting, there was no denying the success of Chamberlain's Birmingham caucus, and he went on to found a National Liberal Foundation (NLF) along similar lines. However, the NLF ran into difficulties getting itself accepted by the parliamentary Liberal Party and their organisers, the party whips, especially when Chamberlain started clashing with Gladstone over Irish Home Rule.

The Conservatives took longer to organise themselves, but they did it very effectively. Local Conservative and Constitutional Associations played the same role that Chamberlain had carved out in Birmingham, maintaining party support at local level and ensuring it was translated into votes at election time. Lord Randolph Churchill set up the popular Primrose League, named after what Disraeli had claimed was his favourite flower, and which proved particularly successful in mobilising Conservative support among women. By the turn of the century the Conservatives combined a strong parliamentary organisation with a widespread network of local associations, overseen by, but not answerable to, a Central Office. Party structure had developed along lines that are familiar today.

Much of the need for this reorganisation had come from the enfranchisement of so many working-class men. Yet neither Conservatives nor Liberals could claim to have been traditionally the parties of urban working people, and they now had to some extent to adapt their political philosophies to appeal to this new section of the electorate. Gladstone's brand of Liberalism placed the interests of the people at its heart, and although it would be quite mistaken to see Gladstone as some sort of proto-socialist, he certainly understood how to mobilise strong popular working-class support for his programme. He did not focus on traditional 'working-class' issues: he launched his first popular campaign against Disraeli over the Bulgarian atrocities in 1875–6, and he mobilised general support again, on a wider range of issues, in his famous Midlothian campaigns of 1879–80. The Conservatives to some extent copied the Liberal line on social reform, though Lord Randolph Churchill claimed, rather grandly, that the new Conservative interest in working-class concerns represented a new philosophy of 'Tory Democracy'. Perhaps more plausibly, Disraeli had helped to mobilise working-class support by presenting the Conservatives as the party of monarchy and empire. Nevertheless, the Conservatives remained a solid party under the leadership of Lord Salisbury and his nephew, Arthur Balfour, though they did discover, to their delight, that there was a substantial section of the working class that would consistently vote Conservative. Whether it did so out of some sense of nostalgic deference to the party of the landed squires, or out of dislike for – or disillusion with – the Liberals (or, after 1900, the new Labour party) was harder to say.

ANALYSIS (1): HOW USEFUL ARE THE CONCEPTS OF 'GLADSTONIAN LIBERALISM' AND 'TORY DEMOCRACY' TO THE HISTORIAN OF THE PERIOD 1867–1892?

The concept of Gladstonian Liberalism has fared rather better at the hands of historians than has that of Tory Democracy. Almost all of the many historians who have written about Disraeli, including his admirers like Blake and Cowling, tend to discount the claim that Disraeli's brand of Conservatism amounted to a coherent philosophy aimed at spreading the appeal of the party into the working classes. The phrase itself starts at a grave disadvantage since it was never, so far as we know, used by Disraeli himself; it seems to have been coined by Lord Randolph Churchill. Churchill had his many strengths, but accurate political analysis was not one of them. (He disastrously over-estimated his own political importance, for example, not to mention his rather grand naming of his group of four Tory radicals as 'the Fourth Party'.) Although much of this makes Churchill very like the young Disraeli, and Churchill often claimed to be following in the great man's footsteps, the fact remains that he had not understood Disraeli well at all. Disraeli did not believe in resigning, and certainly would never have dreamt of sacrificing hard-won office in order to force his views on the Cabinet, as Churchill did in 1886. Perhaps more to the point, Disraeli never had anything as coherent as a policy programme, of the sort Churchill was trying to force on Salisbury.

When Disraeli won the election in 1874 (having briefly headed a minority government in 1868) he took office for the first and last time with a majority in the Commons, but it was soon painfully obvious that he was by no means clear what he was going to do with it: what is there to do, after all, at the top of a greasy pole? John Vincent[1] sees Disraeli's response to what was known as the 'Condition of England Question' as the creation of a sort of rhetoric of national unity – like the later 'Dunkirk spirit' – rather than anything resembling a programme of social reform. Although Disraeli's ministry produced some perfectly competent, even good, social legislation, it was mostly designed to build on the legislation Gladstone had passed between 1868 and 1874 and to clear up some of the areas of ambiguity or controversy it had thrown up. The most obvious example is the law relating to trade union picketing, which had been made illegal under Gladstone's Criminal Law Amendment Act; it was a relatively easy matter to change this to allow peaceful picketing, thereby scoring a point off Gladstone and winning the grateful thanks of the trade unions. Even in new departures Disraeli's legislation was cautious, seeking to avoid antagonising important interest groups, and to keep state intervention to a minimum. So, for example, the Artisans' Dwellings Act, the social reform for which Disraeli's ministry is probably best known, did not suddenly clear the cities of their slums – there were still plenty of these around for the Luftwaffe to bomb seventy years later: it merely *allowed* local authorities, if they so chose, to buy up slum areas and build workers' accommodation. Some chose to; others did not. The Merchant Shipping Act introduced the famous Plimsoll line but allowed the shipping owners to oversee how it was done. Throughout, there was a theme of pragmatism rather than of principle in Disraeli's legislation.

Part of the problem is that it was not, for the most part, Disraeli's legislation. There is no evidence that he took much personal interest in the details of domestic legislation, and it is Richard Cross at the Home Office who deserves much of the credit for whatever domestic policy Disraeli may have had. We should not leap too quickly to judgement on this. Eighteenth-century 'conservatives' were deeply suspicious of change of any kind, and this remained the case well into the nineteenth century. Peel's acceptance of Catholic emancipation and his response to the Corn Law agitation were largely pragmatic; only his conversion to free trade could fairly be called a party policy. The Conservatives had not had a distinctive political philosophy since then, which was one reason why the middle years of the century saw so much coalition politics. Insofar as they had a political philosophy in the 1870s, it was the result of Disraeli's two famous speeches in 1872, in Manchester's Free Trade Hall and in the Crystal Palace, but although these are often quoted, they do not amount to much of a political philosophy, and certainly not to a programme to be followed in office. He said the Conservatives should be in favour of the reform of proven abuses (who isn't?) and that they should stand up in support of the institutions of England. This no doubt sounded grand enough to make his audience's chests swell, but it did not amount to much more than maintaining the *status quo* in practice. In any case, apart from the Church of Ireland not many institutions of the sort Disraeli had in mind were under much threat anyway.

Disraeli's 1872 speeches are usually credited with linking the Conservative Party to the issue of empire, but this too needs to be read with caution. There was no real evidence to support Disraeli's claim that the Liberals had neglected the empire, which is probably why he did not give any; but neither is there much real evidence of Disraeli's enthusiasm for imperialism once he was in office either. In both the major areas of imperial expansion during his ministry, into Afghanistan and into Zululand in 1879, neither move was undertaken with the government's approval (nor, entirely, with its knowledge), and both went disastrously wrong. In 1876 Disraeli passed the controversial Royal Titles Act to make the queen Empress of India, which she already ruled anyway; the year before he had seized the opportunity to buy the shares of the bankrupt Khedive of Egypt in the Suez Canal Company – a bold and no doubt wise move, but not one which required a sense of burning imperial mission to take. The main example usually given of Disraeli using foreign and imperial policy to play to the gallery is the Eastern Question crisis of 1875–8, which spawned the term 'jingoism' for an aggressive, crowd-pleasing foreign policy.[2] What is often forgotten, however, is how *un*popular Disraeli was in the early stages of the crisis, when he steadfastly refused to lift a finger to help the Bulgarians against the Turks, and Gladstone was able to whip up widespread support with his attacks on Disraeli's inaction.

Does all this mean that Disraeli stood for nothing except his own political survival and that the whole idea of Tory Democracy is a myth? Disraeli himself was a complex character, and no term will entirely encapsulate his political ideas and policies; but even if he himself was not a Tory Democrat, that does not of itself deny the term any validity. It will do, for example, very nicely for Lord Randolph Churchill; the only trouble is that when Churchill tried to force his tory democratic ideas on Salisbury's cabinet in 1886 he failed. There was nothing democratic,

Tory or otherwise, about Lord Salisbury, a patrician figure of the loftiest sort. It is true that under Salisbury the party widened its electoral appeal, but this was far more marked among the middle classes than among the workers. Suburban, middle-class toryism even gained its own nickname, 'Villa Conservatism'; working-class Conservative support certainly existed, but Salisbury never went out of his way to foster it, and still less would he alter policy radically in order to gain it. Working-class Conservatives seem to have been motivated by a range of issues, from dislike of Home Rule and pride in the empire to fear of the Socialists or simple dislike of the Liberals; what they were not doing was responding to a Conservative Party policy geared to working-class concerns, for the simple reason that there wasn't one. Salisbury was more than happy to receive the support of local Conservative and Constitutional Associations, many of which had substantial working-class membership, but he took care never to let them influence his decision-making.

Unlike Disraeli and Salisbury, Gladstone was quite unashamed in his pursuit of popular support, though putting it in these terms is to mis-read Gladstone's purpose. In an age of great crowd oratory by religious revivalist preachers, Gladstone deliberately adopted an overtly mission-ary style of politics, and simply carried his message out to the public. Gladstone had a strong sense of mission, whether it was to pacify Ireland or to save girls from prostitution, and although it could backfire and get him disliked by people who encountered it at close quarters, it nearly always worked well with the Victorian public. He used it first in response to the appalling reports of atrocities in Bulgaria, veritable nineteenth-century 'ethnic cleansing'; by 1879 in his Mid-lothian campaigns he was presenting 'Beaconsfieldism' (from Disraeli's ennoblement as Earl of Beaconsfield) as a sort of immoral set of attitudes and policies. In each case Gladstone was able, personally, to create a wave of widespread public support in a way for which the supposed Tory Democrats simply had no equivalent.

Admittedly, the Bulgarian campaign turned sour on Gladstone when Disraeli stood up to the Russians – always a popular move with the Victorian public – but Gladstone was soon able to turn the tables on Disraeli with his Midlothian campaigns, which effectively won the 1880 election a year early. The only time Gladstone failed badly was when he tried to apply the same style of Old Testament prophet approach to Irish Home Rule, and even here he succeeded far more than he is usually given credit for. It is easy to remember that Chamberlain raised a revolt against Home Rule which killed the bill; it is easy to forget, firstly that the majority of the Liberals stayed loyal to Gladstone, secondly that the extra-parliamentary Liberal Party and even Chamberlain's own National Liberal Federation stayed loyal to Gladstone; and thirdly that the second Home Rule Bill passed the Commons and had to be killed in the House of Lords. Gladstone is often accused of wrecking his party over his great missionary obsessions, but the plain fact is that for the most part he carried both his party and the wider public with him.

But was this the work of Gladstone himself or of some wider philosophy called Gladstonian Liberalism? Did Gladstonian Liberalism, indeed, exist beyond the fertile brain of Mr Gladstone, or did it just mean whatever he happened to have thought of most recently? It is certainly clear that the Liberals were dependent on Gladstone to a peculiar degree, far more than the Conservatives were on Disraeli. The best way to see this is to look at the relatively poor showing of the Liberals when Gladstone retired in 1874 and the party was taken over by Lord Hartington, or again in 1894 when it was taken over by Lord Rosebery. Neither could shine in the way Gladstone could, and Rosebery proved particularly ineffectual. Above all, there was no attempt by either man to launch the Liberals on any path of policy in the way Gladstone did, or to deviate from the paths Gladstone had laid down.

This would tend to suggest that Gladstonian Liberalism, insofar as it was a political philosophy at all, was simply what Gladstone believed. Put like this, it sounds like a criticism, but in fact there is no reason why it should be. In practice, except for certain very basic principles, all parties operated as voting fodder for the policies and wishes of their leaders. In the twentieth century, party leaders have become bound by conference votes and party rules, and leaders who lose touch with their parties' wishes can be ignominiously dropped, as Ramsay MacDonald, Edward Heath and Margaret Thatcher were all to find to their cost; but this idea was only just emerging towards the end of Gladstone's time. Up until then a major leader, like Pitt, Fox, Peel or Palmerston, effectively directed policy as he thought fit, and MPs who were unhappy with it had to secede from the party. Even the steady growth of cabinet government did not prevent a strong leader from imposing his views. Peel's fall in 1846 was the exception that proved the rule: he and his cabinet were convinced that their party would have supported them had it not been for Disraeli's sniping campaign; and the Tories promptly took up Peel's policy of free trade after 1846 in any case. If Gladstone did lead his party according to his own particular philosophy, then he was acting fully in accordance with every precedent available to him.

What makes Gladstonian Liberalism so difficult to pin down is that Gladstone possessed a complex mind which people at the time – and afterwards – often found difficult to follow. There are certain basic instincts, such as free trade or individual liberty, but all too often different aspects of Gladstone's beliefs came into conflict, which would lead to apparent contradictions and accusations of hypocrisy. He believed passionately in *laissez-faire* as a general philosophy; yet it was his governments, especially his first, which – by extending their operations into areas like education and local services – set in motion the enormous growth in the power of the state which was to come to full fruition in the following century. Gladstone abhorred Disraeli's imperialism and sought always to pursue an ethical foreign policy, yet he it was who launched the British invasion of Egypt in 1882. Above all, Gladstone's brand of Liberalism was always subject to sudden obsessions which would threaten to overshadow everything else: what would nowadays be called 'single-issue politics' and was known then as 'faddism'. It might be disestablishment of the Irish Church, and later of the Welsh Church, or it might be Irish Home Rule but, whichever it was, it became Liberal Party policy the moment Mr Gladstone decided he was in favour of it. One can sympathise with Joseph Chamberlain's sense of frustration with his leader.

Nevertheless, for all its weaknesses and apparent contradictions, there was a coherence and consistency to Gladstonian Liberalism. Gladstone's – and therefore his party's – belief in setting individuals on their own two feet to give them a fair start in life lay behind aspects as diverse as the 1870 Education Act, his attack on the paper duty, his attitude towards parliamentary reform, his unremitting campaign for Irish Home Rule, even his work with London prostitutes. However, there were two problems with this way of developing policy: in the first place, as the franchise grew wider no political party was going to continue to be content to have its policy decided in effect by its leader as he walked around his garden; secondly, a system based so heavily on one man needs new blood to carry the policy-making role on, and there was no obvious candidate for such a role in the 1880s or 1890s. Without an individual to make it, policy would have to come from the party itself, which would mean that when Gladstone finally retired the internal structure of the Liberal Party would come quickly to assume much more importance than it had before.

In conclusion, then, the terms Tory Democracy and Gladstonian Liberalism are certainly useful to historians, but in different ways. Tory Democracy can be used to describe the views of those – such as Randolph Churchill, John Gorst and, at least in the early days, Arthur

Balfour – who wanted the Tories to appeal more directly to the working classes. In a sense they both failed and won: they failed because they did not persuade Salisbury to make the sort of pitch they wanted; on the other hand, working-class support for the Conservatives certainly did materialise, in large quantities, so that even if Tory Democracy never represented a coherent policy, it can be said to have represented a successful political instinct. It was certainly a reaction to Gladstone's brand of Liberalism, and even more to Chamberlain's style of political operating, and in that sense, perhaps paradoxically, Gladstonian Liberalism, far more than Tory Democracy, can be credited with setting the agenda for the development of policy in both the Tory and the Liberal Party in the era of democratic politics which followed on from the Second Reform Act.

Questions

1. In what ways, and to what extent, did the Conservative Party under Disraeli appeal to a working-class electorate?
2. How important was Gladstone himself to the appeal of the Liberals to the electorate?
3. How convincing is the case that Gladstonian Liberalism had more substance and influence than Tory Democracy?

ANALYSIS (2): TO WHAT EXTENT DID THE 1867 REFORM ACT CREATE THE MODERN SYSTEM OF PARTY POLITICS?

At some point when writing on this issue, historians nearly always find time to quote Gilbert and Sullivan's 1882 comic opera *Iolanthe*, which satirises the parliamentary politics of its day. At one point in the opera a guardsman on duty outside the Houses of Parliament muses in song that

I often think it's comical
How Nature always does contrive
That every boy and every gal,
That's born into the world alive,
Is either a little Liberal,
Or else a little Conservative.

This is usually taken to indicate that by 1882 the two parties actually exercised that degree of hold over the political affiliations of the nation; what gets forgotten is that *Iolanthe* is a satire, and it is in the nature of satire to exaggerate for comic effect. W. S. Gilbert had spotted a trend, but it was not the case in 1882 that the country could be divided in two as neatly as the song suggests: it was not even true of the House of Commons. Nevertheless, a general impression persists that the period following the 1867 Reform Act saw the development of modern-style party politics, dominated by two highly organised parties binding their members in unquestioning loyalty to their leaders. This aspect, too, features in the Guardsman's song, as he explains that MPs, 'If they've a brain and cerebellum too, They have to leave that brain outside And vote just as their leaders tell 'em to'. It was good for a laugh in 1882, but both Gladstone and Salisbury would no doubt have responded, 'If only it were true!'

There is one respect in which this interpretation is fairly accurate: the modern role of party leader, with a strong hold on the party, can be dated from the period of Gladstone and Disraeli. Their colourful personalities, their command of oratory and the personal antipathy each felt for the other lent Gladstone and Disraeli a sort of 'star quality' which made them a gift for cartoonists and helped to personalise politics for the electorate and newspaper readers. Their features were well known, and their names became almost shorthand terms for their parties. Later leaders adopted different styles but their hold on their parties was no less secure. Although Salisbury and Balfour never played for a strong popular image in the way Disraeli did, they saw off a series of challenges to their authority, from Randolph Churchill, to an extent from local Conservative Associations, and very definitely from Joseph Chamberlain. Gladstone, too, outmanoeuvred Chamberlain, though at the cost of both his first Home Rule bill and his third ministry, and his successors proved capable of seeing off challenges to their authority, Campbell-Bannerman outfacing the Liberal Imperialists, and Asquith the supporters of women's suffrage. Not until Asquith crumpled under the strains of the war was a Liberal leader forced to succumb to pressure from within the party, and the circumstances in 1916 were unusual by any standards.

But although this indicates that strong, directional party leadership was in evidence at this time, it also indicates that politics was far from being the straightforward two-party affair of *Iolanthe*. For one thing, there were never just two parties. The Irish Nationalists were a substantial third party, and Joseph Chamberlain's Liberal Unionists a similarly substantial fourth. In the same way as the Unionists were being absorbed into the Conservative Party, the trade union movement began sending Labour MPs to Westminster. For a time the Liberals were able to head off three-party politics by means of an electoral 'Lib–Lab' pact, by which the two parties agreed not to put up rival candidates at elections, but the alliance did not last, and it was breaking up by 1910.

Within the major parties too there were important divisions. The Liberals had split over parliamentary reform in 1866 and would split again over Home Rule and the Boer War. Gladstone's style of leadership proved so divisive that in the general election of 1874 in Bradford and Sheffield Liberal candidates actually stood against each other. Later there were to be similarly serious internal disagreements over the radical 'New Liberal' proposals of Lloyd George and Winston Churchill, and over the battle with the House of Lords that followed. The Conservatives were bitterly divided after they lost the 1868 election; in the 1880s Salisbury had to deal with Randolph Churchill and his 'Fourth Party' of Tory Radicals; in the 1890s and 1900s Salisbury and Balfour tried in vain to contain the disastrous split in Conservative ranks provoked by Joseph Chamberlain's campaign for tariff reform. Although politics had certainly come a long way from the patronage politics of Pitt's day, it was not yet in the age of huge, monolithic parties imposing their will on all their MPs.

What certainly did change was the way the parties were organised. In the days of Peel and Palmerston there was no equivalent of the heavily centralised party organisations of the late twentieth century. The nearest equivalent of a central office were two London gentlemen's clubs, the Carlton Club (founded 1832) for the Tories and the Reform Club (founded 1836) for the Whigs. These clubs acted as semi-formal gathering places for like-minded MPs, but since party allegiance was fairly fluid, membership of a particular club was not necessarily a sure guide to political principles. After the Tory split over the Corn Laws in 1846, for example, many Peelites continued to pay their membership subscriptions to the Carlton Club long after they had gone over to the Whigs. The more mundane work of running elections was undertaken at constituency level by local firms of solicitors who would act as party agents, checking registers of electors to ensure the maximum turnout. Many of these registers survive, and one can still see the handwritten annotations against the long lists of names, indicating who has moved, who is newly eligible, even exasperated comments against persistent absentees like 'Is he alive?'

The wider franchise of the 1867 Act placed severe strains on what was in truth a relatively amateurish system: in Blackburn, for example, the Act increased the electorate overnight from 1,845 to 9,700. To meet new demands of this magnitude, both parties began establishing local clubs and associations. The Liberals founded Working Men's Clubs; the Conservatives responded with local Conservative

Associations and more working-class-orientated Constitutional Clubs, all loosely grouped in an overall federation, the National Union of Conservative and Constitutional Associations (NUCCA). It is a sign of the importance of these associations that Disraeli chose to give his famous Manchester and Crystal Palace speeches in 1872 to meetings of the NUCCA. In due course, politics at local level saw a flowering of groups of this sort. By the 1880s any sizeable town would have its local Liberal Association, often a local Women's Liberal Association, and in university towns there would be a University Liberal Association too. On the Conservative side, as well as the local Conservative or Constitutional Club there would be the formidable 'Buds', 'Dames' and 'Knights Companion' of the Primrose League, which had 2,300 branches and over 1.5 million members by 1900, including a Cycling Corps for contacting voters in isolated areas.

These political associations ran a full programme of social events for their members – picnics, outings, educational lectures, even a Wild West Show in one case, while one enterprising Liberal Club in Lancashire held a dangerous-sounding evening of administering electric shocks! Many of these clubs were designed to attract working-class members: some ran burial and co-operative societies for their members, and one gets a sense of the clientele at the Cambridge Liberal Association from the fact that in the 1880s it was spending more on spittoons than on chairs or tables! But these social functions were always secondary to the clubs' prime purpose: to mobilise support at election times. As well as general elections, this meant local council elections, School Board elections, elections to the (Poor Law) Boards of Guardians, and for really zealous activists it meant parish or district council elections as well.

What this clearly adds up to is a sort of mass mobilisation of a substantial section of the population in political activity in the last quarter of the nineteenth century. This was not necessarily confined to political parties: local debating societies ran 'Houses of Commons' which discussed topical issues within a parliamentary structure, with a 'government' and 'opposition'. This growth of interest and participation in political activity was helped by – indeed it could hardly have happened without – a big increase in the number and circulation of local newspapers, which would carry long, detailed descriptions of political meetings and marches, and verbatim reports of major speeches. The important question at the time, as well as for historians looking back on this remarkable spread of political activity, was the extent to which local activists might influence, and might even come to dominate, the parties in parliament and the formation of party policy.

This was very much what Joseph Chamberlain was after, from his Birmingham base within the Liberal party. He began by working out how to manipulate the complicated voting system for School Board elections so that they returned a Liberal majority, and in 1877 he established the National Liberal Federation (NLF) to do the same in local and parliamentary elections. Interestingly, although the NLF was formidably efficient in turning Liberal voters out on polling days, many in the party leadership, including W.E. Forster and Gladstone himself, were strongly opposed to it. They rightly predicted that such a formidable political machine, or 'caucus' as it was known, would not be content with producing voters for other people's policies, but would want a say in drawing those policies up. Gladstone launched into his vigorous Midlothian campaigns at least partly in order to seize the initiative back from Chamberlain and the NLF and re-establish his authority as party leader, and he cannot have been surprised that, once in the Commons, Chamberlain should have proved difficult to deal with: he tried to push through an 'unauthorised' programme of social reform policies and constantly criticised Gladstone's dealings with the Irish nationalist leader, Parnell.

After Gladstone lost the 1885 election Chamberlain tried to push the party into a radical, anti-landlord policy, but – as John Belchem puts it – Gladstone outflanked him by taking up the cause of Irish Home Rule and making it a test of party loyalty.[3] In fact, the Home Rule crisis was as much a battle for control of the Liberal Party as it was about the future of Ireland, and that side of the battle at any rate Gladstone won: Chamberlain took 78 'Liberal Unionist' MPs with him out of Gladstone's government, and gained some support in Lancashire and Cornwall, but otherwise the parliamentary party, the local Liberal Associations, and Chamberlain's own NLF all stayed loyal to Gladstone. The parliamentary party quickly consolidated its hold on the NLF by having it taken over by the Liberal Central Association, with Francis Schnadhorst operating as secretary to both organisations and effectively bringing the NLF to heel. The NLF was not yet a spent force: in 1891 it forced Gladstone to accept the 'Newcastle programme' of radical social reforms as party policy; but this was an easy victory: Gladstone was old, his relations with the parliamentary party were rapidly reaching snapping point, and many Liberals thought that the party had to have a bit more to its policies than just Home Rule for Ireland. When the Newcastle programme failed to attract voters in the 1895 election, however, Rosebery quickly dropped it, and neither he nor his successors, Campbell-Bannerman and Asquith, would give the party rank-and-file another chance to force policy on the leadership.

On the Conservative side, there was a similar pattern to the growth of the party. Disraeli effectively created the role of full-time party agent, to keep an eye on the growing numbers of local associations, and in 1870 he appointed an efficient and methodical MP, John Gorst, to the post. Gorst established a Central Office for the party, and also became secretary of the NUCCA, which promptly moved into the same building as Gorst's Central Office. The proof of the effectiveness of this new arrangement was the Conservative triumph in the 1874 election. Gorst himself fell out with the party leadership after the Conservatives lost the 1880 election, and joined Lord Randolph Churchill's band of radical Conservative dissidents known as the 'Fourth Party', but the party structure he had established carried on under the leadership of W.H. Smith. Smith, whose name, then as now, was familiar from the high-street stationers' shops, was an example of the new breed of professional politician, doggedly loyal to the party and its leadership, who could be found leading Conservative and Constitutional Clubs up and down the land. In a party of this sort there was no chance for an insubordinate aristocrat like Lord Randolph Churchill to split the party as Chamberlain had done with the Liberals. Chamberlain, whose background lay in industry and who had made his name through local political activity, could mobilise enough support in the party rank-and-file to cause a major split, as he did over tariff reform; but a mixture of loyalty to the party leadership and a deeply-rooted instinct in favour of free trade meant that he could never win the Tories over. It is small wonder that Derek Beales concludes that 'what strikes one most about the history of these [local] organisations, after their initial outburst, is their ineffectiveness'.[4]

In other words, in the case of political parties after 1867, appearances – and *Iolanthe* – are deceptive. Parties undoubtedly grew, in size, in number and in complexity; they developed an increased sense of their own importance, and certain individuals within them had major ambitions both for themselves and for party organisations. But parties had splits and factions within them, and could on occasion cause their leaders serious trouble. Party leaders proved capable of overcoming this trouble, and above all, in both the Conservative and Liberal parties the leadership was usually able to keep the grass-roots party out of policy- and decision-making. Whether or not this means that the 1867 Act produced modern party politics depends on how one views modern politics. In general terms, the answer must, apart from the issue of party leadership, be no, or at least not by 1900; however, when Conservative Associations complained bitterly in 1997 that the election of the party leader to succeed John Major was reserved for the deleted post-election parliamentary party, some of them must have considered that little had changed.

Questions

1. In what ways did the development of party organisation at local level threaten the unity of the Conservative and Liberal parties?
2. Why, by 1900, had the party membership failed to establish a hold on policy-making within the Conservative and Liberal parties?
3. 'It changed their membership, but not their philosophies.' How accurate is this judgement on the effect of the 1867 Reform Act on the Conservative and Liberal parties?

SOURCES

1. TORY DEMOCRACY AND GLADSTONIAN LIBERALISM

Note: To investigate these two historical concepts, this selection of documents is drawn from various historians' accounts of the careers of Gladstone and Disraeli. To help clarify the points they make, the selection and the questions deal with each statesman separately; the last question in the section on Gladstone then brings the two issues together.

Source A: John K. Walton, *Disraeli* (1990).

Disraeli presided over the passing of the [social reform] legislation, without supplying a detailed agenda: his role was to make time available for a programme of this kind, and to supply a benign environment for it. Most of the actual legislation merely emerged: there was no need for an overall plan or set of priorities to identify problems and bring them into the parliamentary arena. And the only distinctly Conservative aspects of the legislation had nothing to do with its status as 'social reform': they were the parts of the Licensing and Education Acts which rewarded or protected Tory vested interests. The only *Disraelian* aspects were rhetorical.

Source B: Robert Blake, *Disraeli* (1966).

The truth is that Disraeli had principles when he led the party and believed in them sincerely, but they were not the 'principles', if that word can be used at all, of Young England. It is easy to underestimate Disraeli's innate conservatism. He believed passionately in the greatness of England – not in itself a Tory monopoly.

But he also believed no less deeply that England's greatness depended upon the ascendancy of the landed class. All the rest was 'leather and prunella'.* This does not mean that he wished to set class against class. On the contrary he proclaimed the doctrine of one nation and asserted that if the Conservative party was not a national party it was nothing. But he did sincerely think that the nation would decline with the decline of the landed interest. Like Gladstone he was an 'out-and-out inequalitarian'.

*a matter of complete indifference

Source C: Paul Smith, *Disraeli* (1996).

That Disraeli, if he had called into being a working-class majority in the borough electorate, had done so with no notion of making it the target of an appeal in the name of some 'democratic' Toryism was made sufficiently obvious when the next [1868] election arrived. . . . He [had] almost casually fashioned an electorate with which he had little desire to communicate and an arena in which he had little aptitude to perform. He had never cared for electors much . . . Characteristic was his response to the 'great mob' which cheered him on Carlisle station while he was on his way to Balmoral in 1868: 'It was an ordeal of ten minutes; I bowed to them and went on reading; but was glad when the train moved'.

Source D: Stanley Weintraub, *Disraeli* (1993).

The term 'Tory Democracy' would later be associated with Disraeli. Its reality is validated by his sympathy and respect for political opponents like Cobden, Bright, and Mill, whose radical views about social and economic change he respected and wanted the Queen to understand.

Source E: T.A. Jenkins, *Disraeli and Victorian Conservatism* (1996)

The middle classes had changed since the 1840s, both in terms of the weaken-ing political affinity with Liberalism on the part of the employers of labour and tradesmen, and in terms of the expansion of the professions and of 'white collar' occupations like clerks and teachers. All these groups may well have found much to approve of in Disraeli's rhetoric about upholding the ancient institutions of the country and maintaining Britain's imperial strength, and perhaps a little sanitary reform would not necessarily have been considerered a bad thing. Disraeli is therefore reasonably entitled to receive credit for having created his own brand of 'conservatism' by the 1870s, although a later generation would prefer to call it 'Tory Democracy'.

Questions

1. Explain what is meant by:
   i 'Young England' (Source B) [2]
   ii 'Cobden, Bright, and Mill' (Source D) [2]
2. On what grounds do Walton (Source A) and Smith (Source C) accuse Disraeli of having no consistent policy of parliamentary and social reform? [4]
3.* What principles are recognised by Blake (Source B), Weintraub (Source D) and T.A. Jenkins (Source E)? [4]
4. In the light of Source D and E, assess the validity of the argument in Sources B and C that Disraeli's political philosophy was fundamentally anti-democratic. [6]

Worked answer: Question 3

Although Blake does not believe that Disraeli kept to his Young England principles, he does see Disraeli as a believer in a traditional, conservative image of England, in which the landed aristocracy played a central part. Weintraub is more impressed by the idea of Disraeli as a radical, essentially because he paid tribute to opponents like Cobden, Bright and Mill (though it is one thing to pay tribute to an opponent, and quite another to take up their principles). T.A. Jenkins takes the themes of social reform, maintenance of institutions, and Empire that Disraeli laid out in his 1872 speeches and suggests that, because – whether or not Disraeli intended this – they appealed to the new, larger, professional middle class, they deserve to be regarded as a set of principles. In this sense, Jenkins is not necessarily suggesting that Disraeli actually had a coherent philosophy, merely that one could be inferred from his rhetoric.

Source F: E.J. Feuchtwanger, *Gladstone* (1975).

The Liberal party as a whole [in 1887] . . . was still a middle-class party, but middle-class radicalism, with its emphasis on religious and civil equality, had largely shot its bolt – it had won its objectives. The party was, however, not ready to allow the politically conscious working class to occupy positions of real influence in its organisation, either locally or nationally. . . . Radicalism within the Liberal party was a ragbag of ideas and causes, disestablishment, local option, electoral reform, the status of the House of Lords, employers' liabilities, shorter hours; the leading Radicals were anti-authoritarian gadflies like Labouchere. Had Gladstone been radical rather than conservative in his views he might have given the Liberal party a new radical impetus. As it was he remained a Peelite

Conservative who gradually reconciled himself to a few items from the Radical ragbag; from a left-wing point of view his sin was one of omission rather than commission.

Source G: H.C.G. Matthew, *Gladstone, 1809–1874* (1988).

Buoyed up by the great Nonconformist revival of the 1860s, Dissenters saw the victory of 1868 as the occasion for an assertion of the political priorities of Nonconformity: general disestablishment, abolition of university tests, a Burials Bill. The disestablishment of the Anglican Church would lead to social and political equality in the same way that Peelite finance had led to fiscal and economic equality. Allied to these proposals were those of the intellectuals, especially demanding educational reform, the abolition of university tests, the ballot, and equality of opportunity in entrance to the Civil Service. Most of these Gladstone regarded with caution, and some with hostility. He particularly disliked the complete repeal of university tests, which he succeeded in avoiding in its extreme form. He also regretted the introduction of the ballot which he came to see as unavoidable but with a 'lingering reluctance', and whose various delays he contemplated with some satisfaction, partly because the issue helped to hold the party together in 1871 and 1872.

Source H: Roy Jenkins, *Gladstone* (1995).

The Ballot Bill was not much more welcome to Gladstone than had been the Elementary Education and the University Tests Bills. It was nearly forty years since he had informed the readers of the *Liverpool Standard* that the fall of the Roman Republic was to be attributed to the corruptions of secret voting . . . [and] he had retained a certain resistance towards the idea that those who deserved the vote also needed the protection of being able to exercise it secretly. His ideal polity was a mass of contradictions. He liked small boroughs with restricted electorates which could nurture statesmen without distracting them from higher things with the squalor of local log-rolling. He also liked the idea of voters as independent gentlemen who strode to the poll with their heads high and the courage to declare their choice without fear or favour. . . . Yet he had also come to believe in the good moral sense of the masses against the classes. The great democracy of Northern England and Scotland, acting like a vast jury, was the best hope of saving Britain from the brittle values of the metropolitan 'upper ten thousand' and their Home Counties hangers-on, of whom Disraeli had made himself the unesteemed mouthpiece.

Source I: Jonathon Parry, *The Rise and Fall of Liberal Government in Victorian Britain* (1995).

[Gladstone's] particular political concerns were with finance, religion and the immorality of coercive or careless government; everything else in politics was to him just mundane administration. His economising zeal, his foreign policy, his instincts about Ireland, his hostility to clumsy parliamentary interference with the doctrine and discipline of his beloved Church of England, all took the form they did because of his drive to eradicate incompetent, boastful over-government. The problem for the Liberal Party was that these attitudes could be very controversial, because of Gladstone's own forcefulness in promoting them . . . His zeal for purification, superimposed on his Peelite inheritance, created a new conception of politics organised around an endless agenda of business. In 1877 he declared that the 'vital principle' of the party was 'action'. This was news to most Liberals.

Questions

5. Explain what is meant by:
    i   university tests (Source G) [1]
    ii Ballot Bill (Source H) [1]
    iii The great democracy of Northern England and Scotland (Source H) [2]
6. What evidence is given by Feuchtwanger (Source F), Matthew (Source G) and Roy Jenkins (Source H) that Gladstone was out of sympathy with the radicals within the Liberal party? [4]
7. How do the differences between Gladstone and his party highlighted by Feuchtwanger (Source F), Matthew (Source G) and Roy Jenkins (Source H) differ from those highlighted by Parry (Source I)? [5]
8.* In the light of Sources F, G and I, assess the validity of the claim in Source H that Gladstone's political philosophy was a 'mass of contradictions'. [6]
9. *(Both sets of documents)* To what extent do these extracts suggest that Tory Democracy and Gladstonian Liberalism were identical sets of political principles? [7]

Worked answer: Question 8

Jenkins sees Gladstone's ideal polity as a mass of contradictions, though the examples he gives do not necessarily merit this description. He hated corruption wherever it came from, and he recognised that it could come as easily through the ballot box as it could through borough-mongers and patronage: this explains the *apparent* contradiction of his faith in the (uncorrupted) masses of the north and his liking for small boroughs that could support able statesmen without bothering them with the need to nurture their constitutencies. This certainly tallies with Jonathon Parry's analysis that, although there certainly was a coherence to Gladstone's policy, it did not necessarily look that way to others, and especially to others in his own party. Parry's final phrase perhaps suggests that the fault lay to some extent with Gladstone for not keeping his party abreast of his thinking. Feuchtwanger and Matthew are, if anything, kinder to Gladstone than Parry or Jenkins, because they point out that there was at least as much inconsistency and incoherence among the radicals (Feuchtwanger) and among the party as a whole (Matthew) as there was in Gladstone himself. Feuchtwanger's analysis of Gladstone, as a Peelite picking up one or two radical ideas along the way, would certainly help explain and correct Roy Jenkins' image of a mess of contradictions; Matthew suggests that if there was any contradiction in, for example, Gladstone's attitude to the ballot and to democracy, it was to some extent necessary in order to keep the party together. In the light of these analyses, Jenkins' description seems too harsh: there was a coherence and consistency to Gladstone's principles, going back to his Peelite days, but it could certainly appear otherwise to others.

SOURCES

2. POLITICAL PARTIES AFTER 1867

Source J: School Board election poster (1876).

Electors of Chatteris
I have just read another smutchy handbill signed by M.A. Gathercole, in which there appears a great repetition of the word

Vicar! Vicar! Vicar!

It is astonishing how proud Mr Gathercole is of a false title, and how haughty he is in a false position. He has ignominiously failed to get on the Local Board, also on the Board of Guardians, and now he is trying to get re-elected on the School Board . . . I should say that Gathercole and his party would only be too glad to shut up the said Schools and support their own; and that W.S. Ruston and his party would only be too good to hang the Vicar, being gentlemen ever desirous of benefiting their parishioners.

Source K: Cambridge Borough election song (1886).

Now that the battle has begun,
Like men we mean to fight,
We'll rally round the Grand Old Man,
And struggle for the right.
For CYRIL DODD we'll do our best;
What's more, we shall not stop
Until the day of polling, when
We place him at the top.

Then we shall see our brother Pat
Commence a peaceful life,
For when he's got what he desires
There can be no more strife.
Loving, honest, brave and true,
He'll prove he does not lack
Real loyalty to England's Queen
And to the Union Jack.

**Source L: letter from Joseph Chamberlain to *The Times*
(13 April 1880).**

Popular representative organizations on the Birmingham model, sometimes called
'The Caucus' by those who do not know what a caucus really is, and have not
taken the trouble to acquaint themselves with the details of the Birmingham
system, exist in 67 of the parliamentary boroughs in which contests have just
taken place. In 60 of these Liberal seats were gained or retained. In seven only
the Liberals were defeated, but in three at least of these cases a petition will be
presented against the return on the ground of bribery.

This remarkable success is a proof that the new organization has succeeded
in uniting all sections of the party, and it is a conclusive answer to the fears
which some timid Liberals entertained that the system would be manipulated in
the interest of particular crotchets. It has, on the contrary, deepened and
extended the interest felt in the contest; it has fastened a sense of personal
responsibility on the electors; and it has secured the active support, for the most
part voluntary and unpaid, of thousands and tens of thousands of voters, who
have been willing to work hard for the candidates in whose selection they have
for the first time had an influential voice.

Source M: Letter from Lord Randolph Churchill to Lord Salisbury (3 April 1884).

The delegates at the Conference were evidently of the opinion that, if the principles of the Conservative party were to obtain popular support, the organisation of the party would have to become an imitation, thoroughly real and *bona fide* in its nature, of that popular form of representative organisation which had contributed so greatly to the triumph of the Liberal party in 1880, and which was best known to the public by the name of the Birmingham Caucus. The Caucus may be, perhaps, a name of evil sound and omen in the ears of the aristocratic or privileged classes, but it is undeniably the only form of political organisation which can collect, guide, and control for common objects large masses of the electors; and there is nothing in this particular form of political combination which is in the least repugnant to the working classes in this country.

Questions

1. Explain the following references:
   i   School Board   (Source J) [1]
   ii Grand Old Man (Source K) [1]
   iii Birmingham System (Source L) [2]
2. From the internal evidence of Sources J and K, which political party are their authors most likely to have supported? [3]
3.* What can be learnt about the state of popular politics in the 1880s from the tone of Sources J and K? [5]
4. What do Sources L and M suggest about the critics of the Birmingham caucus? [5]
5. How far do these documents explain the failure of both Joseph Chamberlain and Lord Randolph Churchill to take over the leadership of their respective parties? [8]

Worked answer: Question 3

It is clear from Source J that School Board elections could be robust affairs. As always with local examples, such as these, their usefulness will depend on the extent to which they are typical. Source J clearly reflects some strong local and personal animosity, though the fact that it appeared at Chatteris does not mean that the same could not be found elsewhere. It is important that such stress is laid upon the fact that Mr Gathercole is the local vicar: the repetition of the word and the repetition of 'false' suggest a sneering, not to say snarling, tone. The accusation that the vicar and his party would be glad to 'shut up the said Schools and support their own' sounds like the sort of enmity between the Church of England and the nonconformist churches that always plagued educational reforms throughout the nineteenth century: each ran their own schools and feared that the others would use School Boards to force Anglican or nonconformist education on everyone.

Source K is less fierce in tone – its rhymes and rhythm suggest a popular song – and contains the usual clichés that tended to come out at election time: 'We'll rally round the Grand Old Man', 'loving, honest, brave and true' and lines of that ilk. The song brings in Gladstone early on, even before the candidate himself is named, which probably indicates that Gladstone was regarded as an electoral asset at this point, just as – unsurprisingly – is the Union Jack with which the quoted verses reach their climax. However, it is noticeable that Gladstone's pet project, Irish Home Rule, takes up the whole of the first half of the second stanza. This could indicate that Home Rule had a popular following, at least in Cambridge, and that it was thought worth putting into a song designed to whip up political support. The wording – 'our brother Pat', 'peaceful life' and so on – make the Irish Question sound like a minor misunderstanding between siblings; either Mr Dodd was a fool who did not deserve to be elected, or this would indicate that at least some of the electorate would swallow this line.

6

THE LABOUR MOVEMENT AND THE GROWTH OF DEMOCRACY

BACKGROUND NARRATIVE

The Third Reform Act of 1884 and the Redistribution Act of the following year were a response to the inequality in the electoral system left by Disraeli's 1867 Act. Taken together, these measures extended the same voting qualifications as existed in the towns to the countryside, and essentially established the modern one-member constituency as the normal pattern for parliamentary representation. Although there was much less controversy over the issues than there had been in 1832 and 1867, passing the measures did provoke a confrontation between the Liberal majority in the House of Commons and the Conservative majority in the Lords. Gladstone had originally introduced only a Franchise Bill, but Salisbury wanted it to be accompanied by a redistribution measure, and he was prepared to use his majority in the Lords to block the Franchise Bill until Gladstone gave way. In the end, the stand-off was solved by negotiation, brokered by the radical Liberal, Sir Charles Dilke, and by the queen: a Redistribution Bill was to be introduced into the Commons the moment the Lords passed the Franchise Bill.

The Franchise Bill certainly extended the vote, but it was still a household-based suffrage, which excluded many of the working classes. Yet by the 1880s the working classes were rapidly becoming more politically active than they had been since the heyday of

Chartism. The trade unions and friendly societies which had in the 1850s and 1860s mostly represented the sort of skilled workmen that the parliamentary reform proposals of that period had been designed to enfranchise, were being joined by a new wave of trade unions representing the much larger, unskilled sector of the workforce. Industrial conflict was spreading, sometimes accompanied by violence, as in the 'Bloody Sunday' confrontation between unemployed workers and the police in 1887. A series of major strikes, including the match girls' strike of 1888 and the London dock strike of 1889, engendered considerable sympathy among the middle classes, but this sympathy was not matched by any willingness to grant the workers the vote. Working people had to find other ways of having a voice in Parliament.

Although in some areas working people, and even trade unions, remained loyal to the existing parties, especially the Liberals, a series of major set-backs to the Labour movement, including the Osborne judgment of 1909 and the Taff Vale judgment, served to disillusion many trade unionists with both the Liberals and the Conservatives. There seemed no alternative to setting up a new political party, specifically to represent the interests of working people. James Keir Hardie had set up a 'Labour Party' in Scotland in 1888, and it had spawned many imitators which all came together in 1893 as the Independent Labour Party (ILP). The ILP worked hard to form a broad alliance with other left-wing groups, particularly the Trade Union Congress (TUC) and the socialist groups like H.M. Hyndman's Social Democratic Federation (SDF), William Morris's Socialist League, and the more moderate Fabian Society. In 1900 these groups all came together to found the Labour Representation Committee (LRC), which in 1906 changed its name to the Labour Party.

The LRC was committed to advancing its cause through parliamentary politics, but there were plenty of figures on the Left who criticised this stance and called for a drive for revolution, including the SDF, and the militant Syndicalist movement, led by Tom Mann and Ben Tillett. In the end, however, it was the more moderate approach which was destined to succeed and eventually to bring Labour to power; historians continue to argue about how inevitable this rise of Labour actually was by 1914.

ANALYSIS (1): WHY DID THE PARLIAMENTARY REFORM ACTS OF 1884–5 NOT CREATE A DEMOCRACY?

The question can come as a surprise. It is often assumed that the 'Third Reform Act' – which actually consisted of no fewer than ten separate Acts – rounded off the work of the earlier, more famous Acts, leaving only women still to be enfranchised. Edgar Feuchtwanger says of it: 'Together with the Corrupt Practices Act . . . the third Reform Bill moved the country almost all the way towards political democracy';[1] but others, such as Clive Behagg, point out that some 40 per cent of the male working class was still disfranchised after 1885.[2] The 1918 Representation of the People Act increased the size of the electorate by somewhere between two and a half and three times, which, even allowing for the exclusion of women before 1918, is an indication of just how far short of a democracy the pre-war system fell. Widescale corruption persisted into the 1880s – the 300 electors of Beverley in Yorkshire were so notoriously venal that they were known as 'rolling stock' – and it was not until 1883 that an effective law was passed to limit candidates' expenditure. Even then, the old ties of patronage could remain very strong, particularly in the countryside, where the old way of life persisted much longer than in the towns. There were still plenty of agricultural labourers hiring themselves out each year at hiring fairs and ploughing the fields behind shire horses, but there was no campaign that they should have the vote.

In the towns too, there was an extensive population which lived in utter destitution and squalor – we see them sometimes in books of old photographs, and their murky world was brought to wider attention in lurid fashion by the 'Jack the Ripper' murders in 1888; outside the most radical ranks, however, there were no serious proponents that such people should be given the vote. Yet there clearly was a sense of momentum in favour of further change to the franchise established in 1867. Disraeli's Act had brought in major changes to the political scene, especially in its impact on political parties, but it had been a compromise measure, cobbled together in the course of its tortuous route through Parliament, and it contained a number of anomalies which had come to fruition by the 1880s. For example, the urban household suffrage carried a one-year residence qualification, but in many working-class areas people were constantly on the move, sometimes from town to town, sometimes from one part of a town to another, moving where there was work to be had. Such men – and in some areas, like Glasgow, there could be a lot of them – were in effect disfranchised by the 1867 Act.

But the most obvious anomaly remained the discrepancy between the straightforward householder suffrage in the towns and the more restricted £12 household suffrage in the counties. The idea behind it had been to mark the distinctive differences between the populations and pursuits of the two kinds of constituency, but this was not a distinction which could be relied upon. Miners, for example, might have been expected to fall into the urban, householder category; but in reality many mines were located in country areas and those miners were subject to the £12 qualification, putting them at a disadvantage compared with other industrial workers. In fact, the whole 1867 Act was based upon a premise which was widely shared when it was passed, that the country could be more or less neatly divided into traditional, rural 'counties' and the more showy and unpredictable towns. Holding down an urban seat in the Commons might require reserves of stamina and courage, but sitting as MP for a county brought respect and prestige: it was the sort of position that fell very naturally to the landed squires of the Conservative back-benches. Yet this clear distinction between town and country was coming under pressure, not so much from the towns as from a new phenomenon: suburbs.

If the 1832 Act is often said to have enfranchised the middle class and the 1867 Act the urban workers, then the 1884–5 Acts marked the point at which Parliament opened its doors to the suburbs. The suburbs, connected to their towns by new railway lines, were overwhelmingly middle-class areas, and as such their inhabitants for the most part had the vote already; more to the political point, it was widely assumed that they would vote Conservative. But these Conservative suburban votes were either being added to county constituencies, where they were usually not needed in order to return a Conservative member, or else they were going into the electoral hurly-burly of urban politics and the Birmingham caucus, where they would not necessarily prevent the election of a Liberal. It was this sort of calculation, rather than any abstract – still less Chartist – belief in equal constituencies that led Lord Salisbury to take up the cause of redistribution with such uncharacteristic zeal.

When, therefore, we look at the motives on both sides in the stand-off that developed over passing parliamentary reform in 1884–5, we find many different factors at work, but we do not, on the whole, find a belief in democracy. Gladstone and the Liberals still saw democracy as a dangerous tendency, which would open government to corruption and to the whims of the fickle populace. There was a paradox here. Gladstone himself had whipped up a fever of popular expectation in his Midlothian campaigns of 1879–80, and would do so again when he set off on the stump to campaign for Home Rule: he did so because he had developed an almost mystical faith in the good sense of the People. He believed in the People as a bulwark against old-style corruption and against the corruption which comes with political power. But for Gladstone there was an important difference between this belief and a belief in democracy. The sort of people in whom Gladstone put his faith were those who had worked hard to better themselves and so had earned the vote as a fitting reward for their labours and self-improvement.

This is why the 1884 Redistribution Act did not introduce a wider franchise as such: it simply said that the same franchise as already existed in the towns should also apply in the counties. The franchise was extended, but the basic thinking behind who should and who should not have the vote had not changed at all since 1867: the residuum was as excluded as it ever had been. The one-year residential requirement was retained: the idea that to be a voter you had to give some evidence of a steady, stable existence still persisted. So did plural votes for university graduates. MPs were still not paid. In short, if Gladstone did not expect the 1884 Franchise Bill to prove controversial, it is easy to see why: there was nothing particularly controversial in it.

Salisbury was in a potentially awkward position on the franchise question. As Lord Cranborne he had opposed household suffrage in 1867 and had even resigned from the cabinet rather than accept it; and after the bill was passed he had launched a scathing attack on Disraeli's political tactics in the press. In 1884, however, he was leader of the Conservative Party, which had done very well out of household suffrage in 1874 and hoped to do so again. Despite his opposition in the 1860s, it was not realistic for Salisbury to oppose it in the 1880s; what *was* realistic was to turn it to his party's political advantage. Salisbury realised the Conservative voting potential of the suburbs, but he also realised that they would have to be separated from both the towns and the counties if they were to increase the Conservative representation in the Commons. This was why Salisbury held out so strongly for a Redistribution Bill to counteract the effects of Gladstone's Franchise Bill.

Gladstone was an experienced enough politician to realise that Salisbury was acting from party motives, but even he was taken aback to hear Salisbury – of all people – arguing for one-member constituencies of roughly equal size. This meant breaking up the old two-member county constituencies, the Conservative heartland. It would also hit the Liberals: they tended to avoid splitting their vote between Radicals and

Liberals in two-member constituencies by putting up one candidate of each sort: single-member constituencies would bring the moderate–radical split into the open. There is a pleasing but almost certainly untrue story that Salisbury masked the full extent of how the Redistribution Bill would benefit the Conservatives and harm the Liberals by making sure Gladstone never saw the map of the new constituencies the right way up: in fact the vehemence with which Gladstone fought to delay a Redistribution Bill suggests he knew only too well what its effect would be. It is Salisbury rather than Gladstone who tends to emerge with the credit for the 1884–5 package of parliamentary reform, and this is essentially on the basis of the Redistribution Bill.

A set of measures put together in a compromise brokered to end a stand-off between the Liberals and the Lords was hardly likely to pay much attention to the principles of democracy. The 1880s were simply too early for the various Labour groups to be able to exercise the pressure that would be necessary to get a democratic franchise out of a government which had no intention of granting one. Popular politics had certainly revived in the 1880s, with a vehemence and intensity that reminded commentators at the time – and historians since – of Chartism at its height. In Parliament, Charles Stewart Parnell's Irish Nationalists adopted blocking tactics so effectively that they held up the entire business of the Commons and forced the Speaker to create the precedent of curtailing debate on his own initiative. Outside Parliament, the unusual figure of a wealthy upper-class businessman, H.M. Hyndman, founded the Social Democratic Federation in 1883 dedicated to fomenting a proletarian revolution which would sweep Parliament and the constitution away, but his movement quickly began to fragment. The poet and artist William Morris left it the next year to found his Socialist League, while Sidney and Beatrice Webb founded the parallel Fabian Society in 1884 whose approach to social revolution was so gradual that it is debatable whether it deserves to be termed socialist at all.

Despite the aspirations of their members, these movements remained essentially intellectual affairs, with little impact in day-to-day politics: indeed, Hyndman's 'Scientific Socialism' took very little interest in the practicalities of social reform or welfare, which he saw as a deliberate attempt by the ruling class to distract the workers from the class war. The few working men who had made it into Parliament sat as 'Lib–Labs', representatives of labour who worked through the parliamentary Liberal Party. The SDF and the Socialist League affected to despise this approach, but others saw the sense in it. Disillusion with the Liberals did not happen overnight, and almost all the major figures of the early years of what would become the Labour Party, such as Keir Hardie, Ramsay MacDonald and George Lansbury, began their political careers as Liberals. Working-class Liberalism lingered for a long time in some areas, and both the important Miners' Federation of Great Britain and the TUC itself were profoundly suspicious of the move towards a separate, socialist party to represent the interests of labour. The TUC even changed its voting system, introducing 'block' votes which favoured big unions like the miners over the smaller socialist ones, specifically in order to prevent the socialists from being able to take it over.

The answer to the question would therefore seem to be fairly straightforward: the 'Third Reform Act' did not introduce a democratic system because Gladstone's government did not believe in it and was likely to suffer from it, because Salisbury's Conservatives did not believe in it either and were pushing for the redistribution settlement which would benefit them the most, and because the bodies who did believe in it were either too small or too divided to have any influence on the outcome of the parliamentary dispute the issue produced. But it is not quite enough to leave the issue there. The 1884–5 measures did change the political nation irrevocably, and the changes they brought do perhaps merit Feuchtwanger's description. The radical feature was not the franchise – this was hardly less restrictive on the working class than it had been before – but the new distribution of seats. Salisbury had wanted to ring-fence Conservative suburbs, and this is indeed what happened, but the move to one-member constituencies had other implications, perhaps less anticipated.

To start with, by breaking up the old county constituencies, it also to some extent broke the traditional bands of patronage and deference which had persisted for so long in the countryside. Secondly, what redistribution did for the suburbs it also did for inner city areas. New constituencies were created in what had become heavily working-class areas of major cities, like Poplar or West Ham in London. This had two further effects. It meant that if and when the Labour movement was able to end its internal differences and settle on a single separate drive for parliamentary representation, these new working-class seats were tailor-made to be represented by 'Labour' MPs. More generally, and more profoundly, the redistribution in effect grouped constituencies by class: middle-class suburbs, working-class inner city areas, landed-class counties and so on.

Of all the factors that had determined voting behaviour in the nineteenth century, social class had usually been the least consistent or useful – it mattered much less, for example, than religion – but after

1885 class rapidly became the single most important, some would say the only, determining factor in elections. Both the Liberals and the Conservatives might strive to pretend this was not the case, or else to get around it, the Conservatives by bandying the term 'One Nation' around as much as they could and grossly distorting the memory of Disraeli to back it up, the Liberals by launching their famous 'New Liberal' social reforms and by taking on the House of Lords: but neither party could escape being identified overwhelmingly with the middle and upper classes, any more than they could pose as better representatives of labour than the party which actually carried its name. By creating the framework for a class-based political system, the 'Third Reform Act' was more of a step towards a democracy than either its framers or its critics ever allowed for.

Questions

1. Explain the reasons why the issue of redistribution of seats provoked a political crisis in 1884–5.
2. 'The Franchise and Redistribution bills of 1884–5 rendered the Liberal Party redundant.' How far would you agree with this verdict?

ANALYSIS (2): HOW EFFECTIVELY DID THE LABOUR MOVEMENT OPERATE WITHIN THE PARLIAMENTARY SYSTEM, 1892–1914?

In 1936 the British historian George Dangerfield published a best-seller with the engaging title, *The Strange Death of Liberal England*. It was written in a florid, rhetorical style which few historians would get away with today, somewhere between a novelist and a rather loquacious barrister addressing the jury. When the book appeared, Hitler was marching into the Rhineland, Franco was landing in Spain and Edward VIII was being forced to abdicate for love of an American divorcee. Dangerfield was far from the only one to look in despair at the way the world was going, and to look back nostalgically to the golden years before the Great War when life seemed to have been so much more straightforward, and to ask: What went wrong? How had that remarkable balance of interests and passions, the England of Mr Gladstone and Queen Victoria, evolved into the England of militant miners and Oswald Mosley's blackshirts? Some people blamed the war, but Dangerfield saw the rot setting in before 1914, in the years between the Liberal electoral triumph of 1906 and the outbreak of war. The symptoms of trouble were easy to recognise: suffragette violence, militant trade unionism and what seemed to be a civil war brewing in Ireland. Deeper analysis indicated a failure – for reasons still unclear – of the fundamental sense of restraint and decent behaviour which had been the hallmark of Victorian England. A 'strange death' indeed.

If a fundamental philosophy dies, then the consequences are, to all intents and purposes, inevitable. This was very much Dangerfield's view and the story of the Labour movement seemed to illustrate his point very well. As more and more unskilled workers joined the 'new' unions, the trade union movement was fast growing into a formidable political force which could only continue to grow bigger still. Representation of labour in Parliament too was bound to continue growing as it slowly but definitely squeezed the Liberals out of the political picture. It was a picture that the Fabians would have agreed with wholeheartedly: they saw Labour as a force that would grow almost organically out of Liberalism, gradually taking over from and supplanting its parent political movement. But this idea has provoked considerable argument among historians.

On Dangerfield's central thesis, that the Liberals somehow 'died' between 1906 and 1914, there have been plenty of historians to argue that, far from dying, the Liberals were thriving in 1914 and had every reason to expect to continue as one of the two largest parties for years to come. In the case of the allegedly unstoppable rise of Labour, some historians have pointed out that just because the Labour Party supplanted the Liberals after the war, it does not necessarily follow that this was already happening before the war, or even that it would have happened without the war. Some historians, like Duncan Tanner, take this a stage further and argue that in fact Labour was in deep trouble by 1914, was possibly even past its peak, and that it was only saved by the war.[3] Others, like Keith Laybourn and Jack Reynolds, argue on the contrary that Labour was progressing well before 1914 as long as she kept close links with the trade unions, which she nearly always did; only in the (relatively rare) cases where these links had become strained or weak did Labour suffer decline.[4]

Implicit in all these arguments is the basic question of how one measures success in political parties. In 1900 there were two Labour MPs, who commanded 1.8% of the vote; by 1914 there were 42, and ten years later 191, commanding a third of the national vote. By 1914 almost the whole trade union movement had come round to Labour, including the miners, and the Lib–Lab alliance was virtually over – it had been prolonged only because of Labour's support for the Liberals in their battle with the House of Lords. This is impressive progress by any standards. On the other hand, there were clear limits to Labour's progress. It was not in government, nor by 1914 did it seem likely to be. It had an electoral pact with the Liberals, but the Liberals had won such a majority in 1906 that they had no real need to make any concessions to Labour. Labour's political organisation was in its infancy: the electoral qualifications were difficult to work with and kept some five million working men – a high proportion of whom must be reckoned as potential Labour voters – disfranchised. Labour had only 12 full-time electoral agents compared with the Liberals' 300. Labour's influence on policy seemed minimal. At a time when the very operation of the trade union movement was under threat in the courts, in the Taff Vale and Osborne judgments, the Liberals seemed unwilling to do anything to help. It is hardly surprising that by the 1910s a number of important voices within the Labour movement felt that the party was heading nowhere and called for an end to the Liberal alliance.

These factors should not obscure more intangible but nevertheless important issues. Labour had established itself as an experienced and respected parliamentary party far more than its number of MPs might suggest. By comparison with the disruptive and obstreperous Irish Nationalists, the ILP and LRC MPs learned the complicated rules of parliamentary procedure quickly, and did not try to bend them. Keir Hardie is well known for having worn his check suit and tweed cap to the Commons; his persistence in pressing ministers on awkward questions is less well known but rather more important. Violent industrial confrontations certainly raised fears of revolution – this is one of the symptoms Dangerfield identifies – but here the split in the Labour movement worked to the advantage of the parliamentary party, who could disassociate themselves from extremist actions while maintaining their attack on the employers. Although the Lib–Lab electoral pact of 1903 undoubtedly worked to the Liberals' advantage, it is a sort of tribute to the importance other parties accorded to Labour that the Liberals should have approached them with it in the first place. The ILP and the LRC managed to fashion the Labour movement from a potentially revolutionary movement into a shape and form which could operate effectively within, and would not seek to subvert, the existing constitutional structure.

But this success came at a price. The most obvious was unity. Labour was not a single party but a coalition of different groups and interests, not all of which were easily compatible. The SDF and William Morris's Socialist League agreed on the need for revolution, but Morris hated the SDF's coldly scientific approach to socialism. The SDF had no time for trade unions, many of which took a long time to wean themselves off the Liberal alliance, and many of whom remained hostile to intellectual socialism. The Fabians thought that socialism was coming gradually anyway, while the few Labour figures who had sat in Parliament, notably Keir Hardie, had no time for theory and wanted pragmatic policy for action on issues like unemployment, health and safety at work, and disability payments. It was clear that some sort of broad socialist alliance was essential, and this is what Keir Hardie was trying to create, first through the Independent Labour Party in 1893 and later through the broader Labour Representation Committee, but these moves had to be compromises.

The most obvious indication of this is the name: 'Labour' was a much more neutral, 'respectable' term than 'socialist', and Keir Hardie took great care to avoid using the 's-word' as a party label. In so far as Labour did use the term 'socialist' it usually changed it into 'socialistic', which suggested a mild tendency towards socialist ideas rather than an out-and-out commitment to Marxism. Hyndman's radical SDF quickly seceded from the LRC (renamed the Labour Party after the 1906 election), and the more radical trade unionists, especially syndicalists like Tom Mann and Ben Tillett, soon took to denouncing the leadership of the Parliamentary Labour Party in only slightly less vehement terms than those they used against the Conservatives and Liberals. This evidence of disunity was not necessarily fatal to the party's long-term ambitions – both the Conservatives and Liberals had long histories of damaging splits – but it did hit the party's credibility in the short term. Labour's whole justification was that it was the only party which effectively represented labour, so that any examples of disunity were bound to undermine that claim, especially in such a young movement.

This disunity mattered all the more as the impression took hold that the working classes were engaged in virtual war with the employers. Not content with dominating both the Conservative and Liberal parties, in 1898 the Employers' Federation set up its own parliamentary committee to co-ordinate the representation of capital in Parliament. The judicial setbacks to the trade unions, like Taff Vale and Osborne, appeared to many trade unionists like part of a concerted attack by the employers and their cronies, but the event which had really aroused a sense of alarm in trade union circles was the 'Bloody Sunday' confrontation in Trafalgar Square in 1887, when the police moved in to break up a sit-in by the unemployed and one man was killed. The unsympathetic attitude of the Liberals through the major conflicts that followed, the match girls' strike of 1888, the gasworkers' and London dockers' strikes of 1889, began the steady process of disillusionment with the Liberals among many labour leaders. This was not halted by the 'New Liberalism' of Lloyd George and Winston Churchill: for one thing the 'New' Liberals were never a majority in the cabinet, let alone the Liberal party as a whole, and for another their proposals still did not directly benefit the whole of the working class. Clive Behagg[5] points out that Old Age Pensions could be withheld from those with a prison record, including imprisonment for union activity, and that since the National Insurance scheme worked on the basis of contributions, it excluded those who could not afford to make them. To most Labour supporters 'New' Liberalism was rather too close to 'Old' Liberalism for comfort.

This was what lay behind the criticism from syndicalists at the time, and from left-wing historians since, that Labour essentially lost precious time by tying itself too quickly, too tightly and for too long to the Liberals. According to this line of argument, Labour's record by 1914 must be accounted a failure because it did so little to advance Britain down a socialist road. To the pragmatists at the time, this criticism simply was not realistic: if the country as a whole had seen Labour as socialist, then the party would never have been allowed to advance to the point it had. Labour was in a position similar to that of the militant suffragettes at the same time: they were no nearer their aim in 1914 than they had been ten years earlier, but whether this was because they had been too forceful or because they had not been forceful enough was much harder to say. Whether measured in terms of concrete achievement or in Marxist terms of substituting the parliamentary system, the answer to the question must be that Labour had largely failed in its various aims by 1914, but this is probably not the best way to judge.

Any examination of Labour's record by 1914 has to be an exercise in tracing 'invisible' success, even to an extent in what Niall Ferguson calls 'counter-factual History'.[6] Think for a moment of how things could easily have turned out. Tolpuddle and Chartism both provided object lessons of how a promising movement can fail. Labour could have torn itself apart in internal arguments; it could have been cowed by police or military action like the celebrated case at Tonypandy in 1911; it could have lost votes to the 'new' Liberals, who undoubtedly won popular support for their social reforms; it could have folded after the ILP gained no seats at all in the 1895 election. It did none of those things. Even if one sees it in decline in 1914, there was – and is – no reason to suppose that that decline need necessarily have been terminal. Even in the far-from-democratic system introduced by the Third Reform Act,

Labour was able to mobilise itself effectively and to establish itself as a permanent feature of the political scene.

Questions

1. 'By 1914 Labour had failed in all its principal political and social objectives.' How far would you agree with this judgement?
2. Why, and with what consequences, was the Labour movement 1885–1914 disunited?
3. Why were the forces of conservative opinion unable to prevent the growth of the Labour movement 1885–1914?

SOURCES

1. THE THIRD REFORM ACT

Source A: *The Times* (2 January 1884).

In the abstract it may be argued with force that a man has no more natural right to be an elector than to be a duke. In practice, and in view of the current of national tendencies, the advocates of a limited franchise will find it useless to attempt to deny him possession of it unless he be disqualified for its use. Their aim should be to prove that a vote is a union of a personal right to be enjoyed with a public duty which the claimant must demonstrate his ability to fulfil.

Source B: *The Times* (17 January 1884).

The Liberals, [Lord Salisbury] says, are anxious to pass a Reform Bill under which they will obtain a permanent dominion in the constituencies 'before this admirable accident* of a House of Commons has separated'. The charge may be not unfairly retorted. The Conservatives are equally anxious to control the redistribution of political power; and they believe that, apart from the general feeling in the country, the small boroughs will not, on the next appeal to the constituencies, give the Liberals the same measure of support as in 1880. This, however, is on practical, though not, perhaps, on moral grounds, as strong a reason for Conservative opposition as any that Lord Salisbury's ingenuity could devise.

*Salisbury habitually referred to the Conservative defeat in the 1880 election as an 'accident'.

Source C: *Gladstone to Queen Victoria* (23 July 1884).

Will Your Majesty graciously forgive his [Gladstone's] observing in the meantime, that so far as he can judge, and certainly so far as his intention is concerned, the Franchise Bill could not rank among measures properly considered Radical, inasmuch as its main enactment is to extend a principle established by a Conservative Government in the towns and working beneficially there, to the counties, where the corresponding class of Householders are certainly more conservative than in the Towns.

Mr Gladstone is convinced that the English rural voters, forming the majority of those to be enfranchised, may prove to be 'conservative' even as matters stand, and would unquestioningly have so voted but for the strange and (as it seems to him) suicidal resistance offered to the Bill of Enfranchisement.

Source D: *The Times* (18 March 1885).

The [Redistribution] Bill must be accepted substantially as it stands or the compromise must be given up ... Sir Charles Dilke has repeatedly asserted his right to make known his personal wish for the settlement of various important questions – such as that of University representation and of the 'one man one vote' principle – in a different way from that adopted in the bill, though officially he is compelled to refuse assent to amendments in that sense. This, according to many members of the Opposition, amounts to an invitation to the advanced Liberals to reopen the question of Parliamentary reform in the next Parliament and to overthrow a settlement the principal recommendation of which, from the Conservative point of view, was that it was likely to be accepted as closing the controversy for, at all events, many years to come.

Source E: Conservative MPs in England.

	Boroughs (total 226 seats)	*Counties (total 239 seats)*
1885	114	105
1886	165	174
1892	132	136
1895	175	184
1900	177	162

from Robert Blake, *The Conservative Party from Peel to Churchill* (1970)

Questions

1.* Explain the following references:
   i 'a vote is a union of a personal right to be enjoyed with a public duty' (Source A) [2]
   ii 'the strange and (as it seems to him) suicidal resistance offered to the Bill of Enfranchisement.' (Source C) [2]
   iii 'the compromise' [1]
2. How far do Sources C and E support the analysis of Salisbury's motives contained in Source B? [6]
3. To what extent do Sources A and D support the view that full democracy was inevitable? [6]
4. 'A Conservative triumph.' How far do these sources, and any other evidence known to you, support this interpretation of the passage of the Franchise and Redistribution bills in 1884–5? [7]

Worked answer: Question 1

i *The Times* is merely quoting the generally accepted view that the vote was not a right but had to be earned by performing some service to the general well-being of the state. However, in this context *The Times* is stressing that this view is under attack, and that opponents of extending the franchise would need to reiterate it. It was the reason behind the restrictive franchise and residence qualification, and also behind the retention of plural votes for university graduates and multiple landholders.

ii The Franchise Bill was defeated by the Conservative majority in the House of Lords. Gladstone refused to call an election at the behest of the Lords, and had Parliament prorogued instead. His astonishment is two-fold: firstly that the Conservatives could jeopardise a measure which embodied their own principles and would almost certainly work to their advantage; secondly because by challenging the Commons on a matter directly relating to itself, the Lords were asking for a constitutional battle which they were bound to lose.

iii After the Lords refused to pass the Franchise Bill without an accompanying Redistribution Bill, Queen Victoria and Sir Charles Dilke worked out a compromise whereby the Lords would pass the Franchise Bill, and a Redistribution Bill would be introduced into the Commons at the same time. Under the terms of the compromise, Dilke was not allowed to call for further changes to the franchise while the bills were progressing through Parliament.

SOURCES

2. THE GROWTH OF LABOUR

Source F: William Morris, *News from Nowhere* (1890).

Note: William Morris' *News from Nowhere* is a fable in which a visitor travels through time to the twenty-first century, when England has gone through a bloody revolution and become a socialist Utopia. He speaks with the people he meets about how this state of society evolved.

On some comparatively trifling occasion a great meeting was summoned by the workmen leaders to meet in Trafalgar Square . . . The civic bourgeois guard (called the police) attacked the said meeting with bludgeons, according to their custom; many people were hurt in the *mêlée**, of whom five in all died, either trampled to death on the spot or from the effects of their cudgelling; the meeting was scattered, and some hundred of prisoners cast into gaol. A similar meeting had been treated in the same way a few days before at a place called Manchester, which has now disappeared . . .

    That massacre of Trafalgar Square began the civil war . . . A so-called 'Liberal' paper (the Government of the day was of that complexion), after a preamble in which it declared its undeviating sympathy with the cause of labour, proceeded to point out that in times of revolutionary disturbance it behoved the Government to be just but firm, and that by far the most merciful way of dealing with the poor madmen who were attacking the very foundation of society (which had made them mad and poor) was to shoot them at once.

* *mêlée* = hand-to-hand fighting

Source G: Ben Tillett's by-election address, *Bradford Observer* (11 July 1895).

I tell every Liberal who votes for a Liberal candidate and does not vote Labour, that he might just as well vote Tory. Every vote lost to Labour will strengthen the hand of the Tory, and if I do not get in Mr Flower* will, and the Liberals will be responsible for returning to Parliament the hereditary enemy of the working class.

*Mr Flower was the Conservative candidate.

Source H: H.M. Hyndman, *The Historical Basis of Socialism* (1883).

Powerful as the Trade Unions have been, and, indeed, to a certain extent still are, Trade Unionists are, all told, but a small fraction of the total working population. They constitute in fact, an aristocracy of labour who, in view of the bitter struggle now drawing nearer and nearer, cannot be said to be other than a hindrance to that complete organisation of the proletariat which alone can obtain for the workers their proper control over their own labour ... The waste of the Trade Union funds on strikes or petty benefits to the individuals who compose them is still more deplorable. Enormous sums have been ... lost, directly, or indirectly, in consequence of strikes which, if applied by Unionists to active propaganda against the existing system ... would long since have produced a serious effect.

Source I: George Bernard Shaw, 'The Transition to Social Democracy' in *Fabian Essays* (1889).

What then does a gradual transition to Social Democracy mean specifically? It means the gradual extension of the franchise; and the transfer of rent and interest to the State, not in one lump sum, but by instalments. Looked at in this way, it will at once be seen that we are already far on the road, and are being urged further by many politicians who do not dream that they are touched with Socialism – nay, who would earnestly repudiate the touch as a taint ... Since 1885 every man who pays four shillings a week rent can only be hindered from voting by anomalous conditions of registration which are likely to be swept away very shortly. This is all but manhood suffrage; and it will soon complete itself as adult suffrage ... A democratic State cannot become a Social Democratic state unless it has in every centre of population a local governing body as thoroughly democratic in its constitution as the central Parliament. This matter is also well in train ... Politicians who have no suspicion that they are Socialists, are advocating further instalments of Socialism with a recklessness of indirect result which scandalises the conscious Social Democrat.

Questions

1.* Explain briefly the following references:
   i   'aristocracy of labour' (Source H) [2]
   ii 'anomalous conditions of registration' (Source I) [2]
2. How factual is Source F? [3]
3. Compare and contrast the arguments against Liberals and trade unions presented in Sources G and H. [6]
4. Assess the validity of the claim in Source I that socialism was being introduced by the policies of the Conservative and Liberal parties. [7]
5. How far do these documents, and any other evidence known to you, support the view that the biggest obstacle to the development of the labour movement before 1900 was its own disunity? [7]

Worked answer: Question 1

i   The term 'aristocracy of labour' was often used to refer to the craft unions, or 'New Model Unions' of the 1850s and 1860s. They set great store on presenting a sober and respectable image, and for that reason they excluded unskilled workers. Hyndman is suggesting that they have not changed, and in this context the term 'aristocracy' would be more of a sneer than a compliment.

ii   The 1884 Reform Act continued the requirement on voters to have been resident in their constituency for a year before they were eligible to be registered. This worked to the detriment of working-class voters, many of whom had to move frequently in search of work, and so were effectively disfranchised by the circumstances of their existence.

7

THE DECLINE OF THE MONARCHY AND THE FALL OF THE HOUSE OF LORDS

BACKGROUND NARRATIVE

It is easy to forget the importance of those ancient institutions, the monarchy and the House of Lords, as we trace the apparently unstoppable rise of the House of Commons. This is not a mistake any nineteenth-century minister would have made. Grey, Peel, Palmerston, Disraeli and Gladstone all had cause either to feel gratitude for, or – more frequently – impatience with, the power of the Crown, but none of them could ignore it. There is a pleasing symmetry about the story, for Asquith found himself having to coerce George V into using his power to create peers in order to pass the 1911 Parliament Act just as Grey had had to do with William IV to pass the Reform Bill in 1832. Disraeli was able to channel Queen Victoria's popularity to his political advantage, while Gladstone found his relations with the queen one of the most difficult aspects of his holding office. Although the Crown's influence on day-to-day politics had declined, it could and did still play an important role both in foreign policy and at moments of political crisis at home, particularly when – as was increasingly happening towards the end of the century – the House of Commons came into conflict with the House of Lords.

No nineteenth-century statute limited the powers of the ancient House of Lords, and it was common for prime ministers and cabinet ministers to sit in the upper house. Russell, Derby, Disraeli (as Earl of Beaconsfield), Salisbury and Rosebery were all prime minister while in the Lords: of the prime ministers in the second half of the century, only Palmerston and Gladstone stayed in the Commons throughout their careers. Practice, aided by Parliamentary Reform Acts, was steadily establishing the principle that the House of Commons embodied the will of the people and that, all other things being equal, the Lords should not frustrate it. However, all other things were by no means always equal, and the Lords were quite prepared to use their prerogative to vote down measures of which they disapproved. The 1884 Franchise Bill provided one ground for confrontation; Gladstone's second Home Rule Bill provided another. By the time Asquith moved to curtail their powers in 1911 the Lords had defeated the 1909 'People's Budget' and were frustrating as many pieces of Liberal legislation as the Conservatives (or Unionists, as they were then usually called) wanted frustrated.

And here lay the essential problem, for the conflict was only partly constitutional, between the two Houses of Parliament: in reality the Lords were acting, in Lloyd George's famous phrase, as 'Mr Balfour's poodle', doing the Conservative leader's bidding on purely party-political grounds. As long as the Lords were so dominated by the Conservatives, no Liberal government could afford to leave them alone. By rejecting the 1909 budget the Lords were going against precedent, but they were not actually in breach of the constitution. Asquith put forward a bill to limit their powers severely, removing their power to reject money bills, and limiting their powers to reject other legislation so that measures passed twice in the Commons should pass automatically into law. Many Conservative Lords seemed ready to fight to the end (or 'in the last ditch', as the phrase of the day had it) and to reject Asquith's bill, regardless of his threat to swamp the House with five hundred Liberal peers if they did. In the end, political realism won the day and the Lords passed the bill, thus retaining their in-built Conservative majority to use another day.

ANALYSIS (1): WHY DID THE CONSTITUTIONAL POSITION OF THE MONARCHY DECLINE, 1785–1914?

Perhaps the most striking aspect of the monarchy during the period was the fact that its actual existence was never under serious threat. Apart from one or two would-be assassins, there were no serious attempts to get rid either of the monarchy or of individual monarchs. This does not mean that the monarchy was immune from criticism: George IV was desperately unpopular for much of his reign, as was Queen Victoria during the years she spent in seclusion after Prince Albert's death, but the monarchy proved quite capable of weathering these storms. George III in the 1800s, Queen Victoria in the early years and again towards the end of her reign, Edward VII and George V all enjoyed periods of immense popularity; and serious illness, like George III's madness or the Prince of Wales' typhoid fever in the 1860s, only increased public sympathy for the monarchy. In any case, as Vernon Bogdanor has pointed out, the complaint was usually that there was too little monarchy on display, as when monarchs went into seclusion, rather than that there was too much.[1]

Genuine republican sentiment is extremely difficult to find. Charles James Fox flirted with French revolutionary republicanism, but never actually proposed an English republic; the Chartists never advocated one either, nor even did the Irish nationalists until the very end of the century; the most that can be pointed to was a short-lived burst of republican writing from the atheist MP Charles Bradlaugh in the 1860s, supported briefly by Sir Charles Dilke and Joseph Chamberlain, both of whom later went back on their views. Part of the explanation for this general acceptance of a need for monarchy seems to be that the monarchy did play an important and recognisable role as a symbol of the nation. Linda Colley has shown how George III fitted into his 'Farmer George' role to symbolise British defiance of Napoleon and all things French;[2] Queen Victoria's role as Empress of India helped to define an idea of empire both in Britain and in the colonies; Edward VII as Prince of Wales made a very successful visit to India and as King famously helped to symbolise the *entente cordiale* during his equally successful visit to Paris in 1904; but perhaps the single most successful venture of this sort was the visit to Scotland undertaken by the much-maligned George IV in 1822, which went a long way towards healing the very deep scars of the eighteenth century and forging a stronger Anglo-Scottish union.[3]

In this sense, there was considerable continuity in the role of the monarchy: George V played a similar symbolic role in the First World

War, for example, to that played by George III in the wars against Napoleon. In the political arena, however, the role of the monarch was increasingly controversial. George III had established an awkward precedent when he sacked Fox and North and replaced them with Pitt: he followed it up by virtually sacking Pitt in 1801 rather than accept Catholic emancipation. His successors tried to emulate him, but were not able to get away with it in the way that he had: William IV sacked the Whigs in 1834, but could not influence the reformed electoral system with the success his father had enjoyed with the old system in 1784, and he had to swallow his pride and accept the Whigs back a year later. Victoria staved off the Tories in the 'bedchamber crisis' of 1839, but only for a couple of years, and on very flimsy ground anyway. Victoria did not give up her prerogative to choose her ministers without a fight: she tried hard to avoid having to send for Palmerston in 1855 and again in 1858–9; in 1880 she tried to avoid Gladstone, in 1885 she tried to keep Salisbury. Nevertheless, for all her spirited action, her list of actual success in getting her own way was short: in 1892 she successfully persuaded Gladstone not to appoint the radical Henry Labouchere to his cabinet; and when Gladstone finally retired a year later, she sent for Lord Rosebery on her own initiative. For a reign of sixty-three years, this is a fairly meagre showing.

The reason for the decline in the exercise of the monarch's right to appoint a prime minister lies very largely in the growth of political parties after the 1867 Reform Act. When politics was still heavily dominated by patronage, and when party allegiance was unclear, as was the case before 1867, then the monarch very clearly had a part to play if the situation was in any way fluid: the best example is the way in 1852, after the first Derby–Disraeli government had collapsed, Victoria and Albert avoided the more obvious names like Russell and Palmerston, and selected Lord Aberdeen to head a coalition government. Once party machines began to operate more efficiently, however, the monarch could no longer ignore the party's own choice of its leader. This was even the case when the party chose to ignore its official leader in favour of another: in 1880, for example, Queen Victoria was prepared, even eager, to appoint the official Liberal leader, Lord Hartington, in preference to Gladstone; unfortunately for her, the Liberal party was adamant that it wanted Gladstone and in the end she had to give way to its wishes. Long before 1914, the right to appoint the prime minister had in effect passed from the Crown, and even from Parliament, to the internal electoral processes of the political parties.

Much of the problem the monarchy faced lay in the nature of the British constitution. Unlike its American counterpart it is not contained in a single document, but consists of a number of written laws passed at different points in British history which lay down aspects of constitutional practice, like the Act of Settlement which laid down the Hanoverian succession to the throne, or the nineteenth-century Parliamentary Reform Acts. This means that major importance is given to what can best be described as 'custom and practice'. For example, the practice of the sovereign presiding over meetings of ministers lapsed in the time of George I, who found better things to do with his time, though the right was never formally revoked or given up. The uncertain constitutional position of the nineteenth-century monarchs owed a lot to the way their eighteenth-century predecessors had fulfilled their role.

Where the Stuarts had taken a very active role in the detail of political life, the first two Hanoverians left much more of the day-to-day running of the state to their ministers. When George III tried to revive the practice of a more active Crown he found himself being accused of acting unconstitutionally, and this helped provoke the American colonies into revolt, even though he never proposed any step that was in any way illegal. When he sacked the Fox–North coalition it was certainly of disputable *fairness* – no-one was in any doubt that the king was acting as he did because he could not stomach his ministers – but, for all Fox's protests, the king was acting entirely within his rights. But what really clinched the crisis for the king was the simple fact that he got away with it – in the election that followed, the king's candidate, William Pitt the younger, trounced the Whigs and governed for another seventeen years. Clearly the Whigs did not *like* what the king had done, but if they wanted to make it actually unconstitutional they would either have to pass a bill limiting or removing the king's powers to dismiss ministries – and with the Tories so firmly entrenched in power there was no prospect whatsoever of such a bill passing – or else, more realistically, they would have to try to change the composition of parliament and of the electorate so that, even if the king were to dismiss a ministry, he would not be able to get away with it. This, as we have seen, was one of the major motivations behind the 1832 Reform Act, and the proof of its effectiveness came two years later, when William IV was unable to keep the Melbourne ministry out of office for more than a few months.

The Great Reform Act of 1832 began a process of change imposed upon the monarchy by changes in the composition of Parliament. By 1867 the change had been noted by the political journalist Walter Bagehot in his highly influential book *The English Constitution*, which was quickly adopted by the royal family as guidance on the Crown's role in politics – Queen Victoria read it, and so did the future Edward VII and George V. Bagehot saw the queen's role as vital to the continuation of constitutional government in Britain, but he saw it in terms which her predecessors would have found rather limited: he argued that 'the sovereign has three rights – the right to be consulted, the right to encourage, the right to warn'. So an experienced monarch might very well be able to give sage advice – and very possibly unwelcome advice – to a headstrong prime minister, and she had a right to expect that advice to be listened to seriously, but not necessarily that it should always be followed.

The sort of example Bagehot had in mind was the role Prince Albert had played a few years previously in leading Lord Palmerston's government away from confrontation with the United States, which threatened to draw Britain into the American Civil War. Although Bagehot's analysis coincided to some extent with the ideals of Prince Albert and Queen Victoria, the monarchy had by no means reached that state willingly or by design. George III had established a precedent by his close co-operation with Pitt the younger and George IV followed it with his similarly close relationship with Lord Liverpool's ministry: the result was that for some forty years the monarch effectively left the prime minister to determine domestic policy as he saw fit, as long as he steered clear of Catholic emancipation (and George IV was even prevailed upon to accept that). By the time of the reform crisis of 1831–2, the Crown was being brought in by the Whigs as little more than a tool for forcing reform on the House of Lords. In effect, blatant political partisanship was reducing the Crown to a cipher when its party was in power, and leaving it open to highly risky temptation when they were out. The young Queen Victoria was blatantly pro-Whig: her close relationship with Melbourne led to the nickname 'Mrs Melbourne', and her anti-Tory bias was exposed very clearly in the bedchamber crisis. Had Peel wished, he could have made matters very uncomfortable indeed for the young queen in 1839, and she was largely saved from her own folly by his chivalrous forbearance.

It is sometimes held that Prince Albert, who married Victoria in 1840, saved the monarchy by instilling in her a clearer view of the Crown as being above party. There is some truth in this. It was certainly Albert who opened Victoria's eyes to Peel's merits, and he gently but firmly guided her away from the sort of partisan approach that had marked her reign so far. But Albert's ideas were not quite as straightforward as they have been portrayed. He relied heavily on his old tutor, the Danish Baron Stockmar, who accompanied him to London and lived at the palace, and Stockmar had a distinctly continental view of the proper role of monarchy: he believed that the Crown should be above party precisely in order to be able to take a more active role in government than had been possible heretofore. The 1840s and 1850s were not a period of clear-cut party politics, and Albert did not live to see the Disraeli–Gladstone era, when there was a more obvious party divide for the Crown to rise above, so we cannot say how this idea would have worked in practice, but it is reasonable to expect that it would have provoked considerable controversy.

As things turned out, Victoria withdrew from public life after Albert's death in 1861, and when Disraeli managed to charm her out of seclusion she emerged an even more fiercely partisan character, determined to play her role to the full. On occasion she could do so constructively, as when she helped to resolve the confrontation between the Lords and Commons over the Redistribution Bill in 1885; for the most part, however, her participation consisted of fierce and futile rearguard actions to avoid having to send for Gladstone, and incessant letters to Gladstone or Rosebery complaining about the tone of public speeches made by one or other of their more radical cabinet colleagues. Although both men were unfailingly courteous in their replies, her blatant bias inevitably limited her influence over their thinking.

Edward VII as Prince of Wales had played so small a part in politics that when he came to the throne any constitutional analyst could have been forgiven for thinking that the Crown's importance was about to disappear. Campbell-Bannerman certainly did not regard keeping the king informed of public business as a major priority, and the king complained that bulletins from the prime minister consisted of vague reports like 'The Cabinet met today and was entirely engaged with arrangements of public business'.[4] Ironically, the Crown was about to play its most central role in public business for years. The confrontation between the Lords and Commons over Lloyd George's 1909 budget thrust the king into a highly delicate constitutional position. Asquith could not coerce the Lords without a guarantee from the king to create 500 Liberal peers in order to break the Tory majority, and this Edward VII resolutely refused to grant in advance of a general election on the issue.

George V fought hard against giving what he regarded, with reason, as a hypothetical guarantee to create the peers: unlike Asquith, he had to consider the possibility that if the Conservatives were to win the December 1910 election, he could appear to have made improperly partisan promises to help the Liberals. The king was also receiving contradictory advice from his two private secretaries, the Liberal Lord Knollys and the Conservative Sir Edward Bigge. In the end he followed

Knollys' advice largely because Knollys, who had been Edward VII's private secretary, persuaded George, not altogether accurately, that his father would have given the guarantee to create the Liberal peers. Three years later, George V was actively considering dismissing Asquith's ministry in order to avert civil war over Irish Home Rule, but the outbreak of war with Germany changed the situation: we will never know whether or not he would have been able to get away with it, still less whether or not it would have avoided civil war.

In foreign policy, the monarchy traditionally had a major role to play. Diplomacy was carried out in theory, and to some extent in practice, between Heads of State. George IV sometimes used his position as Elector of Hanover to circumvent his ministers and at least pretend to pursue an independent policy; he also complained bitterly at having to recognise the newly-independent states of South America. Nevertheless, however much George IV might dislike Canning and his policy, in the end he had to abide by it. More important was the long tussle for control of foreign policy between Queen Victoria and Palmerston. On the face of it, for all Palmerston's showmanship and popularity, the Crown won some important battles: Palmerston was sacked in 1851 when he recognised Louis Napoleon's *coup* in Paris without reference to either the queen or the prime minister, and in 1861 his dispatch to Abraham Lincoln was altered and toned down by the intervention of Prince Albert.

The reality is not so clear-cut: Palmerston was dismissed in 1851 at least as much because he had infuriated Russell, the prime minister, as because of the attitude of the queen; it is by no means clear that in 1861 he and Russell seriously wanted war with the USA, and they seem to have been happy, perhaps even relieved, to accept the prince's amendments. Even if one believes that the Crown had gained an advantage over Palmerston, it is hard to see that it led anywhere: the queen disliked much of Palmerston's foreign policy, particularly towards Austria and Italy, but could not prevent him from following it; she violently disliked Gladstone's policy on Egypt and the Sudan, but had to learn to live with it. Edward VII's role in cementing the 1904 *entente* with France has long been put in its proper perspective: he added lustre, he helped its public acceptability, but the policy was the policy of his ministers and everyone knew it.

By 1914, therefore, the monarchy had more or less arrived at the situation described by Bagehot: to advise, to encourage and to warn the government of the day. This was by no means a foregone conclusion, and it did not come without a fight: Albert had had higher aspirations for the Crown but had not survived long enough to pursue them properly; Victoria had tried but largely failed to influence political appointments; Edward VII had established a strong position in the 1910 crisis but had died before he could carry it through to its conclusion; George V had been induced, largely through his inexperience, to yield his father's position and the outbreak of the First World War had averted a more serious confrontation between the palace and the Commons. Circumstances, and untimely deaths, had largely prevented the monarchy from slowing, still less halting, its decline.

Questions

1. What constitutional questions were raised by the crises of 1783–4, 1834–5 and 1839?
2. To what extent did Prince Albert succeed in elevating the Crown above party politics?
3. What was the significance for the monarchy of George V's guarantee to Asquith to create sufficient Liberal peers to pass the 1911 Parliament Act?
4. 'The Crown was at its strongest when it was faced with a ministry it did not like.' How far do you agree with this statement?
5. How significant was untimely death in the decline of the power of the monarchy?

ANALYSIS (2): WHY DID THE 'PEOPLE'S BUDGET' PROVOKE A CONSTITUTIONAL BATTLE WITH THE HOUSE OF LORDS?

This question works on a number of different levels. The most basic response is that the battle was provoked by the very nature of Lloyd George's 1909 budget. Although there were precedents for nearly all its major features, at least in the form of ideas that had been given serious consideration, taken altogether they did constitute a startlingly radical package, an idea which was reinforced by its popular nickname, 'the People's Budget'. It was the first budget to enshrine the idea of graduated taxation, that is, tax that is heavier on the rich than on the poor: unearned wealth was taxed at a higher rate than earned income, and a supertax was brought in for top earners. Most alarming of all, not least because of the principle behind it, were the proposals to levy a tax on the profits from land sales – which would entail exactly the sort of detailed land valuation which the Lords had just refused to countenance – and the introduction of death duties on landed property.

Lloyd George, it seemed, was not just declaring war on wealth but was specifically targeting landed wealth and the hereditary principle. He could hardly have chosen a set of targets more likely to arouse the wrath and opposition of the House of Lords. Added to this was the whole thrust of Lloyd George's rhetoric, which sounded like a man relishing the prospect of a scrap with the aristocracy. Once the rumour began that the Lords might reject the budget Lloyd George delivered two widely reported speeches, at Limehouse and Newcastle, that became celebrated for his scornful description of the Lords as 'five hundred men, ordinary men chosen accidentally from among the unemployed'; seldom had the Lords had to face such venomous wit coming at them from a minister of the Crown.

Rejecting a budget was always going to be controversial; rejecting this budget in the House of Lords was likely to be even more so, partly because it looked so obviously like the Lords protecting their own self-interest, and partly because custom had been established that they did not reject money bills. The Lords' answer to this was that the idea of a single budget measure was hardly an ancient practice – it only dated back to 1860 – and that this was no ordinary money bill anyway, but an attack on the rights of property: this, the Lords argued, was itself unconstitutional, and went far beyond the mandate the government had received at the 1906 election, so the whole issue should be referred back to the electorate. Asquith had no intention of letting the Lords dictate the timing of the election, especially when the Liberals were losing by-elections, and so he determined to force the Lords into submission.

This explanation covers the immediate events of 1909–11, but it leaves too many questions unanswered. Why, for example, did the Lords embark on a battle they must have realised they would lose? What did they expect to achieve? Here, the problem is one of hindsight: because the Lords lost the battle, it does not follow that they were bound to lose it, still less that they should have known it in advance. In fact, the Lords had every reason to think they might get away with rejecting the 1909 budget. They had almost half a century's experience of frustrating the wishes of the House of Commons and getting away with it, and doing so, moreover, on issues every bit as momentous as Lloyd George's budget. In 1860 the Lords had defeated Gladstone's budgetary measure to abolish the duty on paper; it was this confrontation between Lords and Commons that had led Gladstone to put all his budgetary proposals into one Budget Bill instead of following the standard practice of introducing measures in a series of separate bills. Rather than defeat the whole budget, the Lords in 1860 had backed down, but they could point out in justification of their opposition the undoubted fact that Gladstone's proposal had only passed by a very slim majority in the Commons. In 1884 they had held up Gladstone's Franchise Bill and forced him to introduce a Re-distribution Bill; even more conclusively, in 1892 they had defeated Gladstone's beloved Home Rule Bill, despite its large Commons majority. In each case the Lords could point to considerable public support for the line they were taking.

After the massive Liberal victory of 1906 they began selectively frustrating the government's social reform proposals, including the Education Bill and a proposal to end the practice of plural voting by those who owned land in several constituencies. There was something blatant about the Lords' conduct which seemed almost to be daring the Liberals to do something about it. Gladstone had frequently expressed his frustration with the Lords' tactics, and a 'Mend Them or End Them' clause had featured in the 1891 Newcastle programme; now, Lloyd George attacked them in public speeches and in 1907 the prime minister, Campbell-Bannerman, drew up a proposal to limit their powers, but still nothing had actually developed. Not only had the Liberals not taken action but by 1909 they were clearly losing popular support rapidly: it was all very well to talk of the Lords as Mr Balfour's poodle and to whip up popular feeling against them, but when Asquith went to the country in January 1910 it was not the Conservatives but the Liberals who had a nasty shock awaiting them. Paradoxically, it looked, just as it had on every earlier occasion when the Lords had taken on the Commons, as if it was the Conservative and Unionist Lords, rather than the Liberals in the Commons, who were more in tune with public opinion.

Nevertheless, not even the most blinkered 'backwoods' peer can have seriously thought that he enjoyed public support for the retention of his privileges. There was a useful internal party advantage to taking a stand on the issue: determined opposition to an apparently genuine threat of socialist influence in government seemed a good way to heal the increasingly damaging split in the Unionist camp caused by the tariff reform issue. But even without this party spin-off, the Lords would almost certainly have put up fierce resistance to what appeared to be socialistic ideas under the guise of Liberal reforms. This idea was by no means absurd: the Liberals operated an electoral pact with the Labour Party, and there were clear areas of overlap between Lloyd George's policies and the ideas of the Fabians. Indeed the Fabians were happy enough that Lloyd George seemed to be doing their work for them.

The Lords' fears were not motivated just by a self-interested 'knee-jerk' reaction to any hint of socialism: they genuinely believed in the aristocracy and the aristocratic principle as a force for good. As the landowning class they had acted as leaders of society for centuries, their sons had fought and died for their country, and their role in the country was embodied in their constitutional rights and privileges. By contrast, Asquith's government appeared to be acting as what would today be called – and the phrase began to be used at the time – an 'elective dictatorship'. It was using its massive majority to push through measures such as Irish Home Rule and radical social reform which, the Lords claimed, were not covered by its electoral mandate. It was a similar complaint to those heard in the 1980s about the Thatcher governments and in the 1990s about Tony Blair. To the Liberals, the Unionists' use of the Lords was an unfair ploy by the party rejected at the polls by the electorate; to the Unionists it was a sign of how desperate things had become, that they had to resort to the Lords to fight an arrogant and all-powerful government. Interestingly, the Lords' response was not simply to reject the government measures out of hand, but to demand that they should be submitted to public referendum. This could even be seen as an attempt by the Unionists to outflank the Liberals on the left by appearing even more democratic than they were – Disraeli would no doubt have approved.

These different motives behind Unionist resistance varied in intensity: the Die-Hards or 'Ditchers', like Lord Halsbury or the sporting young Lord Willoughby de Broke, were acting not so much from self-interest as from a sort of class instinct. Lord Curzon, who led the Lords' resistance to the Parliament Bill – until the December 1910 election and the king's promise to create 300 Liberal peers made it clear that the bill would pass – seems to have been motivated by a mixture of genuine fear of the constitutional implications of the government's actions and an acute sense of political realism. Balfour and Lord Lansdowne, the Unionist leader in the Lords, seem to have been motivated at least as much by party considerations as by any wider constitutional concerns. To some extent one's reading of the Lords' motives is bound to be determined by either a charitable or a cynical reaction to their opposition, and Asquith for one always viewed it in the most cynical light. But one only has to see just how long the debates in the Lords were, and to see the arguments they brought up, to see that a straightforwardly cynical view is not sufficient to explain the vehemence of the Lords' resistance to their fate.

On the Liberal side the question is not so much why they took on the Lords, but why they went about it so slowly and reluctantly. They had not acted on the 1907 Campbell-Bannerman plan for curtailing the powers of the Lords, and Asquith went about the business of forcing the Parliament Bill through the Lords with every appearance of reluctance and hesitation. Despite the precedent of 1832, which was inevitably much discussed in 1910, he did not get a guarantee from Edward VII to create the Liberal peers necessary to wipe out the Unionist majority, and circumstances obliged him to proceed very carefully about getting it from George V. Above all, by agreeing to deal with the question by means of a constitutional conference with the Unionists, despite commanding a Commons majority with his Labour and Irish supporters, Asquith seemed to be surrendering unnecessarily to Unionist pressure. Although it seems clear that Asquith was prepared to take on the Lords if it proved necessary, and he certainly moved quickly to introduce a motion of censure once they had rejected the budget, the evidence also suggests, with equal clarity, that he did not relish the prospect and held off from it as long as he possibly could.

Why were the Liberals so slow in confronting their old opponents? Part of the problem lay in the precise circumstances of the 1906–9 period. The Lords had defeated government measures, it was true, but these were on issues like education and the licensing laws: important issues, certainly, but rather narrow ground from which to launch a major constitutional crisis and probably fight an election. It would have looked odd to act on, say, the Licensing Bill when Gladstone had allowed the Lords to get away with defeating Home Rule without trying to curtail their powers. Then there was the question of exactly what should be done about the Lords anyway. Campbell-Bannerman's plan had been to limit their powers so that they might not reject money bills, they might not reject legislation passed three times within a two-year period by the Commons, and to restrict the length of parliaments from seven years to five: this would mean that legislation introduced in the first three years of a government's term of office would pass, regardless of the Lords' opposition. However, not all the Liberals agreed with his plan. The main alternative proposal was to alter the composition of the Lords, most probably by eliminating the hereditary element. The trouble with this idea, as its opponents quickly pointed out, was that by removing the most obvious anomaly within the House of Lords it could actually strengthen it, and give it more of a basis for rejecting legislation, including money bills.

In the immediate aftermath of the Lords' rejection of the budget the cabinet was split between these two approaches, and was also under the misapprehension, which was largely Asquith's fault, that the king had already agreed to create the Liberal peers, which he had not. Quite apart from divisions within his own party, Asquith was also under extreme pressure from the Irish Nationalists and from Labour. Labour insisted on a tough attitude towards the Lords; the Irish needed to be persuaded of the merits of curtailing the Lords' powers rather than changing their composition, and had to be kept sweet with the promise of Home Rule. Keeping the support of Labour and the Irish became even more urgent after the disappointing results of the January 1910 election, when Asquith effectively depended on them for his majority. Asquith may well have wished he could drop the issue: his famous catchphrase 'Wait and See' could certainly be – and was – understood in precisely that manner, but the Irish and Labour were determined not to let him off the hook.

Finally, the fact that the constitutional crisis came to a head must be attributed to some extent to a remarkably comprehensive failure of leadership on all sides. Asquith seemed hesitant and unable to direct events: he called one general election in January 1910 which almost wiped out his parliamentary majority and called another at the end of the year which made little difference except slightly to reduce his support still further. In a famous parliamentary scene he was shouted down in the Commons and unable to address the House, and he seemed quite unable to enforce his authority. The Unionists, however, seemed little better off. Balfour and Lansdowne were unable to control their supporters, many of whom were almost as disillusioned with them as they were with Asquith. Some of the 'ditchers' thought Asquith was bluffing about the creation of peers, and given the extreme reluctance of both Edward VII and George V to agree to it, this was not an entirely unreasonable view to take; Balfour and Lansdowne, however, seemed to think that Asquith was seeking only a limited creation of peers which would leave the Unionists with their majority, though why Asquith should have sought this was never explained. The result was that the rank-and-file, in both houses, were able to operate beyond the control of their respective party leaderships: one sees this not just in Lord Halsbury's 'last ditch' opposition to the Parliament Bill, but also in the Unionists' howling down of Asquith at the despatch box and in the apocalyptic language of the Parliament Bill's opponents. There is throughout the crisis of 1910–11 a sense of the parties getting out of control, a sense which is increased when one remembers what else was happening at the same time: the menacing confrontations in Ireland, the height of suffragette violence, bitter and violent industrial disputes, and a crisis in Morocco that seemed to bring a European war very close. To avert a damaging constitutional crisis over the 1909 budget the parties needed a strong hand, and they did not get it.

There are, therefore, a number of reasons, long- and short-term, why the budget brought about a constitutional crisis. The budget's apparent attack on landed property and heredity aroused the opposition of the Lords, fuelled by Lloyd George's provocative rhetoric; the Lords felt that precedents for conflict with the Commons were encouraging, whereas the Liberals were acting to end a long history of interference by the Lords with Liberal policies. The government's waning public support gave the Lords confidence, and the lack of effective leadership gave the Die-Hards an opening for fiercer resistance than was really politically prudent. But perhaps the real reason for the conflict lies in Lloyd George's famous phrase: the Lords may have been Balfour's poodle, but the Liberals realised, as perhaps the Unionists did not, that poodles are essentially for display: they might snap, but their threats are empty and they will usually submit to a determined opponent.

Questions

1. Why did the Lords reject the 1909 budget?
2. Why, despite their confrontation with the Lords, did the Liberals lose so many seats at the 1910 elections?
3. Why did the Liberals not either change the composition of the House of Lords, or abolish it altogether?

SOURCES

1. THE MONARCH AND THE CHOICE OF MINISTERS

Source A: memorandum by Prince Albert (11 July 1850).

I have often heard it stated as the nature of the English constitution and the Royal Prerogatives, that the Sovereign could not interfere with the Government or the management of Parliament which are left to the sole control of the responsible Ministers, but that he was absolutely free in the choice of his Minister. Now I differed completely from that doctrine. I held the Sovereign to have an immense moral responsibility upon his shoulders with regard to his government and the duty to watch and control it, and *no* choice almost in the selection of his Ministers, if he understood his duties.

Source B: letter from Queen Victoria to Lady Ely (21 September 1879).

I wish it were possible for Sir H. Ponsonby to *get at some of the Opposition*, and to point *out* the *extreme danger* of binding themselves by foolish, violent declarations about their policy beforehand. . . . I never could take Mr Gladstone or Mr Lowe as my minister again, for I never COULD have the slightest *particle* of confidence in Mr Gladstone *after* his violent, mischievous, and dangerous conduct for the last three years, nor could I take the *latter* after the very offensive language he used three years ago against *me*.

Sir H. Ponsonby has so many Whig friends that he might easily *get* these things *known*. In former days *much* good was done by Baron Stockmar and Mr Anson paving the way *for* future arrangements and *preventing* complications at the moment, like Sir R. Peel's failure in '39 about the Ladies.

Ever yours affectionately, VR&I*.

I never *could* take Sir C. Dilke as a *Minister*.

*VR&I = Victoria, Regina [Queen] and Imperatrix [Empress of India]

Source C: Queen Victoria to Sir Henry Ponsonby, her private secretary (8 April 1880).

What the queen is especially anxious to have impressed on Lords Hartington and Granville is, firstly, that Mr Gladstone *she* could have nothing to do with, for she considers his whole conduct since '76 to have been one series of violent, passionate invective against and abuse of Lord Beaconsfield, and that *he caused* the Russian war, and made the task of the Government of this country most difficult in times of the greatest difficulty and anxiety, and did all to try and prevent England from holding the position which, thanks to Lord Beaconsfield's firmness, has been restored to her.

Source D: the Duke of Connaught to Queen Victoria (11 April 1880).

Dearest Mama,

Many thanks for your dear letter which I received this morning. How well I can enter into your feelings at the present moment; the difficulties of a constitutional Sovereign at a moment like the present are indeed very great.

I know how strongly you feel against the line that the Liberals have taken up these last three years, and now they are returned with this very large majority. It is indeed hard for you to bear, dearest Mama, but I know how nobly you can sacrifice your own feelings at the call of duty. I can't understand what is to be done about Mr Gladstone if he is not to be in the new Ministry; won't he be a terrible thorn in their side out of office? I am afraid, from what I can hear and from what I read in different papers, that Mr Gladstone is more popular among the Liberals and Radicals than ever, in fact they are mad about him. It is not pleasant to think, but so it is. I hear that the Duke of Westminster has spent £100,000 to promote the Liberal cause. I hear also that even Lord Derby has spent a lot of money for the Liberals in Lancashire. The amount of money that has been spent at this election, especially by the Liberals, has been something enormous.

Source E: memorandum by Queen Victoria (23 April 1880).

I saw Mr Gladstone at quarter to 7, and told him I understood that he had received my message through Lord Hartington and Lord Granville, to which he replied in the affirmative.

I then said that, according to constitutional usage, I had applied to Lord Hartington as the Leader (which he said was quite correct), but as Lord H. and Lord Granville said they could not act without him, I wished to know if he could form a Government? He replied that, considering the part he had taken, he felt he must not shrink from the responsibility, and that he felt he would be prepared to form a Government.

Source F: Gladstone's account of his meeting with the queen, accepting her invitation to form a government (23 April 1880).

Windsor Castle, April 23 1880

[The queen] asked if I had thought of anyone for the war office, which was very important. . . . I said Mr Childers occurred to me as an administrator of eminent capacity and conciliatory in his modes of action . . . She thought that Mr Childers had not been popular at the admiralty, and that it was desirable the secretary for war should be liked by the army. I said that there was an occurrence towards the close of his term which placed him in a difficult position, but relied on his care and discretion. (She did not press the point, but is evidently under strong professional bias.)

Questions

1. Explain the following references:
   'his violent, mischievous, and dangerous conduct for the last three years' (Source B) [2]
   'Sir R. Peel's failure in '39 about the Ladies' [2]
2. Account for the different opinions in Sources A, B and D on the monarch's role in choosing a prime minister. [7]
3. Evaluate Sources B, C, E and F as evidence of Queen Victoria's view of the Crown's constitutional position. [7]
4.* Using all these documents, and any other evidence known to you, consider the proposition that Prince Albert posed more of a threat to parliamentary sovereignty than Queen Victoria. [7]

Worked answer: Question 4

On the face of it, this must seem an unusual proposition. It was Queen Victoria who took a dubious stand in the bedchamber crisis, and she again who interfered so frequently against Gladstone and in favour of Disraeli and Salisbury; Prince Albert tends to get the credit for having helped her into her constitutional role, taking a more neutral stance between the major parties. Source A seems to confirm this, while the tone of Sources B–E seems to suggest good reasons why he had needed to take this role. But if one looks more closely at Source A, the picture is less clear-cut. What, exactly, did this 'immense moral responsibility' consist of? It is not clarified in the passage quoted, but since it does not refer to the choice of ministers, which Albert sees as the province of Parliament and the electorate, it must relate to the monarchy's role in the more normal business of government. Understood in that sense, and it is hard to see how else it could be read, Prince Albert's constitutional philosophy is not so very different from that of George III. He certainly wanted the monarchy to play a more active role in the administration of government: one sees this in aspects as diverse as his role in organising the Great Exhibition and his frustration at Palmerston's cavalier attitude towards the royal prerogative in foreign policy. It makes it less surprising, perhaps, that he was never a popular or generally appreciated figure in Britain: his one attempt to attend debates in the House of Commons led to protests at his 'unconstitutional' action.

Queen Victoria always took a keen interest in the appointment of her ministers, as these documents show; however, what they also show is that, even when she was determined to resist having someone, as here with Gladstone, and even when her constitutional grounds for avoiding him were entirely solid, as Source E indicates even Gladstone conceded, she could not get her way against the combined will of Parliament and the electorate. In this sense, perhaps paradoxically, Queen Victoria's undoubted and passionate interest in constitutional niceties was actually less of a 'threat' – if that is the right word – to parliamentary sovereignty than Prince Albert's lofty and high-minded disinterestedness. Whether the queen would have tried to establish more of a role in everyday government had Albert lived – and whether or not she would have been successful – we cannot say.

SOURCES

2. THE PEOPLE'S BUDGET AND THE PARLIAMENT BILL

Source G: Lord Lansdowne, the Unionist (Conservative) leader in the Lords, speaking against the budget (22 November 1909).

The case I have to make is, after all, a very simple one. What we have to say about the bill is this. It is a grave and I think I should be justified in saying an unprecedented measure. It has never been before the people of this country. It needs the concurrence of the House of Lords. The House of Lords should not, in our opinion, undertake the responsibility of giving that concurrence until it has become aware that the people of this country desire that this Bill should become law. My Lords, that is our position. What is the position of noble Lords opposite? We understand it to be something of this kind. They expect us to pass this Bill *nemine contradicente**, perhaps after a feeble protest . . .

Oliver Cromwell invented a little House of Lords of his own for the express purpose – as he put it – of protecting the people of England against an omnipotent House of Commons – the horridest arbitrariness that ever existed in the world. I think we detect signs of this horrid arbitrariness in the measure which we are now discussing. In all seriousness, my Lords, we have a right to ask where this kind of thing is going to stop. If you can graft a Licensing Bill and Land Valuation Bills and measures of that kind on the Finance Bill, what is to prevent your grafting on to it, let us say, a Home Rule Bill – setting up an authority in Ireland to collect and dispense all the taxes of that country? There is literally no limit to the abuses which might creep in if such a practice were allowed to go on without restriction. Upon this ground alone I venture to think your Lordships' House might consider very seriously whether you are justified in passing this Bill into law.

*nem. con. = with no-one opposed

Source H: Lord Loreburn, the Lord Chancellor, replying to Lansdowne (22 November 1909).

Now, my Lords, the noble Marquess [Lansdowne] assumed that it was within the rights of this House, unquestionably and indubitably, to reject the Finance Bill of the year. If I am asked whether you can do it lawfully, according to law, I answer undeniably yes . . . But if I am asked whether this House can do it constitutionally, I say – in my opinion, no . . . What would happen if all the estates of the Realm were to carry out in freedom all the powers which the law entrusts to them? The Crown has enormous powers, and by the Constitution some of them for centuries have not been used. My Lords, it is not to the letter of the law itself that those who wish to govern this country as this country has been governed in the past must look. They must look also and even more to custom, usage, convention – call it whatever you please – which by inveterate practice had so modified the hard law itself that we are governed more by custom in this country in great matters than we are even by the law.

Source I: Asquith speaking in the House of Commons (20 July 1911).

The truth is that all this talk about the duty or the right of the House of Lords to refer measures to the people is, in the light of our practical and actual experience, the hollowest outcry of political cant. We never hear of it, as I pointed out, when a Tory Government is in power.

Source J: Lord Halsbury speaking against the Parliament Bill in the House of Lords (20 July 1911).

I have been in politics more than sixty years, and I have never witnessed such an attempt to abolish the Second Chamber and to obtain supreme power, not so much for the House of Commons – for it is idle to pretend that House is independent – as for the Minister in power and the political caucus. It is not a question merely of Party division. It is a question of life and death to the Constitution.

Source K: Lord Curzon speaking on the Parliament Bill in the House of Lords (10 August 1911).

There is no getting away from the fact that this Bill is going to pass. The action of Lord Halsbury and his friends may retard its passage into law for a few days or at most a few weeks, but they cannot prevent its ultimate passage. We have reached a point at which it must be admitted that the powers of effectual resistance have gone from us. Supposing that by your votes you defeat the Government and force such a creation [of peers], what good will you do yourselves, to your Party, to the Constitution, to the country, or to anyone concerned? . . . At the bottom of my heart I cannot help thinking that the country . . . would say that the Peers, who had twice stood out against His Majesty's Government and been defeated, were finally hoisted with their own petard . . . and so far from thinking that ridicule would fall on those shoulders where it ought to fall – on those of noble Lords opposite – I think it might conceivably recoil on the heads of noble Lords on this side of the House.

Questions

1. Explain the following references:
   i 'It has never been before the people of this country.' (Source G) [2]
   ii 'the political caucus' (Source J) [1]
   iii 'we are governed more by custom in this country in great matters than we are even by the law.' (Source H) [2]
2. To what extent do Sources J and K agree on the likely effect of the Parliament Bill? [6]
3. Assess the validity of the constitutional arguments in Sources G, H and I. [7]
4. How far do these documents, and any other information known to you, support the contention that the passage of the 1911 Parliament Act hurt the Liberals more than Conservatives? [7]

Worked answer: Question 3

In Source G, Lansdowne compares the situation in 1911 with the dictatorship of Oliver Cromwell in order to stress the point that the Lords are the ones standing up for the rights of the electorate. The whole language of his argument is couched in terms of defending the liberties of the people against the designs of an over-mighty government in the Commons. So, the budget had 'never been before the people', which was true in the sense that it had not been submitted to referendum, but misleading because the budget was designed to pay for reforms, particularly Old Age Pensions, for which the Liberals certainly did have an electoral mandate. Lansdowne objects to the danger of major issues being slipped past the Lords by being tacked onto money bills which the Lords could not oppose: there was a long history of tacking of this sort, and both sides had employed it on occasion, so that Lansdowne had a point but was hardly in a position to make it. His protest that the Liberals wanted the Lords to pass the budget *nem. con.* would carry more weight if he had not been actively engaged in frustrating Liberal legislation for the previous five years: in the circumstances, the Liberal wish was hardly as unreasonable as Lansdowne presented it.

Nevertheless, in constitutional terms Lansdowne was probably on surer ground than the Lord Chancellor in Source H. It was certainly true that the Lords had every legal right to reject the budget, and it had done so rather more recently (1860) than the comparison with long-disused royal powers would suggest. For the Lord Chancellor of England to place custom and inveterate practice (both of which can change) over the rule of law is certainly odd. Loreburn would have been justified in calling it unwise of the Lords to reject the budget – Edward VII said much the same thing – but his constitutional argument is essentially party politics masquerading as impartial judgement. Ironically Asquith's comment in Source I is as true of his own Lord Chancellor as it is of the Unionists. And it is hard to deny the force of Asquith's argument: the idea of referring the budget to a referendum had not been heard before. However, since in the election which did follow the rejection of the budget – and which was, therefore, in effect the referendum the Unionists had been demanding – the Liberals nearly lost their hold on the Commons, Asquith's argument in Source I may be conceded, but his political analysis looks a bit complacent.

8

VOTES FOR WOMEN

BACKGROUND NARRATIVE

The long fight for female emancipation has become one of the best
known aspects of the story of parliamentary reform. Most historical
coverage concentrates on the role of Mrs Emmeline Pankhurst's
Women's Social and Political Union (WSPU), dubbed 'Suffragettes'
by the *Daily Mail*, and especially on the campaign of violent protest
on which it embarked between 1905 and the outbreak of war.
This began with increasingly disruptive barracking of government
ministers at public meetings, and progressed to petty vandalism,
such as attacking golf courses or smashing windows, protesters
chaining themselves to railings outside public buildings, and eventually to violence against property, including arson and small-scale
bombing. The government reaction was defiant and robust, not to
say brutal: Asquith refused to give way to suffragette violence, while
the suffragettes themselves were arrested and thrown into prison.
Once in prison, suffragette hunger strikers were force-fed through
tubes inserted in the mouth, nose or rectum. The so-called 'Cat and
Mouse Act' of 1913 allowed the authorities to release suffragettes
when their health was too poor to withstand imprisonment, and
then rearrest them when they had recovered.

Within Parliament the issue was complicated by the crises over
Ireland, the House of Lords and the trade unions, and by the need
to address female suffrage in conjunction with other aspects of
parliamentary reform, notably redistribution and the issue of plural
voting. When the war broke out, the issue was further complicated
by the residence requirement, which would disqualify servicemen

from inclusion in the new electoral registers. These different considerations inevitably determined the attitudes of the different parties to female suffrage – the Irish Nationalists, for example, generally opposed it, partly because they felt it would strengthen their opponents on the Home Rule issue, and partly because they opposed anything which might weaken the Liberal government. In this complex situation, Asquith was unwilling to commit the government, the more so since he was personally strongly alienated by the militancy of the suffragettes; and supporters of female suffrage had to resort to a series of private members' bills, none of which were accorded enough parliamentary time to succeed. In 1910 Asquith sanctioned an all-party Conciliation Committee to come up with a bill setting out an acceptable basis for female suffrage, but the committee's proposals were overtaken, first by the December 1910 election and then by Asquith's announcement in November 1911 of a government franchise and registration measure. This government measure made the Conciliation Bill redundant; however, it only applied to men, though Asquith said it would be open to amendment in favour of female suffrage. However, to general surprise in January 1913 the Speaker ruled such an amendment out of order and there, despite spiralling suffragette violence, the matter rested until the outbreak of war.

The standard interpretation of these events holds that, whereas suffragette violence before 1914 had not brought women the vote, the work carried out by women on the home front during the First World War won the respect of Parliament, which in gratitude in 1918 granted the vote to women over 30, putting their franchise on the same basis as that of men ten years later. However, there are many problems with this familiar interpretation. It conveniently ignores the serious splits within the WSPU, especially between the autocratic Christabel Pankhurst and her more socialist-inclined sister, Sylvia. Secondly, it does not take into account the important role played by the non-violent and more experienced suffragist movement, led by Mrs Millicent Fawcett. If it is true that women's wartime role won them the vote in 1918, then it must raise at least two questions: firstly whether anything at all had been achieved by suffragette militancy before 1914, and secondly why the 1918 Franchise Act which extended the vote to the entire male population denied the vote to any woman under 30 – the very women whose work in the factories and on the land had so impressed the politicians. Perhaps most puzzling of all, it does not explain why women were so much more politically active and assertive in the last two decades when they did not have the vote than in the first fifty years when they did.

ANALYSIS (1): WHY HAD THE WOMEN'S SUFFRAGE MOVEMENT FAILED TO ACHIEVE THE VOTE BY 1914?

The standard version of the story of the fight for female suffrage sees it as a straight contest between the suffragettes and a chauvinistic male establishment, headed – not to say embodied – by the prime minister, Asquith, and encompassing blinkered politicians, burly policemen and brutal prison warders. This version has the merit of simplicity, with obvious heroes and villains, which makes it well suited to general public consumption; unfortunately it ignores some of the important paradoxes of the story. The most obvious was that, on the whole, male politicians were by no means opposed to some form of female suffrage. The Labour Party supported it, and leading Labour figures like Keir Hardie and George Lansbury were deeply involved in the issue, Lansbury to such an extent that he voluntarily, though unsuccessfully, put himself up for re-election in his Bow and Bromley constituency on a female suffrage platform. A substantial section of the Liberal Party, quite possibly the majority, supported it, as did many leading Liberals, including Churchill, Lloyd George, and Sir Edward Grey. Although there was more opposition to it among the Conservatives, as was perhaps to be expected, a number of leading Conservatives supported it, including the party leader, Balfour.

The issue had a long and venerable history. Henry Hunt had tried to amend the 1832 Reform Act to apply to women: indeed, one of the planks of the suffragist argument was that – under the unreformed system – women property owners had enjoyed ancient voting rights which, ironically, parliamentary reform had removed. Female suffrage was a long-standing aim on the Left, ever since Mary Wollstonecraft had published her *Vindication of the Rights of Woman* in 1792; though the Chartists, who, as we have seen, took women's rights seriously, nevertheless saw it as a subsidiary issue to attaining full rights for working men. But it was not a peripheral issue, especially after John Stuart Mill's celebrated motion to include it in the 1867 Reform Act. The arguments in favour of it were regularly outlined in Lydia Becker's

Women's Suffrage Journal and in the almost annual parliamentary debates on the private members' bills on the issue from the 1870s onwards, at least three of which made it to second reading.

Even more striking than speeches in Parliament is the evidence of actual steps taken to extend political rights to women. In 1869 single women ratepayers got the vote in municipal elections and in 1870 in elections to the new School Boards; women could also vote under the 1888 Local Government Act and in 1894 they were allowed to sit on local councils. By 1900 there were something like a thousand female elected Poor Law Guardians, including Mrs Pankhurst. Although there were some battles along the way – for example, women's right to sit on local councils and in 1902 on the new local education authorities were both challenged and briefly denied – on the whole the progress towards full female political emancipation compares very favourably with, say, the battles of trade unions for full legal rights, or of the Irish nationalists for Home Rule. The picture is all the more striking when one sees it in the fuller context of female social emancipation, well under way by 1900. Women had begun to establish themselves in the universities and in the learned professions like medicine and the law. The development of new technology provided young women in particular with a whole range of work in typing pools, offices, telephone exchanges, department stores and elementary schools, opportunities which had not existed previously, and which gave them a degree of independence which their mothers and grandmothers had never known.

Marriage was not necessarily as restrictive as it has sometimes been made out to be. The point is often made that, until the Married Women's Property Acts of 1870 and 1883, a wife's property was deemed to belong to her husband, but this seems to have been much more of a technicality than a daily reality: most married women retained control over their own property even before the Acts, and the legal position, when it arose, seems often to have come as a surprise as much to their husbands as it was to them.[1] Nor should we entirely forget the point that for most of the nineteenth century the world's largest empire was ruled by a woman. None of this belittles the very real battles that still remained for women – for equal pay and educational qualifications or against prostitution and abuse – but it does change the image given in the traditional version of the story. The central question would seem to be not so much how it was that men could have been so blinkered as not to accord women the vote, but rather how it was that, with such a tide of emancipation flowing in their favour, and given the deeply ingrained Victorian belief in giving the vote to those who had proved themselves worthy of it, women should have missed their chance so completely that by 1914 the vote actually seemed further off than ever.

Part of the answer lies in the parliamentary problems posed by defining the suffragists' and suffragettes' actual aim. The suffragette slogan was 'Votes for Women', but which women? At the time there was no universal suffrage for men, so only those on the Left who actually wanted genuinely universal suffrage interpreted it to mean Votes for All Women (an aim which in turn raised what was generally acknowledged to be the awkward prospect of an electorate in which women would be the majority). For others, Votes for Women would mean deciding where to draw the line between voting and non-voting women just as earlier generations had done for men. It could be drawn along property lines, but many in the Liberal and especially the Labour parties were opposed to extending the property principle: as Labour tended to put it, it would mean 'Votes for Ladies', and Conservative-voting ladies at that. For this reason, politicians like Lloyd George, who supported female suffrage, nevertheless opposed specific female suffrage measures, such as the property-based Conciliation Bill. There were similar objections to proposals to base female suffrage on taxpaying or ratepaying.

The bottom line was that no party, and certainly no party leader, would support a measure which was likely to harm his own party: thus Balfour, though personally sympathetic to female suffrage, would only support limited proposals likely to enhance the Conservative vote, proposals which, for precisely the same reason, were opposed by the Liberals. In any case, with the House of Lords vetoing government proposals far less controversial than female suffrage, the issue was highly unlikely to get through Parliament even had it enjoyed government support, until after the powers of the Lords had been reduced by the 1911 Parliament Act. Even then parliamentary logistics worked against it. It was established practice that measures affecting the franchise were to be put into practice as soon as possible after they passed into law, which meant drawing up new electoral registers and holding a general election. For this reason parliamentary reform bills were usually introduced towards the end of a parliamentary session, so as to give the government time to get some legislation under its belt before facing another election. Where these measures were likely to meet opposition in the Lords, as female suffrage most certainly would, this would not leave enough time for the measure to go through the Commons the three times required under the terms of the 1911 Act in order to overcome the Lords' veto.

The question of which women should get the vote, and on what basis, had an even more divisive effect on the already chronically divided women's suffrage movement. Millicent Fawcett's National Union of Woman Suffrage Societies was founded in 1889, long pre-dating the suffragettes, but the NUWSS itself comprised no fewer than sixteen separate suffrage groups, though at least it succeeded in holding them together; Mrs Pankhurst's Women's Social and Political Union went through seven bitter splits in the first ten years of its life. The key role of Mrs Fawcett's Suffragists in mobilising working-class support has been stressed by Jill Liddington and Jill Norris;[2] by contrast the suffragette leadership, Emmeline and Christabel Pankhurst, and Emmeline and Frederick Pethick Lawrence, were at best indifferent to working-class support and by 1912 increasingly opposed to it, to the point of expelling the socialist-sympathising Sylvia Pankhurst altogether and trying unsuccessfully to prevent her East End Federation of Suffragettes from including the word 'suffragettes' in its name. In 1907 the WSPU had changed its stated aim from 'Votes for Women on the same terms as it may be granted to men' to 'Tax-paying women are entitled to the parliamentary vote', which convinced Labour and the Liberals, not to mention the NUWSS, that the WSPU was, to all intents and purposes, a stooge for the Conservative Party.

The whole question of female suffrage, both in principle and in detail, was bound to be controversial and divisive, but many of the suffragette tactics seemed deliberately geared to aggravate these divisions. They appeared to go out of their way to heckle and alienate Liberal ministers like Lloyd George and Churchill who were actually in favour of female suffrage; in 1906 at by-elections in Cockermouth and Huddersfield they accepted hospitality from the Independent Labour Party, to whom they were allied, and then promptly spoke strongly against the ILP, splitting its vote and letting the Conservatives in. The increasingly autocratic and dictatorial leadership of the Pankhursts and Pethick Lawrences, who would allow the membership of the WSPU no say at all in decision-making and who demanded absolute obedience from everyone around them, caused intense bitterness among their supporters, who could not avoid the paradox of a cam-paign for democratic rights which took no account of the democratic rights of its own members. In 1912 the Pankhursts even drove out the Pethick Lawrences, and according to Sylvia Pankhurst her sister Christabel expelled her from the WSPU saying 'You have a democratic constitution for your [East London] Federation; we do not agree with that . . . You have your own ideas. We do not want that.'[3] Small wonder that one disillusioned suffragette complained that, although Mrs

Pankhurst 'wishes women to have votes, she will not allow them to have opinions'.[4]

To make matters worse, although the WSPU proved good at mounting impressive processions and pilgrimages to link the cause to noble themes from British history, the good effects of these spectacles was outweighed by the Pankhursts' increasing obsession with issues of sex and prostitution. Concern with these issues was by no means confined to the suffragettes – Mrs Fawcett, for example, believed that female suffrage would reduce prostitution – but the Pankhursts seemed to take the issue to extremes, becoming stridently anti-male, ruthlessly dropping even the most loyal of their male supporters from the WSPU, and claiming, as Christabel did in 1913 in *The Great Scourge*, that men were little more than carriers of venereal disease. This was simply ammunition for those who dismissed the suffragettes as cranks.

But by far the most controversial and divisive aspect of the whole controversy over female suffrage was the suffragettes' use of violence. It began when Christabel Pankhurst and Annie Kenney got themselves arrested after interrupting a speech by Sir Edward Grey in 1905; it continued in 1908 with hunger strikes, and a major battle with police outside Parliament on 'Black Friday', 18 November 1910, closely followed by the 'Battle of Downing Street'; and a *Kristallnacht*-style orgy of window smashing after the Conciliation Bill had been torpedoed by Asquith's Franchise Bill in November 1911. Damage to property caused by the suffragette campaign was extensive, and although the only fatality was Emily Wilding Davison's famous death under the king's horse at the 1913 Derby, which we must assume was a form of suicide, it is hard to ascribe this to suffragette restraint: the violence was orchestrated to increase in intensity and seriousness, starting with windows and progressing through to bombs and arson, which – although initially aimed at empty targets – had ample scope for killing or maiming. There is no ostensible reason to suppose that it could not or would not have have progressed to attacks on persons.

No other issue split the women's movement so decisively. The middle-class activists of the much larger NUWSS were dismayed to see the effects of their hard work jeopardised by the suffragette tactics; even stronger was the disgust of working-class suffragists. One suffragette activist emerged from seven days in Holloway to find she had to run a gauntlet of her suffragist workmates, who spat at her as she walked between them. It was all very well for middle-class suffragettes to get themselves arrested, knowing they had servants at home to see to their children and keep the household running; working-class women, for whom the suffragettes had little enough time anyway, could hardly afford to engage in that sort of behaviour. Even more than the increasingly autocratic, almost paranoid tendencies of the Pankhursts, nothing alienated women from the suffragettes more than this insistence on violence.

The crucial point, of course, is not so much its impact on the suffragists but its effect on the government. Obviously, the WSPU itself justified its use of violence, pointing out that men had used violence in 1831–2 and in 1866–7, and some historians have agreed with them;[5] the weight of evidence, however, seems to be very firmly the other way. The violence which attended the passage of the first two Reform Acts had been in response to the defeat of various of the Reform Bills, and when it looked as if the opponents of reform might defeat the measure altogether: this was very different from an orchestrated campaign of violence directed by Christabel Pankhurst from her refuge in Paris. A much better comparison would be with the violent campaigns of Parnell's supporters in their battles with Gladstone over rents and Home Rule for Ireland, but here too there is a strong case for saying that the violence was counter-productive, merely holding Gladstone back from granting concessions which he might otherwise have given much more freely.

In the case of suffragette violence, it is very hard to see what the suffragettes had to show by 1914 for ten years of campaigning, apart from a stymied government franchise measure which applied only to men. On the other hand, they had hardened attitudes against them in Parliament and in the TUC. There was already concern that, if given the vote, women would swamp parliament with 'female' issues of social reform or education, and considerable resentment at the thought that women might get the vote and yet be exempt from military service. Now the suffragette campaign seemed to justify the widely-held belief that women were not physically or mentally stable enough to be trusted with the vote. Above all, Suffragette violence had very effectively alienated the prime minister, and in a political situation where so much depended on the personal attitude of the prime minister this was a fatal mistake. Asquith had been quite prepared to look at the issue of female suffrage, and no doubt to work out a solution which avoided handing a huge new constituency of voters over to the Conservatives; suffragette violence not only repulsed him personally but made it virtually impossible for him to bend on the issue even had he wished to, since it would make it appear as if he were giving in to threats. Bearing in mind that he was also dealing at the same time with violent industrial conflict and with the threat of civil war in Ireland, this was a precedent he simply could not afford to set. By exactly the same token, he could not allow suffragette violence to deter him from dealing with other aspects of the parliamentary system which needed reform, notably plural voting and redistribution. It may have been, and probably was, a miscalculation on his part to kill the Conciliation Bill by bringing in such a limited Franchise Bill – it was bound to provoke further violence, and it did – but it was perfectly consistent with the logic of his position: he was simply showing that the government would not be dictated to.

The most that can be claimed for suffragette violence, and this is, in effect, as much as its apologists' claims amount to, is that it kept the issue on the political agenda and made it impossible for the government to ignore. One could say much the same of the Chartists, of course, and elicit much the same response: there is little point in keeping something on the agenda if the result is to harden attitudes against it. The suffragettes effectively controlled the agenda on the female suffrage issue, but they did so at the expense of the much larger and more politically mature NUWSS, which tended either to be ignored or seen as a less newsworthy adjunct to the WSPU. Marginalising the NUWSS was perhaps the gravest damage the WSPU did to its own cause. Significantly, historians like David Morgan, who have looked at female suffrage in its political context rather than in isolation, are in no doubt that militancy harmed the women's cause: 'while it kept the Suffrage pot boiling [it] served little real purpose, losing in Parliament more supporters than were gained, and hardening enemies as little else could have'.[6] Even outrage at the treatment of suffragette prisoners had its limits: Edgar Feuchtwanger describes how 'arrests, imprisonment followed by release ossified into a kind of ritual and no longer moved the public'[7] – a sort of 'outrage fatigue'.

Indeed, there is even a danger of overestimating the importance of the issue itself to Asquith's government. Although both he and Campbell-Bannerman met suffragist deputations (though Asquith avoided such meetings once the violence started) and ministers did speak on the issue, the question was not discussed in cabinet until June 1910, well after the cycle of hunger strikes and forced feeding had begun. It is quite clear that the government's main concerns lay with the forthcoming battle with the House of Lords and the showdowns with the trade unions and the Nationalists and unionists in Ireland, not to mention the naval race with Germany and the increasingly unstable political situation in Europe; female suffrage was essentially an issue of major but secondary importance. These other issues also interplayed with the female suffrage issue. Redmond's Irish Nationalists were opposed to it, which meant that Asquith could not support it without alienating the Irish: it amounted to a choice between Home Rule and female suffrage, and the party of Gladstone had no doubts which of the two was more important. While Labour was opposed to partial female suffrage, because it would mean 'Votes for Ladies', many trade unionists were opposed to full female suffrage because it would mean a majority female electorate. It all added up to a good case for delaying a decision on female suffrage until things looked a bit more settled.

On 20 June 1914, eight days before the assassination in Sarajevo, Asquith met a deputation of Sylvia Pankhurst's East End Suffragettes. To them he gave the clearest hint yet that he had come round to the idea of female suffrage and that it would have to be on the same basis as the male franchise – and not the taxpaying franchise the other Pankhursts were clamouring for. The only objection was that this would create a majority female electorate, though once the principle of female suffrage had been accepted, this would presumably either have to be faced or a way round it worked out. There seems to be very little ground for crediting the suffragettes with this change of mind by Asquith: rather, he seems to have been impressed with the persistence of working-class, non-militant suffragists and suffragettes in Lancashire and London, who maintained a dignity and perseverance which clearly won his respect. Obviously, a statement to a deputation did not have the same weight as a statement to the House of Commons, but on such an issue – when Asquith knew his every word would be scrutinised closely – it seems safe to conclude that Asquith was taking the first steps in a move to outflank the suffragettes by enfranchising women more widely than they wished. What would have happened had the war not followed so soon afterwards is, of course, impossible to say with certainty.

In conclusion, therefore, the failure of the women's suffrage movement to attain its objective by 1914 may be ascribed to a number of factors. High on the list must be suffragette militancy and violence, coupled with the personal style of management adopted by the Pankhursts. Unlike the Irish Nationalists, but like the Chartists, neither the suffragettes nor the suffragists succeeded in concluding a firm alliance with either of the major political parties, and the suffragettes squandered their potentially very useful link with the ILP. They were perhaps unfortunate in that Asquith was so personally opposed to women's suffrage, but the depth and strength of his opposition was almost entirely a product of suffragette militancy, to which must also be ascribed the low level of public support and the generally hostile national press. They were also unfortunate in that their campaign coincided with other, more titanic struggles in Ireland and in the House of Lords; on the other hand, the suffragists, who had the political experience and *nous* to exploit the situation, found themselves hampered by the WSPU and tarred with the same militant brush (interestingly, but not entirely surprisingly, the skilful political pressure which actually forced Asquith to address the question in 1916 came entirely from Mrs Fawcett and the NUWSS). The great strength of the women's suffrage movement, and of the suffragettes in particular, lay in presentation and propaganda: it did not hurry the vote along, but it determined that they set the agenda for the version that passed into the history books.

Questions

1. What were the main grounds for refusing women the vote?
2. 'The failure of the suffragists to gain the vote by about 1905 justified the suffragettes' resorting to violent tactics.' How far would you agree with this view?

ANALYSIS (2): HOW DID THE FIRST WORLD WAR AFFECT THE CAMPAIGN FOR FEMALE SUFFRAGE, 1918–1928?

A quick way to find out a generally accepted version of the past is to look in school books. One GCSE textbook sums up the standard version of the achievement of female suffrage succinctly:

> It was impossible to deny the vote to women after their work to help the war. But their voting rights were still very limited: in 1918 all men got the vote at 21, but for women the age was 30, and they had to be householders, or married to householders. . . . Only in 1928 did all women get the vote at 21, on the same basis as men.[8]

The treatment in more academic books can be almost as brief. A.J.P. Taylor's classic *England, 1914–1945*, for example, talks of the 1928 'flapper' vote being introduced 'by the government for no particular reason'.[9]

Yet, as Martin Pugh points out,[10] the way in which women actually achieved the vote as a result of the war, just as much as the way in which they had failed to achieve the vote before it, raises a number of questions. It is at least odd that women aged 21–30, who were in many cases the very munitions and land girls who had so impressed the politicians, should have been the ones specifically excluded from the vote by the 1918 Representation of the People Act. Even if an age bar at 30 for women was acceptable to men, in order to avoid a female majority in the electorate, why was it so calmly accepted by women, especially given the vehemence of their pre-war campaign? Where was the campaigning spirit to right this inequality after 1918? Why, if it comes to that, did Baldwin's government decide to grant the 'flapper'* vote, a vote which, it was widely assumed, would benefit his political opponents, if he was under no particular pressure to do so? Above all, given the fears of the opponents of female suffrage that it would herald devastating changes in society and the natural order of things, what effect did the granting of female suffrage actually have?

The reaction of the female suffrage movement to the outbreak of war is revealing. Taking their lead from the fiercely anti-German Mrs Pankhurst, the suffragettes immediately diverted their energies into fervent support of the war, changing the name of their newspaper from *The Suffragette* to *The Britannia* and launching themselves into campaigns to hand out white feathers to young men out of uniform and to lobby for conscription. The NUWSS was much more equivocal in its reaction to the war, and in 1915 Mrs Fawcett, who herself strongly supported Britain's participation, had to engineer an internal *coup* to force all the other officers and ten of the executive of the NUWSS to resign. Many of those ousted were active in the Women's Peace Movement and the No-Conscription Fellowship, which supported the stand of conscientious objectors. Almost alone among the leading female suffrage figures, Sylvia Pankhurst maintained her opposition to the war throughout.

It seems clear enough that this patriotic spirit on the part of the female suffrage leaders, as well as the work carried out by women in running public services, in agriculture and in industry, especially in munitions, made a deep impression on the minds not just of politicians but of men in general. There is a certain irony here. Nineteenth-century reformers had worked tirelessly to free women from just the sort of heavy manual labour they were now gaining so much credit for undertaking. But the position of women was only one, and by no means the most urgent, of four major constitutional issues the wartime government had to consider. One of them, plural voting, could be

---

*'Flapper' seems to have been a nickname coined in the 1910s, when the fashion was for young women to tie their hair back in large bows which flapped behind them as they walked. The term outlived the fashion and was still applied, rather incongruously, to young women in the 1920s, who wore their hair short under cloche hats.

postponed until after the war, but without a change in the law the next general election, due in 1915, could not, and therefore neither could the two others, redistribution and registration: otherwise, under the one-year continuous residence terms of the 1884 Reform Act, nearly all those serving overseas would be excluded from voting.

In theory Asquith could have passed a measure to extend the life of the Parliament until after the war and drawn up new electoral registers to cover householders away at the front – he could even extend the franchise to cover all adult men – and still leave female suffrage until after the war, and there were strong grounds in 1915 for thinking that that was precisely what he was contemplating doing. It was Mrs Fawcett, writing to Asquith in May 1916 with cross-party support to get him to clarify his plans, who brought him to the point of accepting that any scheme to deal with voter registration would have to include female suffrage. It was also Mrs Fawcett who kept up the pressure when Asquith tried first to pass the issue over to the House of Commons to deal with, and then handed it over to a special committee chaired by the Speaker: she made it clear that, war or no war, if the vote were to be extended to all men without provision for female suffrage then the suffragists would resume their campaign.

Although it is probably overstating things to say that without the pressure from the NUWSS there would have been no votes for women in 1918, it certainly is clear that Mrs Fawcett helped bring the issue to a head. For all the admiration being expressed on all sides, including by Asquith, for women's war work, it was by no means a foregone conclusion that it would result in the vote, still less that it would produce the vote on the same terms as men. As it was, the Speaker's Conference proved a stormy affair, with three Unionist members resigning from it and fierce Conservative and Unionist opposition to its redistribution proposals. On the question of suffrage, while it proposed a simple residence qualification for men, for women the proposal was for a much more limited household suffrage, as already existed for local elections, with an age bar of about 35, brought down by the 1918 Act to 30. David Rolf is quite certain that the outcome of the Speaker's Conference was by no means inevitable, and that the politicians would have avoided the whole exercise if they possibly could.[11] It took, in other words, a combination of the war and of Mrs Fawcett's exploitation of the opportunities it offered to bring the politicians to the point of translating their expressions of sympathy and support into actual legislation.

In the light of this, the NUWSS's acceptance of an age bar set at 30 (to exclude the supposedly more flighty and impressionable) as the price for female suffrage looks more understandable: it was as good a bargain as they were likely to get. In the euphoria that greeted the end of the war in 1918 there was not likely to be much grousing about it, but when things had settled down, campaigns began against this and other inequalities. These campaigns have not received the publicity given to the pre-war suffragette campaigns, partly, no doubt, because the suffragette leadership played no part in them: the WSPU was wound up after the 1918 Act, and the Pankhursts wandered off into different causes, Mrs Pankhurst as a staunch Tory, Christabel as a Millennarist expecting the imminent end of the world, and the younger daughter Adela into Fascism. It was the NUWSS which transformed itself into the National Union for Equal Citizenship (NUEC) and began to campaign on wider issues of female equality, such as differences in pay or the dismissal of female teachers who got married. Alongside this the Equal Citizenship campaign naturally lobbied in favour of equal voting rights.

The precedent of 1918 undoubtedly helped, not so much because it marked a watershed but precisely because it seemed, in retrospect, something of an anticlimax: contrary to fears and expectations, votes for women had not wrought huge changes in the political system. Only one of the militant suffragettes who stood for election, Lady Markiewicz, was elected, and as a Sinn Fein representative she refused to take her seat. Nancy Astor, the first woman MP to sit in Parliament, was a Conservative, elected by what was virtually a family pocket borough in Plymouth, and some of the suffragists who were elected, like Margaret Bondfield and Ellen Wilkinson, went on to reach cabinet level without bringing civilisation crashing down around them. By the late 1920s the sight of women, at least those with money to spend, challenging conventions by smoking or driving had become all too familiar, and the idea of extending the vote to them on the same terms as men did not excite the sort of anxieties it had before the war.

There was a widely-held assumption that young women would vote Labour, but in fact, as Baldwin and MacDonald almost certainly realised, there was no reason to suppose that women would vote along lines of sex rather than of class or interest or any of the other factors that determined the voting patterns of any other group of voters. If they did support MacDonald in the 1929 election they did not do so in enough strength to give him a parliamentary majority, or to break the Conservatives' dominance through the 1930s. None of the parties felt it necessary to make any major adjustment to its image or its policies in order to attract young female voters – or older female voters either, for that matter. Granting the 'flapper' vote, in other words, was a concession which Baldwin could well afford to make, probably at small or minimal cost to his position, in answer to the genuine grievance of the Equal Citizenship movement.

It is difficult to get the effects of the First World War into precise perspective in terms of any particular issue. Obviously, it would be absurd to underestimate its impact on attitudes and society. Paul Fussell and Arthur Marwick have both explored its far-reaching impact on British society, covering everything from high politics through to new schools of humour.[12] The war is rightly seen as marking the effective end of the nineteenth century and the start of a distinctively different twentieth century. However, although the war's impact was huge, it was not necessarily immediate. This is well illustrated by the case of women and of female suffrage in particular. The sight of women carrying out such vital war work, much of it work which had previously been thought unsuitable – or even impossible – for women, certainly helped change fundamental attitudes, but it did not do so overnight. Women took on war work in the full knowledge and understanding that it was for the duration of the war, and that they would be making way for men when the war ended, as indeed they did. They had to accept the terms of the day, which usually included more restricted work rights and lower pay than men enjoyed.

The experience almost certainly sowed a seed, but it was a seed which would take many years to grow. In the same way, although the war, and the NUWSS, brought women the vote, in many ways it left Parliament much as it had been before 1914. Labour continued to grow, as it had done before the war, but immediately after the war the two main parties were still the Liberals and the Conservatives; although most plural voting had been ended by the 1918 Act, it still existed for business premises and for the university seats until 1948; above all, female suffrage had not affected the overwhelmingly male composition of Parliament, nor would it do so in any noticeable sense until the 1980s and 1990s.

Questions

1. Why was it unacceptable to the suffragists for the government to deal with voter registration during the war and postpone female suffrage until after it?
2. How strong was the case for accepting an 'age bar' of 30 in the 1918 Act?
3. How did the First World War change the political role of women?

POSTSCRIPT

The development of parliamentary democracy did not stop with female suffrage. There was still some fine-tuning to do, abolishing university seats, allowing peers to sit in the House of Commons, and in 1969 – a more major step – lowering the voting age to 18. The arguments over the merits of proportional representation, actually proposed by the Speaker's Conference though not adopted, were only just beginning and would grow, until by the end of the twentieth century the terms electoral reform and proportional representation had become virtually synonymous. The House of Lords had its delaying powers reduced in 1949, and admitted its first life peers, including women, in 1958. It grew considerably in size, but no government undertook wholesale reform of the upper house until the Blair government in the 1990s.

By then, parliamentary democracy had long moved into an international dimension. Membership first of the League of Nations and then of the United Nations and its agencies placed restrictions on the operation of foreign policy and, in the case of bodies like the International Monetary Fund (IMF), of domestic economic policy. Permanent military alliances like NATO imposed further limits on member countries' sovereignty. The most far-reaching step, however, was Britain's admission in 1973 to the European Economic Community, later the European Union (EU), followed in 1979 by the first direct elections to a European Parliament, whose relatively limited powers were considerably extended by the 1992 Treaty of Maastricht. As 'Europe' took more of a direct role in daily life in Britain, overruling Acts of Parliament or judgments of the courts, the very role and purpose of Parliament itself was increasingly brought into question. The battle for parliamentary reform has moved on from Whigs, Chartists and suffragettes to the corridors of Brussels.

SOURCES

1. THE CAMPAIGN FOR THE VOTE

Source A: Mrs Pankhurst, speaking from the dock at Bow Street Magistrates' Court (1908).

We believe that if we get the vote it will mean better conditions for our unfortunate sisters. Many women pass through this court who would not come before you if they were able to live morally and honestly. The average earnings of the women who earn their living in this country are only seven [shillings] and sixpence a week. Some of us have worked for many years to help our own sex, and we have been driven to the conclusion that only through legislation can any improvement be effected, and that the legislation can never be effected until we have the same power as men to bring pressure to bear upon governments to give us the necessary legislation . . .

No, sir, I do say deliberately to you that I come here not as an ordinary law-breaker. I should never be here if I had the same kind of laws that the meanest and commonest of men have – the same power that the wife-beater has, the same power that the drunkard has. This is the only way we have to get that power which every citizen should have of deciding how the taxes she contributes to should be made, and until we get that power we shall be here. We are here today, and we shall come here over and over again. If you had the power to send us to prison, not for six months but for six years, or for the whole of our lives, the Government must not think that they can stop this agitation. It will go on. We are going to win.

Source B: letter to *The Times* from Dr Almoth Wright (28 March 1912).

There is mixed up with the women's movement much mental disorder . . . The recruiting field for the militant suffragist is the million of our excess female population – that million which had better long ago have gone out to mate with its complement of men beyond the sea.

Among them there are the following different types of women:–

(a) First – let us put them first – come a class of women who hold, with minds otherwise unwarped, that they may, whenever it is to their advantage, lawfully resort to physical violence . . .

(b) There file past next a class of women who have all their life-long been strangers to joy, women in whom instincts long suppressed have in the end broken into flame. These are the sexually embittered women in whom everything has turned into gall and bitterness of heart, and hatred of men.

Source C: Sylvia Pankhurst, *The Suffragette Movement* (1931).

In the midst of all this a message came from Christabel: Would I burn down Nottingham Castle? The request came as a shock to me. The idea of doing a stealthy deed of destruction was repugnant. I did not think such an act could assist the cause. Though I knew she did not consider it so, I had the unhappy sense of having been asked to do something morally wrong. I replied that I should be willing to lead a torchlight procession to the castle, to fling my torch at it, and to call the others to do the same, as a symbolic act. I was presently sent to speak at a by-election in Nottingham, but no procession had been arranged, and we were obliged to struggle with a hostile audience to procure a public hearing.

Source D: letter from three members of the Cambridge branch of the National League for Opposing Woman Suffrage, printed in the *Cambridge Daily News* (9 June 1913).

It will be remembered that several suffrage ladies recently resigned from the Committee of the Women's Liberal Association in Cambridge, though it could hardly be expected that that body would censure its own Government, because it refused to bring in a Bill to enfranchise women; and we also know of a Conservative lady in another county who has retired from the Primrose League, and though still a Conservative, is to be heard speaking in Radical houses in conjunction with Radicals on the subject of 'Votes for Women', which appears to obliterate their vision on all other political matters.

Source E: reply from four members of the NUWSS, printed in the *Cambridge Daily News* (11 June 1913).

Sir,
The spokeswomen of the Cambridge Branch of the National League Opposing Woman Suffrage have helped us to prove our case by the amazing admissions implicit in their letter which appeared in your columns on the 9th inst. The chief admissions are these:–

(1) Women are qualified to form political judgements. (Your correspondents hold that women do rightly in joining political parties, and are exceedingly wrong in leaving them.)
(2) Many of the women most genuinely interested in political affairs united in considering that the political affair which should come first is the enfranchisement of women . . .

Since the participation of voters in a nation's affairs is much more effective than that of non-voters, your correspondents should logically demand women's suffrage.

Questions

1.* Explain the following terms:
   i 'sexually embittered women in whom everything has turned to gall and bitterness of heart, and hatred of men' (Source B) [2]
   ii 'Primrose League' (Source D) [1]

iii 'National League for Opposing Woman Suffrage' (Source D) [1]

2. How effective is Source E as a rebuttal to the arguments in Source D? [6]

3. Compare and contrast the views given in Sources A, B and C on the suffragettes' use of violence. [7]

4. How far do these documents, and any other evidence known to you, support the view that the campaign for female suffrage was hampered by the Pankhursts' desire for publicity? [8]

Worked answer: Question 1

i   Many men, especially those with a background in medicine or the newly fashionable science of psychology, came up with pseudo-scientific explanations of female unfitness for the vote or explanations of suffragette violence, blaming menstruation or the menopause or other aspects of female anatomy or physiology. However, Dr Wright's specific accusation was widely believed by those hostile to female suffrage, not least because of the stress the Pankhursts increasingly placed on issues of prostitution and venereal disease, especially as the campaign for the vote seemed to be reaching stalemate. The idea that many suffragettes simply hated men did seem to tally with the suffragettes' intolerance of male supporters and with the arguments in Christabel Pankhurst's book, *The Great Scourge and How to End It*.

ii   The Primrose League was a Conservative Party body, which helped to mobilise support at election times and provided social facilities and activities for the party membership betweentimes. Although not actually established as a women-only organisation, it quickly became heavily dominated by women.

iii   There were both male and female organisations opposed to female suffrage. The leading woman opposed to votes for women was the novelist, Mrs Humphrey Ward. The men's and women's organisations amalgamated in reaction to suffragette violence and formed the National League for Opposing Woman Suffrage. The League could never resolve the paradox that the more effectively and eloquently it argued, the less convincing looked its argument that women did not deserve the vote.

SOURCES

2. FEMALE SUFFRAGE AND THE FIRST WORLD WAR

Source F: Ada Nield Chew, a radical suffragist, writing in *Cotton Factory Times* (9 March 1917).

The militant section of the movement . . . would without doubt place itself in the trenches quite cheerfully, if allowed. It is now . . . demanding, with all its usual pomp and circumstance of banner and procession, its share in the war. This is an entirely logical attitude and strictly in line with its attitude before the war. It always glorified the power of the primitive knock on the nose in preference to the more humane appeal to reason . . . What of the others? . . . The non-militants – so-called – though bitterly repudiating militancy for women, are as ardent in their support of militancy for men as their more consistent and logical militant sisters.

Source G: press release from the Minister of Munitions of War (January 1917).

The Minister of Munitions has, in fact, done more for women workers in fifteen months than any other Authority could probably have done in fifteen years. As early as October 1915 he published his famous Circular L2 with its keynote 'Equal pay for equal work'. By this Order, women replacing men were to be paid the same piece-rates as men, with a time-rate of £1, a week . . . A Special Arbitration Tribunal has also been set up by the Minister of Munitions to deal exclusively with women's wages.

Source H: Mrs Millicent Fawcett to Asquith (19 May 1916).

Our movement has received very great accessions of strength during recent months, former opponents now declaring themselves on our side, or at any rate withdrawing their opposition. The change of tone in the press has been most marked . . . The view has been widely expressed in a great variety of organs of public opinion that the continued exclusion of women from representation will . . . be an impossibility after the war.

Source I: Lord Selborne writing to Lord Salisbury (25 August 1916).

Personally I think it would be most unjust to women and dangerous to the State to enfranchise the adult fighting man and no women. Dangerous to the State because I firmly believe in the steadying influence of the women voters in essentials and in the long run. Unjust to women because I believe that the interests of labour women, and of the woman's view of certain social matters, would be ruthlessly sacrificed ... I do not believe that 23 million voters will act any differently to 15 or 12 ... Of course things will be done which I vehemently dislike, but those things were already being done before the war; and the war has confirmed the intense belief which I have had now for a good many years in the instincts and intentions of my fellow countrymen and women.

Source J: Asquith speaking in the House of Commons (March 1917).

My opposition to woman suffrage has always been based, and based solely, on considerations of public expediency. I think that some years ago I ventured to use an expression 'Let the women work out their own salvation'. Well, Sir, they have ... How could we have carried on the War without them? ... But what moves me more in this matter is the problem of reconstruction when the war is over. The questions which will arise with regard to women's labour and women's functions are questions in which I find it impossible to withold from women, the power and the right of making their voices heard. And let me add that, since the War began, now nearly three years ago, we have had no recurrence of that detestable campaign which disfigured the annals of political agitation in this country, and no one can now contend that we are yielding to violence what we refused to concede to argument.

Questions

1. Explain the following terms:
    i   'all its usual pomp and circumstance' (Source F) [2]
    ii 'Equal pay for equal work' (Source G) [2]
2.* Compare and contrast the views given in Sources F and G of the suffragette movement. [5]
3. Evaluate Sources G, H, I and J as evidence that issues of female equality were gaining in importance during the war. [8]
4. Using all these sources and any other evidence known to you, how far would you accept the view that it was wartime militancy rather than reasoned argument that won women the vote? [8]

Worked answer: Question 2

For very different reasons, neither Asquith in Source J nor Ada Nield Chew in Source F have much time for the suffragettes: they both reject suffragette violence, though Asquith does so because he refuses to give in to it, and Ada Chew because she rejects all violence. In fact, the difference would have been less marked than at first appears, for Asquith felt some sympathy for the stance adopted by working-class suffragists like Ada Chew. However, in the circumstances of the time, the two writers would hardly have seen eye-to-eye. Source A follows a pacifist line of argument: it rejects the suffragettes' violence whether aimed at the vote or at victory over the Germans, though it concedes them a certain level of consistency; the real object of its anger are the pro-war 'moderate' suffragists. In other words, Source A completely rejects the positive view of women war workers that Asquith gives in Source E. In the light of the arguments in Source A, Asquith could be accused of hypocrisy, in the sense that he rejects suffragette militancy when it is aimed at his government but encourages it when it is aimed at the Kaiser's, but it was not a line of argument he had to worry too much about at the time.

NOTES AND SOURCES

1. THE UNREFORMED PARLIAMENT

1. A scot-and-lot borough was one where any male poor-rate payer had the vote. The 'pot-walloper' qualification enfranchised male householders who supported a family. The proof of this was owning (and using) a family-sized cooking pot, and these pots were proudly presented – 'walloped' – at election times.
2. D. Beales: 'The Electorate before and after 1832: the Right to Vote and the Opportunity', *Parliamentary History* 11 (1992), pp. 139–50.

Source A: Eric Evans, *The Forging of the Modern State: Early Industrial Britain, 1783–1870* (Longman 1985)

Source B: Evans, op. cit.

Source C: Evans, op. cit.

Source D: Quoted in John Brooke, *The House of Commons, 1754–1790* (Oxford University Press 1968), p. 29.

Source E: *Hansard's Parliamentary Debates*, ii (1 March 1831).

Source F: *Hansard's Parliamentary Debates*, xxv (18 April 1785).

Source G: *Hansard's Parliamentary Debates*, xxviii (4 March 1790).

Source H: *Hansard's Parliamentary Debates*, xxix (30 April 1792).

Source I: *Hansard's Parliamentary Debates*, xxx (2 May 1793).

2. THE GREAT REFORM ACT

1. R. Quinault: 'The French Revolution of 1830 and parliamentary reform', *History* 79, no. 257 (October 1994), pp. 377–93.
2. See N. Lopatin: 'Political Unions and the Great Reform Act', *Parliamentary History* 10 (1991) pp. 78–104; H. Ferguson: 'The Birmingham Political Union and the Government, 1831–1832', *Victorian Studies* III (1960).

3. J. Cannon: *Parliamentary Reform, 1640–1832* (1980).
4. N. Gash: *Politics in the Age of Peel* (1977).
5. N. Gash: *Reaction and Reconstruction in English Politics, 1832–1852* (Oxford 1965).

Source A: *Hansard's Parliamentary Debates*, ii (2 March 1831).
Source B: Doherty, *Voice of the People*, a radical newspaper (1 January, 1831). Quoted in Michael Brock, *The Great Reform Act* (1973) p. 168.
Source C: *Edinburgh Review* (June 1831).
Source D: *Quarterly Review* (February 1831).
Source E: Charles Greville's Diary, edited by P. Whitwell Williams, London 1927.
Source F: *Hansard's Parliamentary Debates*, viii (7 October 1831).
Source G: *Hansard's Parliamentary Debates*, xiii (4 June 1832).
Source H: *Westminster Review*, 1833.
Source I: Charles Greville's Diary, op. cit.

3. CHARTISM: THE DEMAND FOR UNIVERSAL SUFFRAGE

1. G. Stedman Jones: *The Language of Class* (1984).
2. D.J.V. Jones: *The Last Rising: the Newport Insurrection of 1839* (1985).
3. Dorothy Thompson: *The Chartists* (1984).
4. Edward Royle: 'The Origins and Nature of Chartism', *History Review* 13 (1992).
5. Asa Briggs: *Victorian People* (1955).
6. See David Jones: 'Women and Chartism', *History* 68, no. 222 (February 1983).

Source A: The *Northern Star* (5 January 1839).
Source B: Extract from a resolution of the Chartist National Convention, drawn up by William Lovett (5 July 1839). Quoted in *Chartism*, Clive Behagg (Longman/Ethos 1993).
Source C: *Leeds Mercury* (3 August 1839), quoted in *Chartist and Anti-Chartist Pamphlets*, Garland Publishing Inc. (New York 1986).
Source D: Friedrich Engels, *The Condition of the Working Classes in England* (Panther 1976 edition). Published in German 1845; in English 1892.
Source E: UCLES Special Subject Paper 9020/16–21 (27 June 1990).
Source F: Quoted in Clive Behagg, *Chartism*, op. cit.
Source G: *Hansard's Parliamentary Debates*, lxiii (3 May 1842).
Source H: UCLES Special Subject Paper 9020/16–21 (27 June 1990).

Source I: *The Times* (10 April 1848).

Source J: Quoted in Richard Brown, *Change and Continuity in British Society, 1800–1900* (Cambridge University Press 1987).

Source K: H.D. Traill (ed.) *Social England: a Record of the Progress of the People* (1897).

Source L: Mary Ann Walker: address to a Chartist meeting in High Holborn, London, 10 December 1842.

4. DISRAELI AND THE SECOND REFORM ACT

1. Royden Harrison: *Before the Socialists* (1967).
2. Donald Richter: *Riotous Victorians* (1981).
3. Catherine Hall: 'Rethinking Imperial Histories: the Reform Act of 1867', in *New Left Review* 208 (Nov/Dec 1994).
4. John K. Walton: *The Second Reform Act* (1987).
5. Maurice Cowling: *Disraeli, Gladstone and Revolution* (1967).
6. Robert Blake: *Disraeli* (1966).
7. *Saturday Review* (13 April 1867).
8. E.J. Feuchtwanger: *Gladstone* (1975).
9. Roy Jenkins: *Gladstone* (1995).
10. John Vincent: *The Formation of the Liberal Party* (1966).

Source A: *Hansard's Parliamentary Debates*, cliii (1859).

Source B: *Hansard's Parliamentary Debates*, clxxxii (13 March 1866).

Source C: Ibid.

Source D: *Hansard's Parliamentary Debates*, clxxxvi (18 March 1867).

Source E: *Quarterly Review* (July 1867).

Source F: *Quarterly Review* (July 1867).

Source G: *Hansard's Parliamentary Debates*, op. cit.

Source H: *Hansard's Parliamentary Debates*, op. cit. (12 April 1867).

Source I: *Hansard's Parliamentary Debates*, clxxxvii (17 May 1867).

Source J: Ibid.

Source K: Ibid.

Source L: Ibid.

Source M: *Hansard's Parliamentary Debates*, op. cit. (20 May 1867).

5. THE PROFESSIONALISATION OF POLITICS, 1867–1900

1. John Vincent: *Disraeli* (1990).
2. The term 'jingoism' derives from the chorus of G.W. Hunt's 1878 music-hall song:

We don't want to fight
But, by Jingo, if we do,
We've got the ships, we've got the men,
We've got the money too!

3. John Belchem: *Class, Party and the Political System in Britain 1867–1914* (1990).
4. Derek Beales: *The Political Parties of Nineteenth-Century Britain* (1971).
Source A: John K. Walton, *Disraeli* (Routledge 1990).
Source B: Robert Blake, *Disraeli* (Methuen 1984 edition).
Source C: Paul Smith, *Disraeli* (Cambridge University Press 1996).
Source D: Stanley Weintraub, *Disraeli* (London 1993).
Source E: T.A. Jenkins, *Disraeli and Victorian Conservatism* (1996).
Source F: E.J. Feuchtwanger, *Gladstone* (Penguin 1975).
Source G: H.C.G. Matthew, *Gladstone, 1809–1874* (Oxford University Press 1988).
Source H: Roy Jenkins, *Gladstone* (Macmillan 1995).
Source I: Jonathon Parry, *The Rise and Fall of Liberal Government in Victorian Britain* (Yale University Press 1993).
Source J: Cambridgeshire Records Office, 386/21–2. School Board election poster (1876).
Source K: Cambridgeshire Records Office. Cambridge Borough election song (1886).
Source L: *The Times* (3 April 1880).
Source M: Quoted in H.J. Hanham, *The Nineteenth-Century Constitution* (Cambridge University Press 1969), pp. 248–9; originally in H.E. Gorst's *The Fourth Party* (1906).

6. THE LABOUR MOVEMENT AND THE GROWTH OF DEMOCRACY

1. E.J. Feuchtwanger: *Gladstone* (1975).
2. Clive Behagg: *Labour and Reform: Working-Class Movements, 1815–1914* (1991).
3. Duncan Tanner: *Political Change and the Labour Party, 1900–1918* (1990).
4. Keith Laybourn: 'The Rise of Labour and the Decline of Liberalism – the State of the Debate', *History* 80, no. 259 (June 1995); Keith Laybourn and Jack Reynolds: *Liberalism and the Rise of Labour, 1890–1918* (1984).
5. Clive Behagg: *Labour and Reform: Working-Class Movements, 1815–1914* (1991).
6. Niall Ferguson (ed.) *Virtual History: Alternatives and Counterfactuals* (1997).

Source A: *The Times* (2 January 1884).

Source B: *The Times* (17 January 1884).

Source C: P. Guedalla, *The Queen and Mr Gladstone*, vol ii (1933) p. 290.

Source D: *The Times* (18 March 1885).

Source E: Robert Blake, *The Conservative Party from Peel to Churchill* (Fontana 1974), p. 153.

Source F: William Morris, *News from Nowhere* (1890).

Source G: Quoted in J. Schneer, *Ben Tillett* (London, Croom Helm, 1982).

Source H: H.M. Hyndman, *The Historical Basis of Socialism* (1883).

Source I: G.B. Shaw, 'The Transition to Social Democracy', in *Fabian Essays* (1889). Quoted in D. Reisman (ed.) *Democratic Socialism in Britain: Classic Texts in Economic and Political Thought, 1825–1952*, vol. 4 (Pickering and Chatto 1996).

7. THE DECLINE OF THE MONARCHY AND THE FALL OF THE HOUSE OF LORDS

1. Vernon Bogdanor: *The Monarchy and the Constitution* (1995).
2. Linda Colley: *Britons* (1992).
3. The king's visit is still commemorated by a very handsome column in Edinburgh. It was on this visit that George IV became the first English monarch to don the tartan kilt, which had been proscribed after Culloden; apparently he slightly spoiled the effect by wearing flesh-coloured tights as well!
4. Vernon Bogdanor: op. cit.

Source A: Quoted in V. Bogdanor, *The Monarchy and the Constitution* (Oxford 1995).

Source B: G.E. Buckle (ed.) *The Letters of Queen Victoria*, second series, vol iii, 1879–1885 (1928), pp. 47–8.

Source C: Ibid. pp. 75–6.

Source D: Ibid. pp. 78–9.

Source E: Ibid. pp. 84–5.

Source F: H.C.G. Matthew (ed.) *The Gladstone Diaries*, vol ix, January 1875–December 1880 (1986) pp. 506–7.

Source G: *Hansard's Parliamentary Debates (Official Report)* xi (22 November 1909).

Source H: Ibid.

Source I: *Hansard's Parliamentary Debates (Official Report)* xxviii (20 July 1911).

Source J: Ibid. (20 July 1911).

Source K: *Hansard's Parliamentary Debates (Official Report)* xxix (10 August 1911).

8. VOTES FOR WOMEN

1. The point is well discussed in Dorothy K.G. Thompson: *British Women in the Nineteenth Century* (Historical Association 1989).
2. Jill Liddington and Jill Norris: *One Hand Tied Behind Us* (1978).
3. Sylvia Pankhurst: *The Suffragette Movement* (1931; 1977 edition).
4. Paula Bartley: *Votes for Women, 1860–1928* (1998).
5. The arguments are usefully summarised in Paula Bartley, ibid.
6. David Morgan: *Suffragists and Liberals* (1975).
7. E.J. Feuchtwanger: *Democracy and Empire* (1985).
8. Christopher Culpin: *Making Modern Britain* (Collins 1987).
9. A.J.P. Taylor: *English History, 1914–1945* (1977).
10. See, for example, Martin Pugh: *Women's Suffrage in Britain, 1867–1928* (Historical Association 1980).
11. David Rolf: 'Origins of Mr Speaker's Conference during the First World War' *History*, vol. 64, no. 210 (February 1979).
12. Paul Fussell: *The Great War and Modern Memory* (1975); Arthur Marwick: *The Deluge* (1965; 1991).

Source A: Mrs Pankhurst (1908). Quoted in L. Bailey, *BBC Scrapbooks*, 1 (Allen & Unwin 1966) from Donald Reed, *Documents from Edwardian England* (Harrap 1973), pp. 290–1.

Source B: Quoted in Reed, op. cit., p. 287.

Source C: Sylvia Pankhurst, *The Suffragette Movement* (1903), (Virago 1977) p. 396.

Source D: Cambridgeshire Record Office 455/Q37.

Source E: Cambridgeshire Record Office 455/Q38.

Source F: Quoted in Jill Liddington and Jill Norris, *One Hand Tied Behind Us* (Virago 1978), p. 257.

Source G: Public Record Office MUN 5/83/342/113.

Source H: Common Cause 19 May 1916, quoted in Arthur Marwick, *The Deluge*, second edition (Macmillan 1991) p. 141.

Source I: Lord Selborne to Lord Salisbury, 25 August 1916. Bodleian Library, MS Selborne 6, fols 174–6. Quoted in L. Butler and H. Jones (eds) *Britain in the Twentieth Century: A Democratic Reader* vol. 1 (Heinemann 1994), p. 118.

Source J: *Hansard's Parliamentary Debates (Official Reports)* xcii (March 1917).

SELECT BIBLIOGRAPHY

PRIMARY SOURCES

For a topic as broad as parliamentary reform, the potential reading list is vast. Far and away the best sources of primary political material are the relevant volumes of *Hansard's Parliamentary Debates* which contain verbatim accounts and from which the parliamentary extracts in this volume come. It is too bulky for most public libraries, but is usually easily available in university libraries. The various volumes of *English Historical Documents*, particularly volume xi (1783–1832), ed. A. Aspinall and F.A. Smith (Oxford 1959), volume xii (1) (1833–74) ed. G.M. Young and W.D. Hancock (Oxford 1956), and volume xii (2) (1874–1914) ed. W.D. Handcock (Oxford 1956) all contain a wealth of material relating to parliamentary reform, by no means confined to debates or other 'official' types of source. For a more comprehensive treatment of the constitution, placing both parliamentary reform and the growth of party firmly into the context of the period, H.J. Hanham's *The Nineteenth-Century Constitution* (Cambridge 1969) is invaluable. It is also well worth sampling Walter Bagehot's classic analysis *The English Constitution* (Fontana 1978). Chartism, of course, merits a volume to itself. F.C. Mather's *Chartism and Society* (Bell and Hyman 1980) is a very handy anthology, while *Chartism* (Longman/ETHOS 1993) edited by Clive Behagg, is a particularly comprehensive and colourful collection, in loose-leaf form for classroom use and with many documents reproduced in their original form. A number of important texts from early labour history are reproduced in the series *Democratic Socialism in Britain:*

Classic Texts in Economic and Political Thought, 1825–1952 (New York: Pickering and Chatto 1996). On the important and often-neglected role of the monarchy in politics, especially constitutional politics, see *The Letters of Queen Victoria: A Selection from her Majesty's Correspondence (1837–61)* ed. A.C. Benson and Viscount Esher (John Murray 1907) *(1862– 85)* ed. G.E. Buckle (John Murray 1926) and *(1886–1901)* ed. G.E. Buckle (John Murray 1930). *The Queen and Mr Gladstone, 1880–1898* ed. Philip Guedalla (Hodder and Stoughton 1933) contains an entertaining selection of material relating to that difficult relationship, including material on the passage of the Third Reform Act. For the twentieth century end of the period, including the Parliament Act and the campaign for female suffrage, *Documents from Edwardian England* edited by Donald Read (Harrap 1973) has a number of good extracts, and the more recent *Britain in the Twentieth Century: a Documentary Reader Vol.1 1900–1939* edited by Lawrence Butler and Harriet Jones (Heinemann 1994) makes an enjoy- able and fascinating introduction to the period and its issues.

SECONDARY TEXTS

All the major general texts on nineteenth century political history give good coverage to the parliamentary reform issue. Eric Evans *The Forging of the Modern State: Early Industrial Britain, 1783–1870* (Longman 1983) is a readable and authoritative treatment supported by a wealth of useful data. Norman McCord's *British History, 1815–1906* (Oxford 1991) is comprehensive and provocative, telling a familiar story but often challenging accepted versions of events in a way which 'A' level students find stimulating. Sir Llewellyn Woodward's *The Age of Reform* (Oxford 1946), though old, is still valuable, especially in the sheer comprehensiveness of its coverage. Asa Briggs' *The Age of Improvement, 1783–1867* (Longman 1959) covers the first two Reform Acts, and still holds up well in the light of more recent writings. Norman Gash's *Aris- tocracy and People: Britain, 1815–1865* (Edward Arnold 1979) is particularly good on the constitutional issues at stake in 1832. For the later period, Keith Robbins' *The Eclipse of a Great Power: Modern Britain, 1870–1975* (Longman 1985) carries on from where the Evans volume leaves off, with similarly strong data to support it. Donald Read *England, 1868–1914* (Longman 1979), Richard Shannon *The Crisis of Imperialism, 1865–1915* (Paladin 1974), E.J. Feuchtwanger *Democracy and Empire: Britain, 1865–1914* (Edward Arnold 1985), T.O. Lloyd *Empire to Welfare State: English History, 1906–1967* (Oxford 1979) and L.C.B. Seaman *Post-Victorian Britain, 1902–1951* (Methuen 1966) all provide solid and reliable guides to the politics of the Lloyd George and Asquith era.

Essential to any study of the unreformed parliament and the passage of the 1832 Reform Act is Michael Brock's classic work *The Great Reform Act* (Hutchinson 1973), still unsurpassed in its detail and clarity and the obvious starting point for any survey of the issue. Norman Gash's equally venerable *Politics in the Age of Peel* (Longman 1977) needs to be read in conjunction with the criticisms of his analysis in John Cannon's *Parliamentary Reform, 1640–1832* (Cambridge 1980). Frank O'Gorman's *Voters, Patrons and Parties: The Unreformed Electoral System of Hanoverian England 1734–1832* (Cambridge 1989) puts the whole issue in a much longer timescale, as does J.C.D. Clark's *English Society, 1688–1832* (Cambridge 1985). For Chartism, Asa Briggs' *Chartist Studies* (Macmillan 1959) remains an important text, though its stress on regional approaches has been largely superseded by more recent studies such as J. Epstein and Dorothy Thompson *The Chartist Experience* (Macmillan 1982) and Dorothy Thompson's *The Chartists* (Temple Smith 1984). For a good outline of the history of the movement as a whole, see J.T. Ward *Chartism* (Batsford 1973).

On the Second Reform Act, John K. Walton's *The Second Reform Act* (Methuen 1987) is the handiest and most concise treatment, summarising the story and giving a useful overview of the historiographical debate. There is a characteristically entertaining account of the bill's passage through parliament in Robert Blake's biography *Disraeli* (Methuen 1966), which should ideally be read in conjunction with Maurice Cowling *1867: Disraeli, Gladstone and Revolution* (Cambridge 1967); for a less Disraelian view of the episode, see Royden Harrison *Before the Socialists* (Routledge and Kegan Paul 1965). There is good treatment of the Act from the Liberal side, as well as of the 1884–5 crisis, in E.J. Feuchtwanger *Gladstone* (Allen Lane 1975) and in Roy Jenkins' masterly biography

Gladstone (Macmillan 1997). The process by which the extension of the franchise helped the development of the modern party system is well summarised in John Belchem's *Class, Party and the Political System in Britain 1867–1914* (Basil Blackwell/Historical Association 1990). For the Conservative Party the classic work is Robert Blake's *The Conservative Party from Peel to Churchill* (Fontana 1970); for the Liberals John Vincent's *The Formation of the British Liberal Party 1857–1868* (Harmondsworth 1972) remains a penetrating analysis, now rivalled by Jonathon Parry's *The Rise and Fall of Liberal Government in Victorian Britain* (Yale 1993). The story of how the Labour movement developed out of Liberalism and into the Labour Party is well told in Keith Laybourn's and Jack Reynolds' *Liberalism and the Rise of Labour* (Croom Helm 1984). Laybourn also provides a handy summary of the issue in *The Rise of Labour and the Decline of Liberalism: the State of the Debate* in *History*, vol. 80, no. 259, June 1995. Nowhere is the decline of Liberalism described with more panache than in George Dangerfield's *The Strange Death of Liberal England* (Constable 1936) which every student of the period ought to read, if only to see how lively historical writing can be, even though relatively little of its analysis is generally accepted nowadays.

Martin Pugh has done particularly good service to students by producing two short but immensely useful Historical Association pamphlets, *The Evolution of the British Electoral System 1832–1987* (Historical Association: New Appreciations 15, 1988) and *Women's Suffrage in Britain 1867–1928* (Historical Association: G97, 1980). The standard texts on the fight for female suffrage remain the accounts of the Pankhursts themselves, particularly Emmeline Pankhurst's *My Own Story* (Virago 1979) and Sylvia Pankhurst's *The Suffragette Movement* (Virago 1977). A useful corrective to the inevitable pro-suffragette bias of the Pankhursts' own account is Jill Liddington and Jill Norris *One Hand Tied Behind Us* (Virago 1978), which not only places the suffragists back on the centre stage but explores their strong working-class appeal. David Morgan's *Suffragists and Liberals* (Basil Blackwell 1975) is particularly useful in putting the women's suffrage issue into the practical political reality of the 1910s. On the monarchy two classic biographies have stood the test of time: *Victoria RI* by Elizabeth Longford (Pan 1966) and

George V by Harold Nicolson (Constable 1952). For a serious analysis of the political role of the monarchy see Vernon Bogdanor *The Monarchy and the Constitution* (Oxford 1995).

INDEX

Note: Page numbers in **bold** refer
to Background Narratives

Aberdeen, Lord 132
administrative reform 72–3, 79
Adullamites **67**, 70
Afghanistan 92
agricultural interests 10, 17–18,
    70
agricultural labourers 113
Alabama incident 81
Albert
Prince 131, 134–5, 136–7;
    memorandum (1850) 143
Althorp, Lord 32, 37
America, emigration to 58
American Civil War 59–60, 74,
    134
American colonies 11, 113
American political system 54
Anglican evangelical movement
    see Church of England
Anglo-Scottish union 131
Anti-Corn Law League 2, 51, 55,
    59
anti-slavery movement 55
anti-war riots (1790s) 38
aristocracy 3, 10, 16, 38, 54,
    137–8; constitutional rights
    and privileges 140; Disraeli
    and the 3, **67–9**; end of the
    power of the 37, 137–40;
    opposition to reform 17–18
armed forces 10, 70
Artisans' Dwellings Act 91

ASE 71
Asquith, Herbert Henry 100, 138,
    139; bill to limit powers of
    House of Lords (1907) **130**,
    141; and female suffrage **151**,
    152, 158–60, 163; Franchise
    Bill (1911) 157, 159; letter
    from Mrs Millicent Fawcett
    (1916) 170; speech in
    Commons (1911) 148;
    (1917) 171; threat to create
    500 Liberal peers **129**,
    135–6, 140, 141, 142
Astor, Nancy 164
Attwood, Thomas 16, 29, 32, 50,
    51, 52
Australia 71
Austria 136

Bagehot, Walter, *The English
    Constitution* 133–4, 136
Baines, Edward 16, 18
Baldwin, Stanley 162, 164–5
Balfour, Arthur **90**, 95–6, 97, 98,
    140, 142, 153; and female
    suffrage 153, 155; and the
    House of Lords **130**, 139
Ballot Act **88**
'Battle of Downing Street',
    suffragettes (1910) 157
Beaconsfield, Earl of see Disraeli,
    Benjamin
'Beaconsfieldism' 93
Beales, Derek 9–10, 101, 173,
    176

Beales, Edward 74
Becker, Lydia 153–4
'bedchamber crisis' (1839),
    Victoria 132, 134
Behagg, Clive 55, 113, 122, 174,
    176
Belchem, John 100, 176
Belgium 47
Bigge, Sir Edward 135
Birmingham 16, **88**
Birmingham Bull Ring riots 51
Birmingham Liberal Association
    89
Birmingham Political Union 29, 50,
    51
'Black Friday' (1910) 157
Blair, Tony 140, 166
Blake, Robert 76, 90; *Disraeli*
    102–3, 175, 176
Blake, William 58
Blandford, Marquess of 30
'Bloody Sunday' (1887) **112**, 121
Boer War 98
Bogdanor, Vernon 131, 177
boilermakers 70–1
Bondfield, Margaret 164
'boroughmongers' **6–7**, 8, 88
boroughs 9, 20, 29–30, **68**;
    disenfranchised **27**; franchise
    in **28**, 72, 77, 79; voting
    qualifications 8–9
Bournville 58
Bradford 64, councillor's report to
    the Home Office (1848) 62
Bradford Observer 126
Bradlaugh, Charles 131
bribery 9, 10, 16, **88**
Briggs, Asa 48, 58, 174
Bright, John 1, 70, 79
Bristol reform riots 33, 38
Britain: national identity 17;
    relationship with the European
    Union 2, 166
Britannia, The 162
Brock, Michael 29, 30, 174
Brooke, John 20, 173
Brougham, Lord 32, 33, 34–5
Brown, John 53
budgets *see* 'People's Budget'
    (1909)

Bulgarian atrocities (1875–6) **90**,
    92, 93
Burdett, Sir Francis 15, 32
burgage boroughs 9
Burke, Edmund 7, 13, 50

cabinet, changes party 4
cabinet government **6**, 94
Cadbury family 58
Cambridge Borough election, song
    (1886) 108
Cambridge Daily News 168
Campbell-Bannerman, Sir Henry
    97, 100, 135, 139, 141,
    159–60
candidates' expenditure, limiting
    113
Canning, George 7, **26**, 29, 136
Cannon, John 33, 174
capital 70; parliamentary
    representation of 121
'Captain Swing' riots (1830) 38
Carlton Club 98
Cartwright, Major John 15, 18
Castlereagh, Lord 7, 81
'Cat and Mouse Act' (1913) **151**
Catholic Association, O'Connell's
    30, 32
Catholic emancipation **27**, 29, 33,
    132, 134; Peel and 30, 34,
    76, 91
Catholics 11, 79
'caucus' 100
Cave, the **67**
Chamberlain, Joseph **88–9**, 93, 95,
    96, 97, 131; and Gladstone
    100; letter to *The Times*
    (1880) 108; and tariff reform
    98, 101, 139
Charles I 5, 14
Charter **46**, 50, 54
Charterville 57
Chartism 2, 3, 45–66, **45–7**, 69,
    122, 131; achievements of
    56–60; aims 49–50, 53;
    failure of 49, 54–6; and
    female suffrage 153; land and
    education schemes 57;
    National Convention **46**, 47,
    51: resolution (1839) 60;

threat of violence 47–8, 51–3: sources 60–2; wider significance, sources 64–5; and working class 47–54

Chartists: female 55, 58–9; petitions to Parliament (1837–48) **46–7**, 52, 55; radicalism of 49–54

Chew, Ada Nield 170

Childers, (Robert) Erskine 85

Church of England **5**, **6**, 10, 14, 30

Church of Ireland, disestablishment of 79, 92, 95

Church of Wales, disestablishment of 95

churches: Chartists and the 51; nonconformist, work ethic of 58

Churchill, Lord Randolph **68**, **89**, **90**, 92, 95, 97; compared with Disraeli 90–1; 'Fourth Party' 90, 98, 101; letter to Lord Salisbury (1884) 109

Churchill, Winston 98, 122, 153, 156

cities, growth of 12, 91, 117

civil service 70

civil wars 1, **5**, 47

Clark, Jonathan 29

classes see social class

co-operative societies 57–8

coalition politics 92

Cobbett, William 15–16, **26**, 32

Cobden, Richard 1, 51

Coldbath Fields riots (1833) 38

Colley, Linda 17, 131, 177

colonial government 1

colonies: American 11, 133; emigration to 58

Combination Laws, repeal of the 50

Commons **5**, 20, **111**; conflict with House of Lords **129–30**; debate on Charter 56; debate on power of the Crown (1780) 7; as embodying the will of the people **130**; representativeness in 18thC 12; rise of the 37, **129–30**

compound-householders **68**, 72, 76, 77; Hodgkinson's Amendment and, sources 84–6

Conciliation Bill (1910) **152**, 155, 157, 159

Conciliation Committee (1910) **152**

'Condition of England Question' 70, 91

Connaught, Duke of, letter to Queen Victoria 144–5

conscientious objectors 162

conscription issue 162

Conservative Central Office 101

Conservative and Constitutional Associations, local **89**, 93, 97, 98–9, 101

Conservatives **67–8**, 75–6, 91, 101, **111**, 165; dominant in House of Lords **130**, 139; and female suffrage 153; governments (1979–97) 2; late 19thC 90–3; MPs in England (1885–1900) 124; party structure of **89**, 101; and redistribution 116; and Reform Act (1867) 80–1; reform issue (1859) 73–4; splits, (1846) 4, 73; (1868), (1880s) and (1890s) 98; (1990s) 2; working class support for **90**, 93, 96; see also Tories; Unionists

constituencies 11, 50; by class 117–18; distribution of 18thC 8; one-member **111**, 115–16, 117

constitution: balance of the 15, 33, 36, 69; and the monarch 132–4; threats to 17, 49–50; written 13, 132–3

constitutional crisis, (1831–2) 28–34, 37; (1910–11) 142

copyholders **28**

Corn Laws 16, 18, 28, 51, 76, 91; splits Conservatives (1846) 4, 73

corporation boroughs 9

Corrupt Practices Act (1883) **88**, 113
corruption 9, 11, 14, 29–30, 71, **88**, 113, 115
Cotton Factory Times 170
'counter-factual' history 122
counties 8, 12, 50, 69; franchise in **28**, 72, 77, 114, 115; representation 35
Cowling, Maurice 76, 90, 175
Cranbourne, Lord **68**, 78, 115; *see later* Salisbury, Lord
Cranbourne, Viscount 85–6
Crimean War 70, 81
'criminal classes' 71
Criminal Law Amendment Act 91
Cromwell, Oliver 5
Cross, Richard 91
Crown: and choice of ministers, sources 143–5; constitutional position (1785–1914) 131–7; and executive power 16, 56, 69, **129–30**; in foreign policy **129**, 136; relationship between Parliament and **5–8**, 36, 37–8; right to appoint prime minister 132; role in politics 3, 31, 34, 132–7
Curzon, Lord 140; speech in Lords on the Parliament Bill (1911) 148
'custom and practice' 133

Daily Mail **151**
Dangerfield, George, *The Strange Death of Liberal England* 118–19
Darwin, Charles, *Origin of Species* 71
Davison, Emily Wilding 157
de Broke, Lord Willoughby 140
death duties on landed property 137
Declaration of the Rights of Man 13
democracy: American 54, 71; development of parliamentary 166; fear of 114–15; growth of and labour movement 56, 111–28, **111–12**; opposition

to, sources 81–3; and Reform Acts (1884–5) 113–18; use of term 71
Denmark, war with Prussia 81
Derby, Earl of **68**, 72, 73, 74, 76, 77, 78, **130**; reform proposals (1859) 70
Derby (1913), Emily Wilding Davison's death at the 157
Derby-Disraeli government, collapse (1852) 132
Dickens, Charles 70
'Die-Hards' 140, 142, 143
Dilke, Sir Charles **111**, 131
diplomacy 136
Disraeli, Benjamin 70, 74, 78, **89**, **90**, 97, 99, 101, **129** and the aristocracy 3, 37, **67–9**; as chancellor of the exchequer **68**, 78: quoted on Hodgkinson's Amendment 86; as Earl of Beaconsfield 93, **130**; 'fancy franchises' 71–2, 77; foreign policy 92; his style of Conservatism 90–3; legislation 91; Manchester and Crystal Palace speeches (1872) 78, 92, 99; opportunism of 75–9; and Queen Victoria **129**, 135; Reform Bill (1866) **68**, 73; (1867) 72, 77, 82, 84–5; relationship with Gladstone 77–8, 85; and the Second Reform Act (1867) 67–87, **67–9**, **111**; speaking against Gladstone's amendments to Reform Bill (1867) 85; speaking in debate on Reform Bill (1859) 81–2
distribution of seats 20, **28**; *see also* redistribution
'Ditchers' 140, 142, 143
Doherty, *Voice of the People* 40, 174
Dunwich 9, 33

East End Federation of Suffragettes 156, 160
East India Company **7, 8**, 10

East Retford 29–30
Eastern Question crisis (1875–8) 92
economic interests 10
economy (1810s) **26**; and Chartism 55
Edinburgh Review 40, 174
education 141
Education Act (1870) 95
Education Bill (1906) 139
educational qualifications, women and 154
Edward VII 131, 136, 137, 141, 142; as Prince of Wales 131, 134, 135
Edward VIII, abdication 118
Egypt 92, 136; British invasion of (1882) 95
Eldon, Lord 42
elections (1784) 14; (1830) **27**, 31, 38–9, 49; (1831) **27**, 38–9, 48–9; (1837) 49; (1865) 80; (1868) 78; (1874) 91, 98, 101; (1880) 93, 101; (1885) 100; (1895) 100, 122; (1906) 119, 139; (1910) 139, 142, **152**; as communal events 10, 11; contested in England (1784–1820) 19; corruption **88**; direct to European Parliament 2, 166; running of 98; types of 58, 99; uncontested 4, 10, 12
electoral districts, equal **46**, 50, 54
electoral registers 98, **152**, 155, 163
electoral system: Crown and the 16; unreformed, sources 19–20; unrepresentative 12
electorate: after-1832 36, 37; problem of majority female 160, 162; size in England and Wales (1831) 19
Ely, Lady, letter from Queen Victoria 143–4
emigration to America 58
empire 92, 93, 131
employers, war with working classes 121–2

Employers' Federation 121
enfranchisement, and social reform 58–9
Engels, Friedrich 49 *The Condition of the Working Classes in England* (1845) quoted 61
engineers 71
English Civil War 49
entente cordiale 131, 136
Equal Citizenship campaign 164, 165
equality: before the law 13; female 164; of pay for women 154; racial 13
European Economic Community, Britain's admission to (1973) 166
European Parliament, direct elections to (1979) 2, 166
European Union 2, 166
Executive 16–17, 36; Parliament and the 2; power of the **8**, 39, 56, 69

Fabian Essays 127
Fabian Society **112**, 116, 119, 121, 139
factory reform 18
'faddism' 95
Fascism 164
Fawcett, Mrs Millicent **152**, 156, 157, 161, 162, 163; letter to Asquith (1916) 170
female emancipation 151–72, **151–3**; political 154; social 154
female suffrage 2, 51, 59, 151–72, **151–3**; campaign (1918–28), effect of World War I on 161–5; divisions in movement 156–61; failure (until 1914) 153–61; granted to women over 30 (1918) **152–3**; sources 166–8; support for 153, 160; and World War I, sources 170–1
Fenians 81
Ferguson, Niall 122, 176
Feuchtwanger, Edgar J. 79, 113,

117, 159, 178 *Gladstone*
104–5, 175, 176
'flapper', defined 162
'flapper vote' 161–2, 164–5
Flood, Henry, debate on
parliamentary reform 22–3
foreign policy 166; Crown's role in
129, 136
Forster, W.E. 100
'Fourth Party', Lord Randolph
Churchill's 90, 98, 101
Fox, Charles James **7**, **8**, 14,
16–17, 23, 36, 94, 131, 132;
boycott of Parliament (1790s)
12
Fox-North coalition, political crisis
(1783–4) 16–17, 132, 133
France 15, 131, 136: (1830) 47;
(1851) 136; wars with (1793
to 1815) 14, 17, 18, **26**, 28
franchise 2, 75; Disraeli and 71–2,
77; in Great Reform Act
(1932) **28**; male **152**;
property tenure and 71–2;
qualifications (1832) 36;
Russell's bill to extend the
(1866) 56, **67–8**; for
servicemen 163; wider with
Reform Act (1867) 98,
113–14; working class 35,
88–90; *see also* borough
franchise; county franchise
Franchise Act (1918) **152–3**
Franchise Bill (1884) **111–12**,
115–16, **130**; (1911)
Asquith's 157, 159
Franco, General Francisco 118
free trade 91, 94, 95
freeholders 8, 18, **28**, 38
French Revolution **8**, 47, 49, 131;
effects of 13–14
friendly societies 58, 70, **112**
Frost, John 50, 52
Fussell, Paul 165, 178

Game Laws 18
Garibaldi, Giuseppi, invasion of
Sicily 74
Gas-and-Water Socialism 58
Gash, Norman 9, 29, 34, 37, 174

Gaskell, Mrs Elizabeth 70
gasworkers' strike 121
George I **6**, 133
George II **6**
George III **7–8**, 39, 131, 132,
134; political activity 132–3
George IV 31, 131, 134; as
Elector of Hanover 136
George V **129**, 131, 134, 137;
against Asquith's threat of
creation of 500 Liberal
135–6, 141, 142
Germany, war with 136, 159; *see
also* World War I
Gilbert and Sullivan, *Iolanthe* 96
Gladstone, William Ewart **67**,
68–9, 70, 75, 97, **129**, **130**,
138; account of meeting with
Queen Victoria (1880) 145;
address to Queen Victoria
124; as chancellor of
exchequer 81; domestic
policy 93; foreign policy 95;
Franchise Bill (1884) **111–12**,
115–16, 139; on
Hodgkinson's Amendment 85;
and Irish Home Rule 76, 95,
97, 100, 115, **130**, 139, 141,
158; legislation (1868–74)
91; Liberalism **89–90**;
Midlothian campaigns
(1879–80) **90**, 93, 100,
114–15; 'pale of the
constitution' speech (1864)
70–1, 73; political
incompetence 79–81;
relations with Queen Victoria
129, 132, 135, 136;
relationship with Disraeli
77–8; versus Salisbury
114–16
Glasgow 18, 113
Gordon riots (1780) 38
Gorst, John 95, 101
Grand National Consolidated
Trades Union **45**
Great Exhibition (1851) 69, 81
Great Reform Act *see* Reform Act
(1832)
Greville, Charles, diary 42, 43, 174

Grey, Charles (Earl) 1, 16, **27**, 30, 31, 32, 35, 37, **129**; on petition (1793) by Society of Friends of the People 23; Reform Bill (1832) **129**; reform motion (1792) 23
Grey, Sir Edward 153, 157

Halsbury, Lord 140, 142; speech in Lords against the Parliament Bill (1911) 148
Hampden Clubs 14
Hanoverians 133
Hansard (1866) 82; debate on Chartist petition (1842) 64; *Parliamentary Debates* 23–4, 42
Hardie, James Keir **112**, 117, 120, 121, 153
Harper's Ferry (1859) 53
Harrison, Royden 74, 175
Hartington, Lord 94, 132
Heath, Edward 94
Henry VIII **5**
hereditary principle 138, 141, 143
Hitler, Adolf 118
Hodgkinson's Amendment **68**, 72, 85; and the compound-householder, sources 84–6
Home Rule issue *see* Irish Home Rule
House of Commons *see* Commons
House of Lords *see* Lords
household suffrage **28**, **68**, 72, 73, 76, **111**, 113–14, 115, 173: (1918) 163
householders, female 161
Hovell, Mark 48
Hunt, Henry 15, 32, 48, 51, 153
Hurd, Douglas 4
Huskisson, William **26**, 29–30
Huskissonites **26**, 29–30, 32
Hyde Park affair 74, 75
Hyndman, H.M. **112**, 121; 'Scientific Socialism' 116; *The Historical Basis of Socialism* 126–7

ILP *see* Independent Labour Party

imperialism 92, 97
income tax, abolition of 18
Independent Labour Party (ILP) **112**, 120, 121, 122, 156; and suffragettes 156, 160
India: direct rule for 81; Victoria as Empress of India 92, 131
Indian Mutiny (1857–8) 74
industrial conflict 51, **112**, 142, 158
industrial interests 12, 18, 69
Inglis, Sir Robert 20
interest groups 35, 36
interests, representation of 10–11
International Monetary Fund (IMF) 166
Ireland **27**, **28**, **151**; civil war 119, 142, 158; county franchise 30; rebellion (1798) 17; threat of violence in 30, 33
Irish Catholic vote 79
Irish Home Rule 2, **89**, 93, 98, 136, 140; Gladstone and 76, 93, 94, 95, 97, 100, 115, **130**, 139, 141, 158
Irish Nationalists 97, 116, 120, 131, 142, **152**, 159
Italy 47, 136; unification of 81

'Jack the Ripper' murders (1888) 113
Jamaica, rising (1866) 74
James II **6**
Jebb, John 15
Jenkins, Roy 79; *Gladstone* 105, 175, 176
Jenkins, T.A., *Disraeli and Victorian Conservatism* 103, 176
'jingoism' 92, 175–6
Jones, D.J.V. 48, 174
Jones, Gareth Stedman 48, 174
July Revolution 28–9

Kenney, Annie 157
Knollys, Lord 135–6

Labouchere, Henry 132
labour 70; 'aristocracy' 70–1; representation in parliament 119

labour movement: and growth of democracy 111–28, **111–12**; the growth of, sources 126–7; split 120–2; within the parliamentary system (1892–1914) 97, 118–23

Labour Party: in government (1997–) 2, 166; growth 165; and the House of Lords 142; setting up of (1906) **112**, 117, 121; support for female suffrage 153, 160; and the trade unions 119

Labour Representation Committee (LRC) **112**, 120, 121; *see later* Labour Party

laissez-faire 95

Lancashire cotton mills 59

landed classes *see* aristocracy

landlords 38

Lansbury, George 117, 153

Lansdowne, Lord 140, 142; speaking against 'People's Budget' (1909) 147

Latin America, revolution in 47

Laybourn, Keith 119, 176

leadership 94–5, 97, 101, 140, 142

League of Nations 166

leaseholders, long **28**

Leeds 16, 18; political union 51

Leeds Mercury 16, 61

Lib-Lab electoral alliance (1903) 97–8, 116, 119, 120, 139

Liberal Associations, Women's and University 99

Liberal Central Association 100

Liberal Democrats 2

Liberal Party: and female suffrage 153; origins of **67**; and proportional representation 2; *see also* Liberal Democrats

Liberalism: Gladstonian **89–90**, 93–6: sources 104–6; Lloyd George's style of 48, 98, 122; working class 117

Liberals 76–7, 79–80, **89**, **111**, **130**, 139, 165; election campaigning 100–1; and the House of Lords 140–1; late

19thC 93–6; and redistribution 115–16; and rise of Labour 119; split (1866) 98; 'tea-room revolt' 79; Working Men's Clubs 98

licensing laws 141

Liddington, Jill 156, 178

Lincoln, Abraham 59–60, 136

Liverpool, Lord 29, 134; government (1812–27) **26**

Livesey, John, on 'Mechanics' churches' 65

Lloyd George, David 48, **130**, 153, 155, 156; 'New Liberals' 98, 122; 'People's Budget' (1909) 2, **130**, 135, 137–43; speeches at Limehouse and Newcastle 138

local activism 99

local councils: elections 58, 99; women allowed to sit on (1894) 154

local education authorities, women's right to sit on (1902) 154

Local Government Act (1888), women's vote in 154

lodgers 71–2

London Corresponding Society 15

London dockers' strike (1889) **112**, 121–2

London Working Men's Association **45**

Long Parliament (1653) **5**

Lords 2, **5**, 29, 30, 34, 37, **111**; and the Crown **7**, 134; defeats People's Budget (1906) **130**, 135, 137–43; delaying powers reduced (1949) 166; fall of the 98, 129–50, **129–30**, **151**; first life peers (1958) 166; importance in 18thC 3; Liberals and the 116, 119–20; as 'Mr Balfour's poodle' **130**, 139, 143; Pitt swamps 16; power of the **130**, 155; proposal to limit power (1907) 139, 141; and the Redistribution Bill (1885) 135; Whigs in **27**

Loreburn, Lord, reply to Lord Lansdowne's speech against 'People's Budget' (1909) 147–8

Louis Napoleon, coup (1851) 136

Lovett, William **45–6**, 50, 52; resolution (1839) 60

Lowbands settlement, Gloucestershire 57

Lowe, Robert **67**, 71, 80; speaking against Reform Bill (1866) 82

Lowther, Sir John **6**, **7**

Maastricht, Treaty of (1992) 4, 166

Macaulay, Thomas Babington 64; speech on first Reform Bill (1831) 34, 39–40

McCord, Norman 29

MacDonald, Ramsay 94, 117, 164

Major, John 2, 101

male suffrage **46**, 51, 59, **152–3**

Manchester 16, 18; mill workers' appeal to Abraham Lincoln 59–60

Manhood Suffrage Associations 59

Mann, Tom **112**, 121

manufacturing interest 12

Markiewicz, Lady 164

Married Women's Property Acts (1870, 1883) 154

Marwick, Arthur 165

Marx, Karl 47, 49, 53, 59

Marxism 121

match girls' strike (1888) **112**, 121

Matthew, H.C.G., *Gladstone* 105, 176, 177

Mayhew, Henry 71

'Mechanics' churches' 65

Melbourne, Lord 32, 36–7, 134; ministry dismissed by the king (1834) 49, 133

Merchant Shipping Act 91

Methodism 14

middle classes 16, 18, 32, 36, 59, 93, **112**; franchise for 114; and suffragettes 157–8

Midlothian campaigns, Gladstone's (1879–80) **90**, 93, 100, 114–15

Mill, John Stuart 59, 153

Millenarianism 164

miners 114, 117, 119; strike (1984) 55

Miners' Federation of Great Britain 117

Minister of Munitions of War, press release (1917) 170

ministers, obligation to stand for re-election before accepting office 37

monarchy, decline of the 129–50, **129–30**; *see also* Crown

Moore, D.C. 10, 36

Morgan, David 159, 178

Morocco 142

Morris, William **112**, 116, 120; *News from Nowhere* 126, 177

Mosley, Oswald 118

MPs: absenteeism 12; accountability of 14; Conservative in England (1885–1900) 124; payment of **46**, 50, 54, 115; property qualification for 49, 50, 54, 55; Scottish 18; selection by 'boroughmongers' **6–7**; traditional role as representatives 50; in Victorian times 1–2; who change party 4; women 164

municipal authorities 58

Napoleon Bonaparte 131, 132

National Convention, proposed 15

National Insurance 122

National League for Opposing Woman Suffrage 168

National Liberal Foundation (NLF) **89**, 94, 99, 100

National Union of Conservative and Constitutional Associations (NUCCA) 99, 101

National Union for Equal Citizenship (NUEC) 164

National Union of Woman Suffrage
Societies (NUWSS) 156,
157–8, 159, 161, 162,
163–4, 165; defence in
Cambridge Daily News
(1913) 168
National Union of the Working
Class (NUWC) 32
New Jerusalem 57, 58
New Lanark 57
'New Liberals', Lloyd George's 98,
122
New Model Unions 58
Newcastle, political union 51
Newcastle, Duke of **6**
'Newcastle programme', of social
reform 100, 139
Newport rising 48, 49, 51–2
newspapers, local 99
Nightingale, Florence 70
No-Conscription Fellowship 162
nobility *see* aristocracy
Norris, Jill 156, 178
North, Lord **7**, 16–17, 132, 133
North Atlantic Treaty Organisation
(NATO) 166
Northcote-Trevelyan report (1853)
70
Northern Star 51, 60
Nottingham reform riots 33, 38

Oastler, Richard 18
O'Brien, Bronterre **46**, 50, 52
O'Connell, Daniel **27**, 30, 32
O'Connor, Feargus **46**, 48, 50, 51,
52, 57, 60
O'Connorville 57
O'Gorman, Frank 9, 10, 11
Old Sarum 9, 33, 36
opposition, tradition of 14
Osborne judgement (1909) **112**,
120, 121
Owen, Robert **45**, 50, 57
Oxford, Earl of *see* Asquith,
Herbert Henry
Oxfordshire 18

Paine, Tom 15, 18
Palmerston, Lord 32, 47, **67**, 70,
72–3, 94, **129**, **130**, 132,

134–5; death (1865) 75; Pax
Britannica 80–1; sacked
(1851) 136
Pankhurst, Adela 164
Pankhurst, Christabel **152**, 156,
157, 158, 160, 164
Pankhurst, Mrs Emmeline **151**,
154, 156, 157, 158, 160,
162, 164
speech at Bow Street Magistrates'
Court (1908) 166–7
Pankhurst, Sylvia **152**, 156, 157,
158, 160, 162; *The
Suffragette Movement* 167–8,
178
paper duty 95, 138
Paris Commune (1870–1) 53, 55
Parliament: in 18thC **6–8**, 8–13; in
20thC 2–4; changes in
composition 133–4; fire
(1834) 37, 50; 'purified'
36–7; reformed (19thC) 56;
relationship between Crown
and **5–8**, 36, 37–8; role in
1530s **5**; role and purpose
2, 166; sovereignty of 2–3,
5–6, 38; and suffragettes
158; in Victorian times 1–2;
see also unreformed
Parliament
Parliament Act (1911) **129**, 155
Parliament Bill (1911), and the
'People's Budget' (1909)
139–42, 147–9
Parliamentary Labour Party 120,
121
parliamentary reform (1785–1815)
opposition to 17–18: sources
22–4; support for 13–17:
sources 22–4; crisis
(1831–2) 28–34; origins of **8**
parliaments: annual, demand for
46, 48, 49, 54; mediaeval **5**;
proposal to shorten length of
31, 141
Parnell, Stewart 100, 116, 158
Parry, Jonathon, *The Rise and Fall
of Liberal Government in
Victorian Britain* 106, 176
participation: in elections,

after–1832 36; mass in politics 48, 99
party, changing meanings of 3
party politics, modern, and Reform Act (1867) 96–102
patronage **6–7**, 9, 29, 50, 54, 70, 113, 117, 132
Pax Britannica, Palmerston's 80–1
Peel, Sir Robert 4, **26**, **27**, 35, 36, 37, 47, 73, 78, 81, 94, **129**, 134; and Catholic emancipation 30, 34, 76, 91; letter to on 'Mechanics' churches' 65; opposition to 1832 Reform Act 3
Peel, General (Robert's brother) 73
Peelites **67**, 98
peers: allowing to sit in House of Commons 166; Asquith's threat of creation of 500 Liberal **129**, 135–6, 140, 141, 142; first life in Lords (1958) 166
Penryn 29–30
pensions, old age withheld from those with a criminal record 122
'People's Budget' (1909) 2, 135; defeated by House of Lords **130**, 137–43; and the Parliament Bill 139–42: sources 147–9
Peterloo massacre (1819) 2, **26**, 38
Pethick Lawrence, Emmeline 156
Pethick Lawrence, Frederick 156
petitions, parliamentary **46**
picketing, law on trade union 91
pikes 53
Pitt, William, the Younger **7–8**, 12, 14, 81, 94, 132, 133, 134; Parliamentary Reform Bill (1785) 14, 22; reply to Grey's reform motion (1792) 23; swamps House of Lords 16
Place, Francis 29, 50
plantation owners 10
Plimsoll line 91
'Plug Plots' 51, 52

plural voting 9, 115, 139, **151**, 159, 162–3, 165
pocket boroughs 7, 8, 9, 36
political crisis (1783–4) 16–17
political parties: growth after 1867 Reform Act 132: sources 107–9; local clubs and associations 98–9; organisation of **46**, **88**, 98
Political Register (Cobbett) 15
political unions 29, 32, 51
politics: popular 116; professionalisation of (1867–1900) 88–110, **88–90**; 'single-issue' 95; two-party 96–7
Ponsonby, Sir Henry, letter from Queen Victoria 144
Poor Law Amendment Act (1834) **45**, 50
Poor Law Guardians, female 154
Portland, Earl of **8**
Portugal, civil war 47
'pot-walloper' boroughs 9, 173
prime ministers: Crown's right to appoint 132; in the House of Lords **130**
Primrose League **89**, 99
private members' bills, on female suffrage **152**, 154
privilege, abolition of 13
professionalisation of politics (1867–1900) 88–110, **88–90**
professions, women in 154
property: attack on rights of 137–8, 143; franchise and the principle 155; women and 154
property qualification, abolition of **46**, 50, 54, 55, 71–2
proportional representation 2, 166
prostitution 93, 95, 154, 157
Prussia, war with Denmark 81
public morals 14
Pugh, Martin 161, 178
Punjab, annexation of the 81

Quarterly Review 41, 75–6, 83, 174
Quinault, Roland 29, 173

Radicals 11, 13, 14–16, **26**, 28, 50, 115; support for Whigs 31–2
ratepaying **68**, 77; and female suffrage 59, 154, 155
redistribution 35, 36, 56, 74, **111**, 114, 117, **151**, 159, 163
Redistribution Act (1884) 111, 115–16, 135, 139
Redmond, John (Edward) 159
referendum, Lords' suggestion of public 140
reform, changing concepts of 35
Reform Act (1832) 2, 26–44, **26–8**, 56, 69, 114, 133; constitutional implications 37; and female suffrage 153; impact, sources 42–4; measures **27–8**; preservation elements 34–9
Reform Act (1867) consensus on 69–75; Conservatives and 80–1; Disraeli and Gladstone and the 75–81; Disraeli's Second (1867) 50, 67–87, **67–9**, **88**, **111**; and female suffrage 153; and the modern system of party politics 96–102; wider franchise 98, 113–14
Reform Act (1884) **111**, 113, 114, 163; and democracy 113–18; sources 123–4
Reform Bill, first (1830), Chandos clause 31
Reform Club 98
reform crisis (1831–2) 31, 134; sources 39–41
Reform League 59, **68**, 74
Relief Act, Catholic emancipation **27**
religion 30
representation 8–13, 56, 69; in 18thC 8–13;of capital in Parliament 121; direct versus virtual 10–11, 13; of House of Commons (1831) 20; of labour in parliament 119
Representation of the People Act (1918) 113, 162, 163–4, 165

republicanism 131
residence qualification 77, 115, **151–2**, 163; for urban household suffrage 113
'residuum' 71, 115
resignations of ministers and governments 4
revolution 1, 53, 74 (1848) **46**, 55; fear of 13–14, 28, 34, 120
Revolution Settlement (1688) **6**, 9
Reynolds, Jack 119
Rhineland, Hitler's invasion of the 118
Richmond, Duchess of 30
Richmond, Duke of 32
rights: democratic 156; of husbands over wives 59; of women 58–9, 153
riots over parliamentary reform (1830s) **27**, 33, 38
Rochdale Pioneers 57–8
Roebuck, John 50
Rolf, David 163, 178
Rosebery, Lord 94, 100, **130**, 132, 135
rotten boroughs 33, 35, 36
Royal Titles Act 92
Royle, Edward 48–9, 174
'rump' see Long Parliament
rural areas 10, 113
Russell, Lord John 18, 31–2, 35, 47, 56, **67**, 73, **130**, 136; reform bill (1854) 70; (1866) 56, **67–8**, 70, 74, 76, 80; reform proposals (1849) 69, 70; (1852, 1860) 70, 72
Russell, William Howard 70

Sadler, Michael 18
Salisbury, Lord **90**, 92–3, 96, 97, 98, **111**, **130**; letter from Lord Randolph Churchill (1884) 109; letter from Lord Selborne (1916) 170–1; Queen Victoria and 132; versus Gladstone 114–16
Salt, Titus 58
Saltaire 58
Sarajevo (1914) 160

Saturday Review 79, 175
Schnadhorst, Francis 100
School Board elections 99, 100:
    poster (1876) 107; vote for
    single women ratepayers in
    (1870) 59, 154
scot-and-lot boroughs 8–9, 173
Scotland **27, 28, 112**; devolution
    2; George IV's visit to (1822)
    131, 177
Scottish MPs 18
SDF *see* Social Democratic
    Federation
seats, parliamentary (1801) 20,
    27–8
Second Reform Act *see* Reform
    Act (1867)
secret ballot **46**, 50; introduced
    (1872) **88**
Selborne, Lord, letter to Lord
    Salisbury (1916) 170–1
servicemen, disqualified by
    residence qualification **151–2**,
    163
Settlement, Act of 133
settlements, Chartist 57
Shaw, George Bernard, 'The
    Transition to Democracy' 127,
    177
'Sheffield outrages' 71
Sicily, invasion by Garibaldi 74
Sinn Fein 164
slave trade 10
slaves 11
slums 91
Smiles, Samuel, *Self-Help* 58
Smith, Paul, *Disraeli* 103, 176
Smith, W.H. 101
Snig's End settlement,
    Gloucestershire 57
social class, and voting behaviour
    117–18
Social Democratic Federation
    (SDF) **112**, 116, 120–1
social reform 16, 72–3, 79, 91;
    enfranchisement and 58–9;
    and the House of Lords 139,
    140; 'Newcastle programme'
    of 100, 139
social revolution 116

socialism, fear of 92, 93, 117,
    120–1, 139
socialist, use of term 121
Socialist League **112**, 116, 120
Society of Friends of the People
    16; petition (1793) 23
South America 136
sovereign, rights of the 134
sovereignty: of nations 166; of
    Parliament 2–3, **5–6**, 38
Spa Fields riot (1816) 38
Spain, civil war 47
Speaker 116
Speaker's Conference (1918) 163,
    166
state, growth in power of the 95
Stephens, J.R. 50
Stockmar, Baron 134–5
strikes 55; (1880s) **112**, 121–2;
    Chartist 51
Stuarts **6**, 133
suburbs, Conservative 114, 117
succession 133
Sudan 136
Suez Canal Company 92
suffrage *see* female suffrage;
    household suffrage; male
    suffrage; universal suffrage
Suffragette, The 162
suffragettes 3, 97, **151–3**; aims of
    155; hunger strikes **151**, 157,
    159; militant 119, 122, 142,
    157–9, 160–1; support for
    war 162; tactics 156–9
'Swing' rioters 32
Syndicalist movement **112**, 121,
    122

Taff Vale judgment **112**, 120, 121
Tanner, Duncan 119, 176
tariff reform 98, 101, 139
taxation: graduated 137; of profits
    from land sales 137
taxpaying, and female suffrage
    155, 156, 160
Taylor, A.J.P. 161, 178
television, in Parliament 2
'ten minute bill' (1867) *see*
    Disraeli, Benjamin, Reform Bill
    (1867)

tenants-at-will **28**, 31
Test and Corporation Acts, repeal of 30
Thatcher, Margaret 2, 94, 140
Third Reform Act *see* Reform Act (1884)
Thompson, Dorothy 48, 49, 174, 178
Tillett, Ben **112**, 121; by-election address (1895) 126
Times, The 64, 123, 124, 167; Chamberlain's letter to (1880) 108
Tolpuddle case (1834) 38, **45**, 122
Tonypandy (1911) 122
Tories **27**; and the Crown 31, 132, 133; origins of **6**; splits 28, 29, 31, 34, 98; two groups in 1820s **26**; *see also* Conservatives
'Tory Democracy' **68**, 90–3, **90**; sources 102–3
towns 10, 36, 113–14
trade union movement 97, 119–20
trade unions **46**, 58, 70, **112**, 121, **151**, 159; and female suffrage 158, 160; legal status 71; militant 119
Trades Union Congress (TUC) **112**; block votes 117; and suffragettes 158
Traill, H.D., *Social England* (1897) quoted 65
Trent incident 81

'Ultra-Tories' **26**, 30, 33
Unionists **130**, 139, 140, 142; absorbed into Conservative Party 97
United Nations 166
United States 81
universal suffrage 2, 15, **26**, 32, 51, 54, 59, 155; demand for 45–66, **45–7**
universities, women in 154
university seats, abolishing 166
unreformed Parliament 5–25, **5–8**; representativeness of 3, 8–13

Victoria, Queen **129**, 131, 134, 135, 136, 137; 'bedchamber crisis' (1839) 132, 134; Disraeli and **129**, 135; as Empress of India 92, 131; and Gladstone 132, 135, 136; Gladstone's address to 124; letter from Duke of Connaught 144–5; letter to Lady Ely (1879) 143–4; letter to Sir Henry Ponsonby 144; and Melbourne 134; memorandum (1880) 145
Victorians 1–2, **45–7**, 118–19
'Villa Conservatism' 93
Vincent, John 79, 91, 175
violence: reforming (1866) 74; suffragette 142, 157–9, 160–1; threat of Chartist 47–8, 51–3
Voice of the People (Doherty) 40
vote by ballot 31, 49, 54; *see also* secret ballot
votes for women 151–72, **151–3**
voting: in the open 11; *see also* plural voting
voting age: lowered to 18 (1969) 2, 166; male 163–4; for women **152–3**, 161–2
voting qualifications 8, 36, 71–2, **111**, 120
voting rights: equal 164; holders of ancient **28**; *see also* franchise

Wales 2, **28**; *see also* Church of Wales
Walker, Mary Ann, address to a Chartist meeting (1842) 65
Walpole, Sir Robert **6**
Walpole, Spencer 74
Walton, John K. 75, 175; *Disraeli* 102, 176
War Office 70
Waterloo, Battle of 18, **26**
weapons, access of Chartists to 52–3
Webb, Sidney and Beatrice 116
Weintraub, Stanley, *Disraeli* 103, 176

Wellington, Duke of **26–7**, 28, 29–30, 31, 34, 37, 48
Westbury 30
Westminster Review 43
Wetherall, Sir Charles 38
Whigs 3, 14, 28, 31, 31–2, **67**, 73, 76–7; approach to reform 16–17, 35, 38–9; creation of fifty peers **27**; crisis (1783–4) **7–8**; and the Crown 132, 133; Grey's government (1830–4) **27**; origins of **6**; resigned (1832) 31; *see also* Liberals
Wilkes, John 14
Wilkinson, Ellen 164
William IV **27**, 31, 32–3, 36–7, 49, **129**, 132, 133
William and Mary 6
Wilson, Ben, *The struggles of an old Chartist . . .* (1887) 62
Winchilsea, Lord 30
Wollstonecraft, Mary, *Vindication of the Rights of Women* 153
women: Chartism and 51, 55, 58–9; political rights for 58–9; right to vote in elections to the local school boards (1870) 59, 154; right to vote in municipal elections (1869) 59, 154; support for Conservatives **89**; votes for 151–72, **151–3**; voting rights (1918) 113, 161; voting rights of property owners 153; *see also* female suffrage
Women's Peace Movement 162
Women's Social and Political Union (WSPU) **151**, **152**, 156–7, 158, 159, 161, 164

Women's Suffrage Journal 154
workers: mobile 113; new industrial 15; skilled 58, 70–1; unskilled 119
workhouses **45**, 50
working class (1880s) **111–12**; Chartism and 47–54; Disraeli and the 3, **67–9**; franchise 3, 35, 56, **88–90**, 114; Liberalism 117; and the 'pale of the constitution' 70–1; respectable and unrespectable 71, 73, 75; and suffragettes 157–8; support for Conservatives 93, 96; support for female suffrage 156; support for reform 15, 18, 38–9, 50; support for universal suffrage **26**; war with employers 121–2
working class movements, Victorian **45–7**, 57–8
Working Men's Clubs **45**, 98
World War I (1914–18) 97, 119, 131–2, 137, **151**; effect on female suffrage campaign (1918–28) 161–5: sources 170–1; women's work in **152**, 163, 165
'W.R.', informer on Chartist meeting in Bradford (1848) 64
Wright, Dr Almoth, letter to *The Times* (1912) 167
Wyvill, Christopher 14, 52

Yorkshire Association 14–15, 18, 52

Zululand 92